US HEALTH POLICY
AND
MARKET REFORMS

AN INTRODUCTION

James C. Capretta

AMERICAN ENTERPRISE INSTITUTE

Distributed by arrangement with the Rowman & Littlefield Publishing Group, 4501 Forbes Boulevard, Suite 200, Lanham, Maryland 20706. To order, call toll-free 1-800-462-6420 or 1-717-794-3800. For all other inquiries, please contact AEI Press, 1789 Massachusetts Avenue, NW, Washington, DC 20036, or call 1-202-862-5800.

ISNB-13: 978-0-8447-5045-3   Hardback
ISNB-13: 978-0-8447-5046-0   Paperback
ISNB-13: 978-0-8447-5047-7   eBook

American Enterprise Institute
1789 Massachusetts Avenue, NW
Washington, DC 20036
www.aei.org

Contents

Foreword

Health care has been a prominent topic in the US national political conversation for decades, with no end in sight. The status quo, even before the COVID-19 pandemic exposed flaws in the nation's public health system, has been too dysfunctional for the issue to fall far down the list of voter priorities. Among other things, a large segment of the US population remains uninsured, and the relentless annual increase in medical care costs in excess of income growth is placing increasing financial strain on households and governments.

While these problems have fueled a strong desire for change, there is a divide over how to proceed, which has made reaching consensus elusive.

Most Americans are familiar with the views advanced by one side of the debate. Medicare for All, which would have the federal government run a public insurance plan for the entire country, is the paradigmatic reform advanced by those who favor full governmental control. It and similar reforms have been discussed widely in recent years in high-profile political campaigns.

The alternative—more reliance on market forces—is less well-known or understood, partly because there is less consensus among those who favor it on what it would entail.

This volume attempts to describe in some detail one version of such a plan. It also explains the major features of current US health policy and the relevant history of how we arrived at this point, because the proposed reforms are best understood in relation to the incumbent system. In general terms, the recommended changes would inject more discipline and consumer choice into what already exists rather than replace it with something entirely new.

The chapters that follow were originally released as individual reports, but they share several common themes, which made publishing them together in a single volume (with modifications and updates) a natural choice. The reforms reinforce one another and will work most effectively when they are advanced simultaneously rather than as stand-alone concepts.

The focus of the recommendations is not on better readiness for the next pandemic or public health crisis. That certainly should be a priority for Congress. However, even if such improvements get approved, the nation's underlying system of insurance and care provision will remain mired in dysfunction. The focus of this volume is on reforming that system to better deliver services that patients need regardless of whether a pandemic is creating global turmoil.

The US has resisted joining other advanced economies in embracing full public control of its health system. That might change if no viable alternative is ever presented. I hope the recommendations that follow demonstrate that there is, indeed, another way forward, as market incentives—channeled by effective public regulation—could deliver in the health sector the same benefits seen elsewhere in the economy—that is, innovation and ever-improving productivity that lowers costs and improves the quality of what is being provided to consumers.

1

The Structured Markets Framework

A dvocates of market-driven medical care have a difficult task. They must convince voters that competition and consumer choice in the health sector will deliver better results than full governmental control will. It will not be easy, but it will certainly fail if voters believe market advocates do not appreciate the dangers to patients from a dysfunctional system.

For instance, in a fully deregulated market, sicker patients will have difficulty securing insurance coverage. Government policy must intervene, one way or another, to ensure this vulnerable population has access to effective medical services.

Some distinctions are necessary, however, as not all regulation is beneficial. Many existing rules are ineffective or counterproductive, and the answer to every health system problem is not extending the government's reach.

Further, competition and incentives can play important roles in the health sector, too, if they are allowed to function in the right context.

Market advocates thus have a clear assignment. They must find the right mix of public regulation and private incentives that will deliver better results than the fully regulated alternative. The starting point for building such a market is understanding why health care will always require public oversight to be accessible to all citizens on an equitable basis.

Grappling with Market Failure

Nobel Prize–winner Kenneth Arrow was one of the most acclaimed American economists of the 20th century. His 1963 assessment of the sources of market failure in medical care was immediately influential and remains relevant today.[1]

Arrow offered a clear and precise description of why medical care is ill-suited to an unsupervised market. He focused on the understandable and unavoidable preference among consumers to secure expansive insurance to pay medical bills and the substantial information imbalance between patients and their professionally trained caregivers. These characteristics lead to distortions that make the medical services market challenging for consumers to navigate without government assistance and oversight.

Personal medical expenses can be large relative to annual incomes and highly unpredictable, so it is natural for consumers to seek insurance to protect themselves against expensive episodes. Most patients trust their physicians' judgments more than their own when making care decisions, especially when the stakes can be existential. The uncertainty of the value of medical care, with so many unknowable factors determining outcomes, reinforces consumers' preference to shift the financial risk off themselves and onto public or private insurance.

The dominance of third-party payment for services introduces additional distortions. Patients are often price insensitive when they seek and use services because their out-of-pocket costs will not increase with higher-priced care. Insurance plans have deductibles and cost-sharing requirements, but, beyond a certain threshold, all expenses usually are covered by the insurance policies, not the patients.

Aggregate health spending is also heavily concentrated in high-cost cases. In 2016, patients with annual expenses in the top 10 percent accounted for two-thirds of all health costs, and those in the top half for 97 percent. The average annual spending was nearly $50,000 for persons in the top 5 percent.[2] Few consumers want insurance with deductibles large enough to meaningfully influence consumption of such expensive care.

Further, while all patients are vulnerable to unpredictable and costly health problems, some consumers with expensive chronic conditions know at the beginning of the year that they will need services with costs exceeding their annual deductibles even if they avoid other problems. So, when paying for services out of pocket, these consumers tend to be price insensitive because no amount of price shopping will substantially alter their final annual bills.

The consumer preference for insurance and the tendency toward risk segmentation in health insurance markets compel additional public regulation. Private insurers can identify high- and low-risk customers based on their ages and medical conditions and charge premiums accordingly. The divergence in consumer costs can become so extreme that high-risk individuals are priced out entirely. Federal and state regulation imperfectly corrected for this tendency before the Affordable Care Act (ACA) outlawed health status in insurance pricing altogether.

The US has a large uninsured population by the standards of high-income countries but for reasons that often are not well understood. While 28 million US residents went without health insurance in 2021, two-thirds of the uninsured were eligible for either coverage subsidized by the federal government or Medicaid and children's health insurance that is entirely free for participants. (Recent legislation expanded the generosity of the government's support for this coverage to further boost take-up.)[3] In addition, about 17 percent of the uninsured are residing in the US unlawfully, which makes them ineligible for the ACA's publicly subsidized coverage.[4]

As in other countries, the US is striving for population-wide insurance coverage because most Americans want a safety net in case they need it and because they want to ensure their fellow citizens can get needed services irrespective of their ability to pay. The political impulse in support of this outlook is bolstered by federal and state laws—along with societal norms and ethical obligations on providers—requiring care for sick patients even without insurance. The net effect of these policies is the provision of some care to the uninsured (albeit at levels below those provided to the insured population), which increases insurance premiums for those who are paying for it and further incents support for policies that can achieve population-wide coverage.

The imbalance in knowledge about medical care also hinders enforcement of standards. Low-quality practitioners may be difficult for average consumers to identify on their own or without risking substantial harm to themselves. Regulation of medical practice, mainly by the states, offsets this vulnerability but also erects barriers to market entry that push costs up for consumers and protect the incomes of incumbent providers. Even high-quality practitioners will provide more care than is optimal because of the low cost to patients from ordering more precautionary tests for low-probability events.

Why a Market?

The constraints on a functioning market identified by Arrow and others compel public regulation and subsidies for coverage, but that does not mean full governmental control is the only option. While Arrow himself favored a single-payer plan, he did not rule out that a combination of private incentives and regulation might deliver acceptable results.[5]

Arrow left the door open to a regulated market because strong outcomes in a health system depend on the details of key policies. In theory, full regulation (such as with single payer or government rate setting) can deliver the best outcomes and beat a regulated market, but only if public officials and institutions can reliably identify and implement sound rules while avoiding others that impose costs in excess of their benefits. (The possibility of regulation outperforming markets is not unique to the health sector; other industries have distortions that could be corrected with precisely targeted governmental interventions. However, doing so requires an ability to collect and use essential information that is beyond the competency of most governments.)

Choosing between full regulation and a mix of regulation and incentives is thus a matter of judgment, informed by assessments of the suitability of existing political processes and government institutions for running the health system directly or channeling private incentives and initiatives toward public goals.

Empirical research can and should inform this debate, but it is unlikely to settle the matter entirely. Among other factors, comparing the relative merits of market incentives or regulations is difficult because of the complexity of the policy designs required for each approach and because public officials are reluctant to subject their constituents to experimentation.[6]

What should be decisive when comparing reform concepts is an assessment of which is capable of delivering more rapid productivity improvement in the health sector. Higher productivity allows health systems to deliver better results while using fewer resources. The relative absence of productivity improvement leaves patients unsatisfied with the costs they must pay when receiving care (including through their premium payments to insurers). Put differently, there is wide agreement that medical care in the US is far too expensive because of rampant waste and inefficiency, and the quality of care delivered is too often below what should be acceptable.

The added value from productivity can reduce prices for consumers and thus raise the standards of living of those using and providing medical care. With productivity improvement, cost discipline would be possible while maintaining or improving the quality of medical services provided to patients. Without productivity improvement, cost controls, imposed by either the government (through price limits) or private payers (with benefit restrictions), will, by definition, lead to an erosion in quality, likely in the form of waiting lists for care, undercapitalized facilities, less innovation, and more restricted access to beneficial treatments.

Under the right circumstances, regulation can improve productivity by offsetting the distortions introduced by market failure. While possible, this occurs only when regulators successfully identify and correct market deficiencies. The opposite situation, one that involves imposing new burdens on consumers or taxpayers through regulation, is not uncommon. For instance, regulations that are difficult to change once in place can inhibit productivity-enhancing innovation. Regulation also can protect market incumbents, who use their favored positions (and protected incomes) to advocate for more generous reimbursement for their services and higher regulatory hurdles for potential competitors.

Critics of US health care point out that the tighter payment controls imposed by governmental systems in other countries are effective at lowering overall costs for patients and taxpayers. In 2018, Canada spent 10.7 percent of gross domestic product on health care, which was 36 percent less than the US total of 16.9 percent.[7]

While more constrained governmental systems tend to devote less of their incomes to health care than do those with looser controls, strict regulations on pricing are not necessarily preferable or more efficient. In Canada, the UK, and many other countries, costs are lower than in the US because the central governments impose price limits on what can be charged for services. (In the UK, the government essentially owns the hospitals and employs the physicians, which allows for an even higher level of control.)

Price setting lowers observable costs but does not translate automatically into improved productivity. Indeed, in many cases, measured health spending falls but efficiency suffers because of hidden costs. Among other things, price limits frequently push some suppliers out of the market, as the regulated prices are no longer attractive enough for some firms to continue operations. With fewer suppliers, patients sometimes must wait to get the care they need.

More than one million people are on official waiting lists in Canada. The average time to see a specialist after a referral from a general practitioner is now 10.1 weeks, up from 3.7 weeks in 1993.[8] For an MRI, the average wait is 9.3 weeks. And these are the official measures, which may understate the extent of the problem because practitioners have an incentive to avoid scrutiny from regulatory authorities.

Patients wait for care in the US, too, but not as long as they do in Canada. Before the COVID-19 pandemic, more than 60 percent of Americans requiring surgery could schedule it within a month of being advised that they needed the procedure. In Canada, only 35 percent of patients could get surgery performed as quickly.[9]

When patients wait for care, there are costs, in the form of unnecessary suffering from untreated symptoms and prolonged anxiety about whether problematic conditions will be successfully addressed. One way to understand this cost is to consider what patients would be willing to pay for more timely care. If patients could speed up the care they receive in Canada and the UK by spending their own money, the cost differential with the US would narrow.

Price and regulatory controls also limit innovation and quality improvement. Investors may pull back from putting capital into risky ventures, such as new drug and medical device products, if their returns depend entirely on payments set by the government rather than private payers. Moreover, with price controls, firms that otherwise might enter the medical services market with disruptive ideas or products might forgo doing so, as the potential returns might be too uncertain to take on the risk of failure.

By contrast, there is substantial evidence from many sectors that market competition induces productivity gains by incentivizing innovation and technological improvements. A UK government review of the country's domestic economy found vigorous competition was central to improved performance.[10] Similarly, in the 1990s and early 2000s, the McKinsey

Global Institute analyzed the economic performance of 13 countries across a dozen years.[11] The principal finding was that countries that opened their markets to competition saw the largest gains in living standards (from productivity gains) and countries that tried to protect industries with regulations and barriers fared much worse.

Competition fosters productivity improvement because it allows new firms to introduce innovation, which in turn forces incumbents to react with their own efficiency gains. In well-functioning markets, costly and inefficient enterprises fail because customers can take their business elsewhere.

In relative terms, the United States's less regulated payment system for new biopharma products has made it the world's leader for research and development and the introduction of new therapies.[12] While the multinational manufacturers that dominate the industry are focused on worldwide revenue and have global supply chains, the US undoubtedly plays a vital role in fostering an environment that encourages product innovation. The US represents a disproportionate share of total industry revenue and is financing biopharma advances for much of the world.[13] The financial burden is not trivial, but it must be weighed against the alternative. The predictable result of US convergence with the policies of other high-income countries would be less innovation and fewer breakthrough therapies.[14]

Wrong Prescriptions

An obstacle to implementing effective market-driven reform is misdiagnosis of the problem.

Some market advocates observe the density of federal and state regulations now imposed on the insurance market and the delivery of medical services and conclude that a policy of undifferentiated deregulation is the solution. They equate pulling back on governmental rules, especially on private insurance, with allowing the market to emerge and flourish as it does in other sectors.

This impulse is what drove the design of the bills to replace the ACA in 2017. The primary authors of those measures viewed the ACA's imposition of new federal insurance rules as its main offense and wanted replacement legislation to eliminate those restrictions or at least partially roll them back.[15] In particular, they believed the ACA's federal rules mandating what is covered by insurance plans and restricting what plans can charge high-risk consumers distorted the market and needed to be repealed or substantially altered.

These views created divisions among ACA critics, some of whom wanted to retain protections for consumers with preexisting conditions while trimming the law's other excesses, most especially its emphasis on public coverage expansion. Further, the push to roll back insurance protections was successfully portrayed by the law's supporters as leaving sick Americans vulnerable to high premiums or no coverage at all. The controversy over these questions sapped the momentum for repeal and replace, and no bill made it through Congress.

Government rules stipulating minimum coverage requirements for private insurance plans and restricting the use of health status in setting premiums raise costs for some consumers, but they also lower them for others. Overall, the net effect is minimal. Their value is in reducing the premium burden on a relatively small number of very sick patients who will need to consume significant levels of medical care irrespective of the cost of the insurance they obtain. Repeal of these rules would not materially lower overall health spending, but it would leave some Americans more vulnerable to high personal expenses.

The primary force behind high overall costs is a system for providing care that is inefficient and wasteful, along with a culture that emphasizes giving patients with insurance unrestricted access to services with little oversight or cost management. The aim of market-driven reform should be to impose more discipline on how medical care is provided to all patients, not to shift a portion of the financial burden from one group to another.

The Structured Market Options

To put dramatic, systemic, and continuous productivity improvement into motion, the consumer role is essential and decisive. With consumers directing resources, enterprises must manage their costs to keep prices competitive and innovate to provide more value.

While consumers are essential, they will not be able—or willing—to fulfill their role if they perceive that their involvement in decision-making would invite added financial risk or possibly worse health outcomes. Their reluctance can be addressed only by putting structure around their choices to minimize the possibility of such bad outcomes.

Advocates for consumer-focused reform have developed two conceptions of a better-functioning market, with different expectations of how competition can be leveraged to deliver better results.[16]

Plan-Focused Competition. The value proposition of managed care insurance plans, especially health maintenance organizations (HMOs), is that they can control costs for their enrollees better than unmanaged fee-for-service (FFS) insurance can. With plan-level competition, consumers would hire agents—HMOs and other types of managed care—to control costs on their behalf. Health plans that successfully keep expenses in check could charge lower premiums than their competitors could and thus attract more enrollees.

The premise is that high overall costs are concentrated in a relatively small number of expensive cases and only trained experts with deep knowledge and supporting data can influence the care protocols of hospitals and physician groups. The patients themselves are in a weak position to manage their own expenses because of insufficient knowledge of medical care.

In the 1970s, Paul Ellwood and Alain Enthoven championed a version of plan-level reform, dubbed "managed competition." (See the sidebar for a brief history.) In managed competition, consumers are given the circumscribed role of selecting (usually annually) from among competing health plans. Insurers would be expected to do the hard work of building networks of affiliated hospitals and physician groups and creating organized systems of care that control overall costs. Consumers would have an incentive to enroll in lower-premium options to reduce their costs because their employers (and the government) would subsidize coverage in ways that do not reward expensive plans. HMOs would use their oversight of the entire care process to improve productivity, just as enterprises under competitive pressure do in other industries.

An example can illustrate the consumer's role. Potential plan enrollees would be presented with competing coverage options charging differing

A Brief History and Summary of Managed Competition

Managed competition is the moniker Paul Ellwood and Alain Enthoven used to market their vision for health reform, beginning in the 1970s. Their influence on health policy has been significant and underappreciated.

Ellwood's contribution came first and was derived from his experience as a practicing physician in Minnesota in the 1950s and 1960s. His central conviction was that medical care, especially for patients needing expensive interventions, is best delivered in organized systems—health maintenance organizations (HMOs)—that have the capacity to systematically assimilate and implement emerging evidence of what works, and does not, in clinical practice into protocols that would govern how HMOs cared for their patients. In his view, providing complex medical services is a process that can be studied, improved, and managed to take out unnecessary costs, much as businesses continuously improve the efficiency with which they make other products or deliver services. By contrast, care provided in fee-for-service settings is difficult to coordinate and manage because fragmented and unaffiliated practitioners have little incentive to work with each other to aggressively eliminate unnecessary expenses.

Ellwood's most significant policy victory came with the groundbreaking Health Maintenance Organization Act of 1973. He convinced the Nixon administration—and then Congress—that imposing cost control in the US context required widespread enrollment in HMOs, which were at that time located mainly on the West Coast. The HMO Act is credited with rapidly expanding the reach of the managed care industry from the 1970s through the 1990s.

Enthoven combined Ellwood's advocacy for organized systems of care with a market structure that would allow managed care plans to thrive. His focus was on getting the incentives right, for both the HMOs that would be in charge of patient care and consumers who would be choosing their insurance coverage from among competing managed care plans.

(continued on the next page)

(continued from the previous page)

A key element of their reform framework, which had many iterations over the years, was marketplaces in which large numbers of consumers would get to select from among competing HMOs. (This vision was partially adopted in the Affordable Care Act.) Employers would help finance the coverage but would no longer choose the plans for their employees. The federal and state governments would set rules for insurance offerings, including required benefits. With standardized insurance coverage, the HMOs would compete based on how well they could keep premiums in check while meeting quality benchmarks.

Managed competition requires premium-sensitive consumers. Ellwood and Enthoven urged policymakers to reform Medicare, Medicaid, and employer coverage to convert subsidies for insurance enrollment into defined-contribution payments that would incentivize economizing. For job-based coverage, this meant converting the existing federal tax subsidy into tax credits under the control of workers that would not increase with the expense of the plans chosen. In Medicare, the push was for "premium support," with the government converting its financing into payments that beneficiaries would use to offset the premium costs of the plans they would choose for their coverage.

Managed competition was purposely positioned in the center of American politics. The Clinton administration borrowed heavily from it in developing the Health Security Act of 1993 (which Congress did not pass), and the George W. Bush administration used it when devising Medicare drug coverage. The ACA's exchanges also borrow from Ellwood and Enthoven's vision.

monthly premiums based on their varying capacities for cost control. The sponsoring organization (an employer, a state insurance exchange, or Medicare) would provide a fixed level of support toward enrollment, perhaps tied to the average cost plan.

If, for instance, the average premium was $500 per month, consumers selecting a plan with a $550 premium would pay the additional

$50 themselves. Alternatively, if they chose a plan with a $450 per month premium, they would save $50 monthly. The employer or the government could set its support at any level (such as $400 or even $500 monthly) so long as it is fixed and does not change with the price of the plan an individual consumer selects.

Government policy is essential to making plan-level competition work. Public funding for insurance enrollment must provide the right incentives to consumers. Insurers must offer coverage with standardized benefits, to ensure premium differences are due entirely to their differing abilities to manage costs.

Ellwood and Enthoven stressed the importance of competition based on sound management of costs, not restrictions on covered benefits, because they believed consumers are unequipped to decide the premium consequences of including or excluding certain services. The complexity would obfuscate the choices and undermine the reform's effect on cost control.

Provider-Focused Competition. An alternative competition model rejects the premise that consumers are ill-equipped to shop directly for medical services. Advocates of provider-focused competition have long contended that patients would seek low-priced and high-value care if given financial incentives to do so. Health savings accounts (HSAs) and high-deductible insurance plans have been advanced as policies that would allow consumers to play a prominent role in disciplining the costs of the services they receive.

The push for stronger consumer financial incentives has been combined more recently with efforts to make pricing for medical services more transparent. Up to this point, consumers with HSAs and high deductibles have been inclined to use fewer services before satisfying their annual out-of-pocket payment requirements, but they have not engaged in active price shopping for care, even when paying for services with their own money.[17]

A major obstacle has been the absence of meaningful price information. Hospitals, physicians, and other service providers have no reason to make their pricing information easily accessible to consumers because most of their revenue comes from insurers and the government, not patients. Further, the prices patients pay are usually decided by negotiations between insurers and medical service providers; as long as care is in network, patients expect that what they will owe is below what they could secure if they were shopping on their own.

Advocates for direct consumer purchasing have sought to overcome these obstacles through transparency tools deployed by insurers and third-party companies and through broad disclosure requirements in federal regulations.[18]

Promising Evidence

While neither plan-level competition nor direct consumer shopping for services has been tested on a large scale in the US, there is evidence from more limited experiments that consumers will opt for lower-priced options if the rules governing their selections give them confidence that they can make such choices free of significant risk.[19]

In Medicare, the drug benefit created in 2003 legislation was designed to foster competition at the insurance-plan level. Beneficiaries have the option of selecting from among competing drug plan offerings each year, and the government's contribution is determined entirely by competitive bids submitted by the plans. Importantly, in each geographically defined market, the government's subsidy for the benefit is fixed at the enrollment-weighted average of the submitted bids and does not increase or fall with the plans enrollees select. Thus, the beneficiaries are exposed to the marginal premium cost—or savings—of their chosen plans. If they pick drug coverage with monthly premiums above the benchmark paid by the government, they must pay the added cost out of their own pockets.

This design has worked to control premium growth. Insurers have competed vigorously to attract drug benefit enrollment by keeping their monthly premiums as low as possible. The result has been remarkable premium stability for 15 years.[20]

There is also evidence that managed care plans are more effective at controlling overall per-patient costs, including for expensive inpatient hospital services and physician care. In Medicare, beneficiaries can elect to get their coverage through private managed care plans called Medicare

Advantage (MA), which are paid fixed monthly rates by the federal government. The MA plans have an incentive to control costs because the government's payment is not reduced when they eliminate unnecessary expenses. This is not true in the traditional FFS program because the government pays when services are rendered, and providing more services leads to more payments. Thus, providers that control utilization in FFS are penalized with reductions in their Medicare revenue.

These diverging incentives are seen in MA plan bids, which are generally well below the measured costs of FFS. (Most MA plans supplement this coverage with added benefits, such as vision and dental care.)

For some services, direct price competition among medical care providers can work too. There should be no expectation that patients with conditions requiring ongoing evaluation and care adjustments, such as those with many cancers or those in the midst of an acute emergency, will be able to meaningfully price shop for the services they need. But a substantial portion—perhaps 35 to 45 percent—of medical care does not have these characteristics.[21] "Shoppable services" are those that can be scheduled in advance and are routine enough to be required by many patients with similar clinical profiles.

Diagnostic tests (such as MRIs) are often cited as examples of services that should be price competitive. Most MRI exams can be scheduled by patients within time frames (such as multiple days or weeks) established by their physicians, and many markets have numerous competing providers offering the service, including stand-alone facilities. Quality distinctions for MRIs are minimal; value, then, would seem to be tied closely to price (although convenience is likely an important factor too).

The benefits of price shopping, when the conditions are right, are encouraging. Several large employers have tested versions of reference pricing, which ties insurance payments to benchmark rates for certain well-defined services. Plan enrollees who select plans with pricing below the benchmarks share in the savings, while those selecting higher-priced service providers must pay most of the added costs themselves. The average cost reduction from these schemes is about 15 percent. If applied across all commercial insurance, the savings would exceed $100 billion annually.[22]

Challenges

While both plan- and provider-level consumer choice have potential, there are sound reasons not to rely solely on one approach or the other.

Plan-level competition works best when the competing health plans are truly integrated—that is, they perform both the insurance and service delivery functions directly—and not overlapping. In other words, they are tightly managed HMOs, with more or less exclusive affiliations with their hospitals and doctors. With such tight control, these HMOs can change the care delivery process for their patients.

Fully integrated HMOs are not the industry norm, however. Most insurers, even those considered "managed care plans," do not have such direct control over costs. Their networks are loosely structured and contractual. Many hospitals and physician groups have relationships with multiple insurance plans and thus are not particularly inclined to bend to the wishes of any of them. Managed care of this type can influence overall costs to a degree, but its oversight of the care process is more attenuated than Ellwood and Enthoven envisioned and preached.

A major impediment to plan-level competition is consumers' indifference to rising premiums. In job-based plans, workers often do not face the full cost of more expensive insurance and thus are more interested in getting access to a wide range of physician services.

Consumer price shopping faces hurdles too. While reference pricing and reward programs can put downward pressure on costs, there is evidence that consumers are not highly motivated to participate in these efforts. One obstacle is the deference patients show to their physicians' recommendations, even when it extends to the location for tests and procedures for which there is no discernible quality difference among competing providers.[23] In this context, online price transparency tools may be insufficient motivators for changing behavior.

Starting Points for Progress

Bringing market-driven discipline to a $3.8 trillion industry will be complex and difficult and involve changing many different aspects of current law and practice. Even so, the needed changes, for both plan- and provider-level competition, generally fall into two categories: strong consumer incentives and standardization to simplify price comparisons.

Incentives. Markets cannot work without rewards and penalties. Consumers must see a financial upside from decisions to economize, or they will gravitate to higher-cost options. In medical care, current policy insulates patients from the significant cost consequences of their choices.

For job-based insurance, the federal government confers a large financial benefit on employer-paid premiums by exempting them from workers' income and payroll taxes. This policy encourages firms to weight compensation toward health coverage, and it means that federal taxpayers partially finance each additional premium dollar paid for insurance. Predictably, this subsidization encourages overconsumption.

In Medicare, program beneficiaries can enroll in private MA plans or stay in traditional FFS. Many MA plans offer benefits beyond what is required by law, which encourages take-up. However, even when FFS is more expensive than MA, beneficiaries do not face higher premiums when they opt for the traditional program.

For plan-level competition to work, both employer coverage and Medicare need to change to provide their participants with strong incentives to economize.

Similar adjustments are needed to encourage direct consumer price shopping of common services. Many plan enrollees today could not reduce their costs by opting for lower-priced care because their insurance plans cover all their medical expenses beyond an annual deductible. Insurers need to adopt reference-based payments (or at least financial rewards) for services that are amenable to price shopping to give their plan enrollees incentives to seek low-priced providers irrespective of other cost-sharing rules.

Standardization. For both plan- and provider-level competition, the goal is to take the complexity and risk out of the consumer decision-making process through standardizing what is being provided.

For insurance, that means plans offering uniform benefits. The plans would compete on how well they control the costs of care, not on whether they will pay for certain services.

The ACA established a minimum benefit package for insurance, but even this requirement is too loose to facilitate easy premium comparisons because competing insurers are only required to offer benefits covering the main categories with a total actuarial value that is equivalent. To find high-value insurance, consumers must weigh the relative value of higher or lower deductibles—and adjustments in cost-sharing rules across multiple benefit categories—against differences in the premiums charged by the plans. The complexity of these comparisons means consumers often select plans that are suboptimal for the care they need.

Strict standardization—with exactly the same deductible and cost-sharing for each covered service—would allow consumers to focus solely on the premium differences among the competing plans.

Similarly, provider-level competition for "shoppable care" requires standardization of the clinical services consumers need. The objective should be to make certain high-volume and routine services, such as testing and common surgeries, as much like commodities as possible. The main difference between getting an MRI or other diagnostic from one provider or another should be just the prices they charge. The same holds for common physician services and routine surgeries. The pricing should be based on clear definitions of the clinical interventions being provided so consumers can readily see the price differences among those offering standardized services.

With standardization of what is being priced, consumers would have confidence that the competing providers are not offering differing packages of clinical services.

A High Ceiling on Better Results

Without public regulation and encouragement, consumers cannot perform their necessary role in the medical services market, which is to discipline low performers by moving limited resources elsewhere. Current government policy does not come close to satisfying what would be required to overcome the inherent barriers to a functioning marketplace for either insurance or individual services.

That need not be the case, however. There are good reasons to be wary of relying exclusively on government regulations to control medical care costs. The evidence of recent decades is that pricing decisions by the government are often arbitrary and lacking in compelling supporting data. The result is a payment system rife with distortions and misallocated resources. Some service providers are starved of resources, while others are swimming in funds they do not deserve.

A functioning market would do better. It would identify the right prices to be paid for high-value services and push premiums to levels that consumers would find acceptable relative to what they receive in return.

There also is ample reason to expect the cost savings from effective reforms to be substantial. Some estimates place the amount of waste in US health care at nearly one-third of total spending, or well over $1 trillion annually.[24] Consumers, armed with the right information and allowed to share in the savings they identify, would be a far more powerful force for rooting out inefficiency than would the federal or state agencies that have been charged with that mission for decades—with disappointing results. That is reason enough to pursue the reforms necessary to build a functioning market, despite the admitted political challenges of doing so.

Notes

1. Kenneth Arrow, "Uncertainty and the Welfare Economics of Medical Care," *American Economic Review* 53, no. 5 (December 1963): 941–73, https://web.stanford.edu/~jay/health_class/Readings/Lecture01/arrow.pdf.

2. Bradley Sawyer and Gary Claxton, "How Do Health Expenditures Vary Across the Population?," Peterson-KFF Health System Tracker, January 16, 2019, https://www.healthsystemtracker.org/chart-collection/health-expenditures-vary-across-population/.

3. Congressional Budget Office, "Cost Estimate: Reconciliation Recommendations of the House Committee on Ways and Means," February 17, 2021, https://www.cbo.gov/system/files/202102/hwaysandmeansreconciliation.pdf.

4. Congressional Budget Office, "Federal Subsidies for Health Insurance Coverage for People Under Age 65: CBO and JCT's July 2021 Projections," July 2021, https://www.cbo.gov/system/files/2021-08/51298-2021-07-healthinsurance.pdf; and Congressional Budget Office, "Who Went Without Health Insurance in 2019, and Why?," September 2020, https://www.cbo.gov/system/files/2020-09/56504-Health-Insurance.pdf. Chapter 6 discusses in more detail the reasons for the persistence of large numbers of uninsured Americans and what might be done to enroll many more in coverage.

5. Asher Schechter, "'There Is Regulatory Capture, but It Is By No Means Complete,'" Promarket, March 15, 2016, https://promarket.org/2016/03/15/there-is-regulatory-capture-but-it-is-by-no-means-complete/.

6. As an example, a demonstration testing the value of a market-enabling reform in Medicare ("premium support") that was authorized in the Medicare Modernization Act of 2003 and scheduled to begin in 2010 was never conducted because of opposition from elected leaders. Congress eventually repealed it. See Beth Fuchs and Lisa Potetz, "The Nuts and Bolts of Medicare Premium Support Proposals," Kaiser Family Foundation, June 2011, https://www.kff.org/wp-content/uploads/2013/01/8191.pdf.

7. Organisation for Economic Co-operation and Development, "Health Expenditure and Financing," February 2020, https://stats.oecd.org/Index.aspx?DataSetCode=SHA.

8. Bacchus Barua and Mackenzie Moir, "Waiting Your Turn: Wait Times for Health Care in Canada, 2019 Report," Fraser Institute, 2019, https://www.fraserinstitute.org/sites/default/files/waiting-your-turn-2019-rev17dec.pdf.

9. Kevin Pham, "America Outperforms Canada in Surgery Wait Times—and It's Not Even Close," Foundation for Economic Education, July 17, 2019, https://fee.org/articles/america-outperforms-canada-in-surgery-wait-times-and-its-not-even-close/.

10. Competition and Markets Authority, "Productivity and Competition: A Summary of the Evidence," July 9, 2015, https://assets.publishing.service.gov.uk/government/uploads/system/uploads/attachment_data/file/909846/Productivity_and_competition_report__.pdf. For an overview of the benefits of competition in various US industries and internationally, see Edith Ramirez, "The Relationship Between Competition, Productivity, and Economic Growth: The Case of the United States," Federal Trade Commission, September 3, 2013, https://www.ftc.gov/system/files/documents/public_statements/579931/140902lacfperuspeech.pdf.

11. William W. Lewis, "The Power of Productivity: Poor Countries Should Put Their Consumers First," McKinsey Quarterly, no. 2 (2004), https://econfaculty.gmu.edu/pboettke/workshop/spring05/Lewis.pdf.

12. Arthur Daemmrich, "Where Is the Pharmacy to the World? International Regulatory Variation and Pharmaceutical Industry Location" (working paper, Harvard Business School, Boston, MA, 2009), https://www.hbs.edu/ris/Publication%20Files/09-118.pdf.

13. Dana Goldman and Darius Lakdawalla, "The Global Burden of Medical Innovation," University of Southern California, Leonard D. Schaeffer Center for Health Policy & Economics, January 2018, https://healthpolicy.usc.edu/wp-content/uploads/2018/01/01.2018_Global20Burden20of20Medical20Innovation.pdf.

14. Prescription drug pricing is discussed in more detail in Chapter 7.

15. Dave Weigel, "Freedom Caucus Backs ACA 'Repeal and Replace' That Counts on Private Coverage," Washington Post, February 15, 2017, https://www.washingtonpost.com/news/powerpost/wp/2017/02/15/freedom-caucus-ready-for-obamacare-replacement-that-expands-hcas-bans-abortion-funding/.

16. For a more detailed description of the competing conceptions of the consumer role presented here, see Bryan E. Dowd, "Coordinated Agency Versus Autonomous Consumers in Health Services Markets," Health Affairs 24, no. 6 (November/December

2005), https://www.healthaffairs.org/doi/abs/10.1377/hlthaff.24.6.1501.

17. Amelia M. Haviland et al., "Do 'Consumer-Directed Health Plans' Bend the Cost Curve over Time?" (working paper, National Bureau of Economic Research, Cambridge, MA, March 2015), https://www.nber.org/system/files/working_papers/w21031/w21031.pdf.

18. Chapter 2 provides a more detailed discussion of using price transparency to improve provider-focused competition.

19. Both the Netherlands and Switzerland have insurance systems built on privately administered coverage, but insurers have limited ability to negotiate their own rates with facilities or practitioners. See Robert E. Leu et al., "The Swiss and Dutch Health Insurance Systems: Universal Coverage and Regulated Competitive Insurance Markets," Commonwealth Fund, January 2009, https://www.commonwealthfund.org/publications/fund-reports/2009/jan/swiss-and-dutch-health-insurance-systems-universal-coverage-and.

20. See Chapter 3, on Medicare, for further discussion of the effects on competition on premiums.

21. American Academy of Actuaries, "Estimating the Potential Health Care Savings of Reference Pricing," November 2018, https://www.actuary.org/sites/default/files/files/publications/ReferencePricing_11.2018.pdf.

22. James C. Robinson, Timothy T. Brown, and Christopher Whaley, "Reference Pricing Changes the 'Choice Architecture' of Health Care for Consumers," *Health Affairs* 36, no. 3 (March 2017): 524–30, https://www.healthaffairs.org/doi/pdf/10.1377/hlthaff. 2016.1256.

23. Michael Chernew et al., "Are Health Care Services Shoppable? Evidence from the Consumption of Lower-Limb MRI Scans" (working paper, National Bureau of Economic Research, Cambridge, MA, January 2019), https://www.nber.org/system/files/working_papers/w24869/w24869.pdf.

24. William H. Shrank, Teresa L. Rogstad, and Natasha Parekh, "Waste in the US Health Care System: Estimated Costs and Potential for Savings," *Journal of the American Medical Association* 322, no. 15 (October 2019): 1501–09, https://jamanetwork.com/journals/jama/article-abstract/2752664.

2

Price Transparency

Market advocates have long believed that US health care would be less expensive and of higher quality if price competition among providers—hospitals, physicians, clinics, labs, and all the rest—were more intense and if consumers played the same price-sensitive role they do in so many other sectors of the American economy.

It is an attractive vision, though it has proved elusive. Even as consumers have been exposed to higher deductibles, prices in the sector have continued to rise rapidly for enrollees in commercial insurance plans.

There is reason for optimism, however. Market advocates have begun to agree on what the main obstacle is: opaque pricing. Consumers rarely know what price will be charged before they receive medical care. Meaningful price information is hard to come by, and, when it is available, it comes in a format that makes it difficult for consumers to use.

Agreement that this problem needs to be addressed has allowed a spate of promising regulatory changes to move forward in recent years. Better results will depend on taking the next crucial steps to allow consumers to easily shop for services when their circumstances allow.

Long-Standing Impediments

Interest in price transparency has grown alongside the advent of consumer-driven health care. As increasing numbers of Americans enrolled in high-deductible health plans (HDHPs) over the past two decades, it was expected and hoped that this trend would put downward pressure on costs through two channels.[1] First, HDHP enrollees might forgo some services while satisfying their annual deductibles. Second, some suppliers of services might lower their prices to become more attractive to price-sensitive consumers. This latter effect—the supply response to the consumer movement—could deliver much more efficiency in the health sector.

Unfortunately, the actual market effects have been modest. While research confirms consumers with high deductibles use fewer services, there is less evidence of price shopping.[2] If a transformation were underway, one would expect more consumers to access the many price comparison tools that have been developed and made available to them (by their insurers and others) or to see more price concessions from providers seeking to improve their competitive position in the market. Neither has occurred. More than 15 years after Congress created health savings accounts, price shopping remains uncommon, and, when it does occur, it is focused on services that account for a small share of overall expenditures.[3] A recent survey found that only 13 percent of enrollees who were facing out-of-pocket costs researched prices before getting care, and only 3 percent compared prices from multiple providers.[4]

While numerous efforts (public and private) are underway to make pricing clearer and more transparent, those providing the services to patients are, for the most part, being pulled along reluctantly. Without a forceful push from the government, hospitals and physician groups are not willing to offer consumers clear pricing information that would facilitate direct comparisons with their competitors.

The record of the past 20 years demonstrates that price competition among providers will not occur spontaneously. Too many impediments stand in the way. Policymakers need a clear understanding of the existing obstacles and what might be done to overcome them.

Current Efforts

As more Americans have moved into HDHPs, both the private and public sectors have launched various initiatives, summarized here, that are aimed at making medical prices more transparent and user-friendly.

The Private Sector. Most employers and large insurers now routinely make available price estimating tools of some kind, with varying levels of sophistication. In a Mercer-sponsored survey, 77 percent of employers reported offering a price transparency tool to their health plan enrollees.[5] These employers, and their insurers, have been helped by a growing number of technology companies refining software applications to deliver understandable pricing information to consumers.[6]

The most sophisticated tools attempt to give plan enrollees a specific estimate of their out-of-pocket expenses based on their selection of provider or product. Other tools use average pricing across procedures and providers to calculate estimated pricing that may or may not match what patients actually will pay when using services.[7]

When built by an insurer or employer, price transparency tools generally focus just on the out-of-pocket costs for plan enrollees, which is related to the total prices negotiated by the insurer on behalf of an employer, mainly for in-network providers. Because these prices are usually confidential, the prices identified for enrollees in one employer-sponsored plan cannot be assumed to be relevant for enrollees in different insurance arrangements. Thus, private-sector transparency tools usually are tailored to the specific parameters of a single insurance plan and thus have been too narrow to this point to improve the functioning of the entire market. That may change when new federal rules are implemented starting in 2023 (as discussed below).

States. As of March 2017, 28 states had passed price transparency laws of various types.[8] Some of these laws require providers to make pricing information available in certain formats to allow for the production of comparison reports. Others require service providers, when asked by patients (or, in some cases, only uninsured patients), to disclose their prices before providing care.

The most prominent state initiatives are those tied to all-payer claims databases (APCDs). As of March 2018, 16 states had up-and-running APCDs, with another four in various stages of development.[9]

APCDs are repositories of medical and pricing data pulled from insurance claims paid by Medicaid, Medicare, and state-regulated insurance plans. States use APCDs for various purposes, including identifying trends relevant to public health efforts, comparing state Medicaid program spending for specific services with costs reported by private coverage, identifying patterns of prescription drug abuse, and lowering costs by targeting services with abnormal use patterns (such as pockets of excessive reliance on emergency room services).[10]

Some states have taken the additional step of using their APCDs to build price transparency tools for their residents, including through publicly accessible websites. Importantly, because APCDs include the actual prices paid by insurers for services, rather than the list prices hospitals and other providers make available, they allow for more accurate estimation of costs for consumers.

Although APCDs house significant amounts of pricing data, it remains difficult to apply those prices to patient-specific insurance designs. Further, accurately estimating what consumers will pay for a given service usually requires knowledge of a patient's year-to-date spending. To avoid this complexity, most states provide only average pricing information to give consumers a sense of the relevant pricing factors without guaranteeing that the price information is predictive of what they will pay.

The exception is New Hampshire, which built a transparency tool that allows residents to get real-time price estimates based on their insurance plans and potential service providers. While analysts consider New Hampshire's website the most advanced of the state-based tools, it is resource-intensive to provide accurate pricing in an environment with ever-changing insurance plan designs, and New Hampshire has found it challenging to keep up with the modifications.[11]

The Supreme Court also curtailed the effectiveness and reach of APCDs in *Gobeille v. Liberty Mutual Insurance Company*.[12] In that ruling, the court held that states lack the authority to compel employers with self-insured plans to submit their medical claims data to state-administered APCDs because the Employee Retirement Income Security Act (ERISA) exempts these plans from state regulation. Consequently, pricing data for the 60 percent of working Americans (and their families) who are enrolled in self-insured employer plans are omitted from the databases, thus undermining their accuracy and usefulness.[13]

The Federal Government. Extracting meaningful price information from the health sector is an unusual reform initiative because at the national level, both parties support it, even in the face of intense opposition from the affected hospitals and insurers.

The Obama administration began the process by forcing more price disclosure by hospitals in accordance with a provision enacted in the

Affordable Care Act (ACA). The Trump administration followed this up with significant new requirements on both facilities and insurers. The Biden administration has signaled it plans to stay the course with this agenda and may expand on it in the future.

The new federal requirements began with a modest first step, which forced hospitals to post their pricing information online, effective in 2014. Hospitals responded most often by placing their "chargemasters" on their official websites. Chargemasters are the list prices hospitals assign to the voluminous billing codes used for insurance payments and are usually well in excess of the prices paid by insurers, or even most uninsured consumers. Even though the information was irrelevant for most patients, many hospitals resisted disclosing it, and compliance was uneven.

The Trump administration started by imposing a requirement, effective in 2019, that hospitals post their chargemasters in formats that allow for automated capture and processing. While this may seem insignificant, it has opened up new possibilities for technology firms to mine the data and identify potential sources of savings for payers and consumers.

Far more consequential changes, promulgated in a 2019 rulemaking and going into effect in January 2021, are now rolling out, albeit unevenly.[14] Effective with these new rules, hospitals must post online, in a readable format, pricing information across a number of relevant dimensions:

- Pricing as reflected in hospital chargemasters,

- Pricing that is used when individuals pay out of pocket for services,

- Contractual pricing that has been negotiated with insurers, and

- The minimum and maximum prices paid by insurers for a hospital's services (with the identities of the insurance plans removed).

Further, hospitals are required to disclose pricing in a consumer-friendly format, available online through a pricing tool, for 300 common services that are amendable to comparison shopping. The Centers for Medicare & Medicaid Services (CMS) has identified 70 of the services that must be on this list, and hospitals are free to select the other 230.[15]

Although hospitals were required to comply with these new disclosure terms starting in January 2021, many have not yet done so. One early 2021 survey of the country's 102 largest hospitals found that only 34 percent had complied with the requirement to disclose all insurer-specific rates in a machine-readable format.[16]

One reason hospital price disclosure remains uneven is the low penalty for noncompliance. Under the Trump administration rule, hospitals could be fined up to $300 per day when they are found to be in violation of the disclosure requirements, which, over a year, would total $109,500.[17] That was not a significant penalty for many facilities that have annual revenue of tens of millions of dollars.

The Biden administration has moved forward with a stricter penalty. For hospitals with more than 30 beds, a new rule will impose a maximum fine of $2 million annually.[18]

In October 2020, the Trump administration also finalized new disclosure rules for the health insurance industry. Beginning in 2023, insurers will be required to make available price comparison tools that can provide precise out-of-pocket cost implications for individual customers. To begin, the tool must cover 500 common services, and then it will be extended to all coverage in 2024.[19]

The new rules that have been promulgated in recent years to force more pricing disclosure may prove valuable, but they have limitations that likely will inhibit their effectiveness too. In particular, the rules imposed on hospitals affect only physicians who are directly employed by the facilities. Physicians with independent practices are exempt, which means the pricing from many hospitals will be partial and not cover the full cost of caring for a patient.

Further, the rules do not define shoppable services in ways that match the typical consumer's experience. Patients might price shop more if it were easy to compare prices for the full bundle of services needed to address their condition. For instance, when needing a common surgery, patients would want to know the all-in price of care. The federal rules issued during the Trump administration fell short of taking that step.

Congress tried to make a correction in the No Surprise Act of December 2020, which had as its primary objective protecting consumers from high out-of-network bills but also advanced price transparency. A key provision requires all providers of medical services to work with affiliated facilities and clinicians to calculate all-in pricing information for full bundles of care. The providers of care must work with all the relevant parties to deliver good-faith estimates of the full prices they will be charging for their services.

The law called for implementation of this provision effective in January 2022, but the Biden administration has announced a delay in enforcing it, to January 2023.[20]

Limited Price Shopping to Date

Several studies in recent years have examined current price transparency efforts and found their effect on consumer price shopping and overall costs to be minimal.[21] As noted, a recent survey showed that only 13 percent of consumers had attempted to ascertain the cost of any of the care they had received in advance, and only 3 percent had attempted to compare pricing from alternative suppliers before seeking out care.[22]

Further, price shopping does not appear to be denting costs even in plans that advertise and encourage transparency tools. The California Public Employees' Retirement System engaged an industry leader in price transparency technology, Castlight, to build a price-shopping tool for its health insurance enrollees starting in 2014. The tool compared prices for in-network outpatient services that lend themselves to consumer-driven decision-making, including physician office visits, lab tests, and imaging services. Only 12 percent of eligible enrollees used the tool, despite much effort by the plan to promote its use, and its effect on overall spending was negligible. Some patients saved modestly on imaging costs but not enough to make a difference in overall spending by the insurance plan.[23]

A recent study interviewed consumers about their views on price shopping, and the results are illuminating.[24] Many consumers simply forget to price shop before getting care because it is still a novel concept in health care. Time and repetition could lead more consumers to automatically consider price shopping in the future, but that is not certain. Further, as noted previously, even with rising deductibles, many patients correctly deduce that price shopping will not lower their total costs because they have satisfied, or will satisfy, their plan deductibles even if they seek out some lower-cost providers early in the year. Once they satisfy their deductibles, they are price insensitive when getting services.

Some consumers are skeptical of shopping because they believe the prices quoted by competing suppliers will not be comparable because of variability in the services included in the prices. For instance, a patient might be quoted prices for a procedure by two competing physicians, but one quote might include lab tests, and the other may exclude them.

Many patients also report that price is less important to them than are the relationships they have with their personal physicians. They rely on those physicians to guide them through the care delivery system, with less attention to the prices of the care recommended for them.

An Instructive Model

Because the use of pricing by average consumers to make care decisions is so uncommon in US health care, there is some skepticism about the potential benefits from disclosing more usable information. An example of how pricing already puts downward pressure on costs helps illustrate the potential of better information and the form that information should take to be most useful.

Certain segments of the Amish and Mennonite religious communities that live in sections of Indiana, Ohio, and Pennsylvania go without some modern conveniences, including the purchase and use of health insurance to pay for medical care.[25] But even without insurance, these communities participate fully in the medical care system and have developed a process for pooling their resources to pay directly for care, in cash, in lieu of traditional insurance coverage.

As they have gained experience as purchasers, the leaders of these communities have become sophisticated in their negotiations with providers of medical services.[26] In particular, they have developed a deep appreciation for getting, in advance of needing actual care, clear, all-in pricing from competing suppliers of services.[27]

One hospital system in Pennsylvania has provided to Amish and Mennonite communities a list of 300 relatively common medical interventions with associated cash prices.[28] The prices include all the costs associated with caring for the patients, with no additional charges or surprise bills after the fact. It took one hospital system nine months to determine the appropriate all-in prices for some of the services on the list because it had never attempted to determine pricing in this fashion before and its accounting systems were not set up to allow for an easy assessment of the relevant input costs.

Many employers and insurers represent large groups of consumers, too, but their objectives and levels of control are different from those of the Amish and Mennonite leaders. For the most part, employers and insurers have as a first objective satisfying the preferences of their plan enrollees, and those enrollees tend to resist restrictions on their choices of care providers. Moreover, the Amish and Mennonite leaders are highly sensitive to costs because they pay for care without any assistance from the government. By contrast, employer-paid health care is heavily subsidized through federal tax law, which undermines the incentive for cost control.[29] Further, enrollees in job-based coverage are price sensitive only to the point when they have fully paid their deductibles.

The Amish and Mennonite example points toward two basic lessons. First, providers of medical services can produce clear pricing when it is required of them, and there is value in forcing them to do so instead of using technology to assemble estimated prices from lists of procedural codes. Most price transparency tools try to help consumers by working with the data that are already available instead of forcing the providers to provide new pricing for packages of services that are designed with boundaries that are useful for consumers.

Second, even usable pricing will be relevant only if those making decisions about where and when to get care bear the cost consequences of their choices. For the Amish and Mennonites, the leaders have that incentive and act accordingly. In a consumer-driven system, the patients need to have strong incentives to care about the prices of the services they use irrespective of the design of their insurance plans.

The Rationale and Framework for Federal Leadership

While some patients could gradually become more accustomed to using price tools as they gain experience, the numerous barriers to a stronger consumer role in medical care make it unlikely that comparison shopping will become routine and effective without fundamental changes to how the market operates.

For the Amish and Mennonite communities, their leaders imposed a structure that allowed for effective price shopping as a group. The federal government needs to do something similar on behalf of all US consumers.

Federal leadership is necessary because no other entity can fix the problem. The private sector can develop innovative approaches to price transparency, but it is too fragmented and disorganized to impose a systemic solution. Further, insurers and employers have incentives that reinforce the current, unsatisfactory status quo.

Some states are making progress with APCDs, but their price transparency tools are insufficiently refined to make a difference. Moreover, states have limited regulatory reach, as they do not control Medicare or the self-insured plans governed by ERISA.

The limited effectiveness of price transparency efforts in today's market should temper expectations of what stronger federal leadership can deliver. Nonetheless, there is sufficient evidence of price sensitivity among consumers, when the circumstances are right, to provide optimism about what might be accomplished with a better and more far-reaching set of rules.[30]

The federal government should focus its efforts on two steps that could intensify price competition: populating the market with pricing for standardized services and interventions and universal reference-based payments by insurers.

A Focused Intervention

The market for medical care is now being flooded with pricing information from providers, as government rules and employer plan requirements compel price disclosure by hospitals, physicians, and others. Most of this information is not useful for consumers, however, because it comes in formats that do not allow for comparison price shopping. Further, some of the pricing data are only available to certain plan enrollees and thus have limited potential to control overall costs.

As discussed previously, some states are attempting to provide tools that allow all their residents to price shop for care. But, so far, those efforts cover only a small portion of the nation's population and have limited value even within the states that have developed them because they mainly provide average prices, not actual pricing for consumers, and they exclude provider data associated with self-insured employers.

The federal government should take and accelerate its leadership role in the price transparency effort by requiring all providers to disclose meaningful, consumer-friendly pricing based on the following framework.

Standardized Pricing

Although some medical care is not amenable to price shopping, nearly half is, as noted previously. Price shopping is possible when (1) the care patients need is packaged into discrete, self-contained purchases and (2) there is sufficient time to make price and quality comparisons before deciding when and where to get services. Services and procedures that can be scheduled by the patient are usually amenable to price comparisons.

Building the List. The federal government would greatly facilitate price shopping in health care by assembling (and continuously updating) a pricing list that all facilities and practitioners must contribute to by disclosing what they will charge and working with other providers to build all-in pricing for full episodes of care.

Standardization is essential for meaningful pricing of medical care. Robust price shopping by consumers will be possible only when apples-to-apples comparisons can be made with minimal effort. Even small differences in the services provided by competing suppliers will undermine the effects of price disclosure because consumers will be unable to assign dollar values to the differences in covered services. Therefore, the federal government should provide a detailed and complete description of the clinical services that must be included within each item on the standardized pricing list. The goal should be to ensure that consumers, when making purchase decisions, get all the appropriate care they need to address whatever it is that is the focus of the service or intervention.

The standardized list should of course include primary care, diagnostics, and laboratory services, but it should reach well beyond those services too. For primary care, the government should include not only discrete fee-for-service (FFS) care but also standardization for services covered in monthly fee models (sometimes called "direct primary care"). Physicians not participating in direct primary care would not be required to provide pricing in this manner. However, for those physicians who do provide a direct care option, they should be required to provide pricing for a standard model of this care, as defined in the federally issued list. For instance, the standard option might include no cost sharing for office visits, unlimited electronic communications (by email and phone), and free preventative care (such as vaccinations). Direct primary care providers would be allowed to offer other monthly fee packages so long as one of them complied with the federally defined standard option.

In primary care, there also should be standardized packages of pediatric and obstetric services, including (for those who want to offer it) a monthly fee model for children and a fixed fee covering the entirety of a pregnancy (but not childbirth itself, which can be priced separately). Similarly, practitioners caring for patients with chronic conditions (such as those with diabetes and heart disease) should be required to post prices for standardized disease management services, both on a FFS basis and in a monthly fee model. Again, the federal government should carefully specify the full range of services required in the monthly fee option.

Beyond primary care, the list should cover other common services and clinical interventions, such as natural and C-section childbirths, joint replacement surgery, and other common surgeries (e.g., repairing a torn labrum in the shoulder). The prices for these services should cover the full episode of care and all the associated services, including post-surgery follow-up and rehabilitation. There should be no surprise bills after the care is provided.

The standardized list could go still further and include other common clinical interventions that allow for discrete pricing and, at least in certain circumstances, consumer decision-making. A good starting point for these items is the 300 discrete packages of care priced by the medical community for Amish and Mennonite patients. In addition, the federal government is pursuing bundled payment initiatives within Medicare, which replaces FFS payments with single, episode-based payments for relatively common medical procedures.[31] These, too, could be added to a standardized pricing list. Some private-sector insurers and employers also are using bundled payments to compensate providers and could contribute their recommended entries.[32]

Required Participation. The federal government should require all providers to participate in this pricing effort, through Medicare regulations. The majority of hospitals, physicians, and other providers accept Medicare patients because the financial loss from opting out would be significant. Current law allows CMS to stipulate requirements for Medicare participation, and compliance with this price transparency effort should be one of the obligations because of its importance to the fair treatment of patients, including those enrolled in Medicare.[33]

Providers would be required to post prices only for services or interventions on the standardized list that are relevant to their clinical focus. For services that involve multiple parties (such as those that entail hospital care and services from more than one physician specialist), providers should be required to participate in coordinated pricing, even if that means establishing contractual relationships that would not exist absent this requirement.

Walk-Up Availability. The prices posted by providers for the services and interventions on the standardized list should be considered walk-up prices available to all consumers. (This would be a more liberalized definition of who is eligible to pay it than is provided in the No Surprises Act.) That is to say, these are the prices consumers would be allowed to pay irrespective of their insurance status. These prices would not preclude providers from maintaining separately negotiated rates with insurance plans, which the enrollees in those plans would always have the right to access if they are more favorable than the walk-up prices available to all consumers.

Pricing for Medicare Patients. The government should require providers to establish separate pricing for two groups of consumers: those not eligible for Medicare and those eligible and enrolled in the program. This differentiation would allow for a major risk factor (age and disability) to be reflected in the overall prices charged for the services and would facilitate incorporation of the prices charged for Medicare patients into a Medicare-specific reference-based pricing model (described below).

Handling Risk. Fixed-sum payments for medical care always raise concerns about risk differentiation. Service providers worry they will attract patients with higher-than-average risk profiles, which would prevent them from offering prices for their services that are as low as those posted by competitors. While the concern is legitimate, risk-adjusting payments for individual medical services would add significant and needless complexity to the initiative.

The negative effects of risk segmentation can be minimized in two ways. First, as mentioned, providers would be allowed to set separate pricing for Medicare-eligible and non-Medicare-eligible patients, which should reduce the magnitude of risk differences among providers. Second, providers will be free to set pricing at whatever level is necessary to ensure they can provide appropriate services to their patients within their available resources. Providers with a healthier-than-average patient population, and lower prices, are likely to attract more patients including those with higher-risk profiles, which may force upward price adjustments over time.

The government might also consider allowing differential pricing based on the ages of patients for some of the services on the federal list. For instance, providers might be allowed to set a price for hip replacements for those age 50–64 that is higher than the price charged for those under age 50. Pricing services, when it is salient, based on age would build into the pricing system an important determinant of risk—the patient's age—and thus lessen the likelihood that some providers would be undercompensated when taking on higher-risk patients.

The Insurance Role: Reference-Based Pricing

A program of mandatory reference pricing by all insurers would multiply the benefits of a standardized pricing list.[34] Reference pricing is the practice some insurers and employers use to provide strong incentives to patients to use lower-cost, higher-value care. In a typical design, the insurer examines the prices charged by competing providers for a standardized intervention, such as hip replacement surgery, and sets the amount of insurance reimbursement based on those posted prices.

For instance, reference pricing could use the average of the submitted prices to determine what an insurance plan will pay, or it could use the lowest or second-lowest priced option. The insurance plan's enrollees are usually free to select any provider offering the service. However, the plan payment is fixed at the reference price and does not change based on the price charged by the patient's selected provider. Patients thus have strong incentives to select lower-cost providers; otherwise, they must pay out of pocket for any price differential above the reference amounts.

Reference pricing is a proven strategy for controlling costs. Studies of various versions of the concept have documented savings ranging from 14 to 32 percent relative to spending for the same services without a reference-pricing design. With reference pricing, consumers migrate toward lower-priced options. Moreover, and perhaps more importantly, the providers of the services covered by a reference-pricing scheme lower their prices in response to the competitive pressures these plan designs impose on the market.[35]

The creation of a federally designed reference-pricing scheme would open an opportunity to vastly expand the practice in commercial and publicly sponsored insurance.

Requirements on Commercial Insurers. The federal government should require commercial insurers to incorporate reference pricing on all the services and interventions on the federally determined standardized pricing list. Insurers would be free to continue to negotiate rates directly with in-network providers, and enrollees in their plans would have access to those providers at those negotiated rates. However, the insurers also should be required to disclose standardized prices on all services on the federal list. The amounts for each insurer should be based, at a minimum, on the average amount paid by the insurer when supplied by in-network providers. (Insurers would be allowed to set reference amounts above the required minimum payment amounts.) With the minimum reference payments tied to average in-network rates, insurers would be protected from losses from their enrollees selecting providers irrespective of network status.

The most straightforward path to implementing this requirement would be to amend current federal laws regulating the commercial insurance market. In the ACA, the federal government created minimum standards for commercial insurance sold in state-regulated markets. Congress should update those standards to require all qualifying insurers to participate in the reference pricing program. In addition, the federal government regulates self-insured plans through ERISA; it too could be amended to extend reference-based pricing to the entire employer-sponsored market.

The reference amounts payable by insurers should be disclosed publicly to make that a point of plan differentiation in the market.

Consumer Incentives. Reference payments work because they give consumers a strong incentive to avoid providers that will leave them with high out-of-pocket costs, which in turn leads the providers to lower their prices to avoid erosion of their market share. Thus, the consumer role is crucial. A federal reference pricing initiative must require consumers to shoulder the costs of choosing high-cost care and reward them with the benefits when they migrate to lower-cost options. In particular, when consumers choose options with posted prices below the reference amounts payable by their insurers, the insurers must be required to provide to the consumers the excess in the form of a cash payment.

It might seem unlikely that an insurer would have in-network rates that would push their reference payments above the prices charged by unaffiliated providers, but that is not a sure thing. In today's market, with so much opaqueness and dysfunction, it is not out of the question that some out-of-network providers are, or could be, less expensive than those in insurers' preferred networks. Moreover, in the new market dynamic that disclosed pricing and reference payments would create, providers would have strong incentives to lower their prices to attract patients. That might be enough to push pricing for some of them below the in-network rates negotiated by insurers.

Implementation of a Shared Savings Scheme in Medicare. Medicare enrollees typically do not face deductibles that match those of commercial insurance plans. Current law requires a patchwork of expensive cost sharing (including separate deductibles for in-patient hospital stays and physician services), but most beneficiaries are either enrolled in a Medicare Advantage plan, with lower cost-sharing requirements, or have supplemental insurance that covers expenses not paid by Medicare. Still, a federal effort aimed at promoting price transparency and a stronger role for consumers would be highly relevant in the Medicare context too.

In traditional Medicare, the government does not negotiate pricing with hospitals, physicians, and other providers of medical services. Instead, the government bases what it will pay for services on a series of complex regulations that get updated periodically—and often annually. In most cases, these regulated rates are below what would be charged by providers in an unregulated market. Further, Medicare does not have in-network and out-of-network providers as that concept is implemented in commercial insurance. Instead, hospitals and physicians that agree to participate in Medicare are all paid based on the same regulations, and most providers fall into this category.

Even so, reference pricing is still a promising reform for Medicare because it would reveal the instances when the government is paying above the prices that would apply in a competitive market. A Medicare reference pricing scheme should be built on calculated reference amounts tied to current regulated rates. The government would need to take the current FFS payments and translate them into pricing for the services covered in the standardized list. (The government should make these calculations annually and post them as part of the regulatory process.)

Medicare beneficiaries enrolled in the traditional FFS program should have the right to get services from providers based on the Medicare-specific pricing required as part of the standardized list. Medicare beneficiaries would not be at risk of paying higher costs because they could always get the services included in the standardized list at Medicare's regulated FFS rates, with no added costs due to higher prices stipulated by the providers.

In other words, Medicare's current payment systems provide a ceiling on the expenses faced by beneficiaries.

However, some providers could post Medicare-specific pricing for services on the federal pricing list that would be below the calculated reference amounts tied to Medicare's payment regulations. In these cases, Medicare beneficiaries should share in the savings (a reasonable amount would be half the total) that would occur from seeking out lower-cost care.

It would not be appropriate to provide all the savings to the beneficiaries because, unlike payments by commercial insurers, the reference amounts paid by Medicare are difficult to modify in the short term, as doing so involves a lengthy and cumbersome regulatory process. Consequently, if the government is overpaying for some services, a Medicare reference pricing scheme would expose the overpayment and allow it to be exploited by some enterprising providers that set their prices below the reference amounts. The beneficiaries should benefit from the savings when this occurs, as should the taxpayers financing Medicare.

As in the commercial market, Congress should put the Medicare reference pricing program into law, to ensure the provider community sees it as a permanent reform around which it can plan its business strategies. However, CMS also has authority under current law to test payment models in the Medicare program to determine if they reduce program costs without lowering the quality of care provided to the beneficiaries. Testing a Medicare reference pricing model would be an appropriate use of that authority and could proceed quickly without further action in Congress.

Would It Work?

It is reasonable to question whether this approach to price transparency would make much of a difference. Today, health plans secure discounted rates with a preferred network, and plan enrollees have strong incentives to stay in that network to avoid unexpected costs. Consumers assume that out-of-network providers are unlikely to offer them reduced out-of-pocket costs compared to what they pay for services from their insurers' participating network of facilities and clinicians. Consequently, they rarely bother to ascertain prices before getting needed services.

Standardized pricing and reference payments are designed to pave the way for disruption of this status quo by lowering barriers to vigorous competition in the medical services market. An entrepreneurial provider could capture market share by breaking away from the insurance-driven networks and offering walk-up prices that are lower than the prices negotiated by competitors tied to insurance plans. The prices offered by enterprising facilities and clinicians would be publicly available and easily compared to prices offered by competitors because of the standardization of what is being priced.

Further, insurers would be obligated to make payments to out-of-network providers at their prevailing in-network rates, which would also be publicly available information. Consumers would thus be armed with easily obtainable information that would allow them to pocket 100 percent of the savings from any provider able to offer pricing below the prevailing in-network rates paid by insurers. The incentives would be fully aligned with rewarding service suppliers that would be willing to offer low prices, which would increase the pressure on competitors to lower their prices as well, in terms of both what they agree to with insurers and their posted walk-up prices for out-of-network consumers.

A Promising, If Partial, Reform

Not all medical services are amenable to consumer price shopping, but a significant portion could be, under the right circumstances.

In recent years, there have been many efforts, public and private, aimed at improving the transparency of pricing for medical services so consumers can make better decisions about where and when to get care. Some of those efforts are providing valuable information to certain segments of the market. Overall, however, these initiatives are too small and fragmented to make a real difference in overall cost trends.

Further, the broader market will not self-correct and spontaneously become more accommodating of an active consumer role because current incentives and public polices reinforce the status quo. The only entity with the capacity to push the market in a new direction is the federal government.

The government could support a more active role for consumers by forcing those providing medical care to patients to disclose pricing for all care that might reasonably be amenable to comparison shopping. Those prices could then be incorporated into insurance plan design to give patients strong incentives to seek out low-cost, high-quality providers and thus reduce their out-of-pocket costs. Over time, the combination of clear pricing for standardized services and the use of those prices in a reference payment system would finally allow consumers to become a powerful force for a higher-value medical care.

Notes

1. In 2018, 46 percent of the privately insured population under age 65 was enrolled in a high-deductible health plan (HDHP), up from 17 percent in 2007. Paul Fronstin and Edna Dretzka, "Consumer Engagement in Health Care: Findings from the 2018 EBRI/ Greenwald & Associates Consumer Engagement in Health Care Survey," Employee Benefit Research Institute, December 20, 2018, https://www.ebri.org/docs/default-source/ebri-issue-brief/ebri_ib_468_cehcs-20dec18.pdf. For an example of the case for HDHPs in combination with health savings accounts (HSAs), see John C. Goodman, "HSAs Force Health Care Providers to Compete," *San Francisco Chronicle*, September 29, 2012, https://www.sfgate.com/opinion/article/HSAs-force-health-providers-to-compete-3905150.php.

2. Zarek C. Brot-Goldberg et al., "What Does a Deductible Do? The Impact of Cost-Sharing on Health Care Prices, Quantities, and Spending Dynamics" (working paper, National Bureau of Economic Research, Cambridge, MA, October 2015), https://www.nber.org/papers/w21632.pdf.

3. In 2003, Congress created HSAs, which facilitated the shift to HDHPs. Employers offering HDHPs can contribute to HSAs on behalf of their employees, and HSA balances can then be used to pay for expenses, including deductibles, not covered by insurance. Although the HSA legislation helped accelerate the shift to HDHPs, not all HDHP enrollees also have HSAs. In 2016, about 58 percent of HDHP enrollees also had an HSA. See Jeffrey T. Kullgren et al., "A Survey of Americans with High-Deductible Health Plans Identifies Opportunities to Enhance Consumer Behavior," *Health Affairs* 38, no. 2 (March 2019), https://www.healthaffairs.org/doi/abs/10.1377/hlthaff.2018.05018.

4. Ateev Mehrotra et al., "Americans Support Price Shopping for Health Care, but Few Actually Seek Out Price Information," *Health Affairs* 36, no. 8 (August 2017), https://www.healthaffairs.org/doi/pdf/10.1377/hlthaff.2016.1471.

5. Mercer, "Cost Transparency Missing Link in Health Care Consumerism," January 28, 2015, https://www.mercer.us/our-thinking/healthcare/cost-transparency-missing-link-in-health-care-consumerism.html.

6. Paul Keckley, "Price Transparency in Healthcare: What We've Learned, What's

Ahead," Keckley Report, July 9, 2018, https://www.paulkeckley.com/the-keckley-report/2018/7/9/price-transparency-in-healthcare-what-weve-learned-whats-ahead.

7. For an example of a misestimate, see John Tozzi, "Priced Out of Health Insurance, Americans Rig Their Own Safety Nets," Bloomberg, August 22, 2018, https://www.bloomberg.com/news/features/2018-08-22/priced-out-of-health-insurance-americans-rig-their-own-safety-nets.

8. National Council of State Legislatures, "Enacted State Legislation: Transparency and Disclosure of Health Costs," March 2017, http://www.ncsl.org/research/health/transparency-and-disclosure-health-costs.aspx#Legislation.

9. Katie Gudiksen, "Are APCDs the Solution to Price Transparency in Healthcare?," Source on Healthcare Price & Competition, April 16, 2018, https://sourceonhealthcare.org/are-apcds-the-solution-to-price-transparency-in-healthcare/.

10. California Health Care Foundation, "The ABCs of APCDs: How States Are Using Claims Data to Understand and Improve Care," November 8, 2018, https://www.chcf.org/publication/the-abcs-of-apcds/.

11. Joel Ario and Kevin McAvey, "Transparency in Health Care: Where We Stand and What Policy Makers Can Do Now," Health Affairs Forefront, July 11, 2018, https://www.healthaffairs.org/do/10.1377/hblog20180703.549221/full/.

12. Gregory D. Curfman, "All-Payer Claims Databases After *Gobeille*," Health Affairs Forefront, March 3, 2017, https://www.healthaffairs.org/do/10.1377/hblog20170303.058995/full/.

13. Kaiser Family Foundation, "Employer Health Benefits: 2018 Annual Survey," October 2018, http://files.kff.org/attachment/Report-Employer-Health-Benefits-Annual-Survey-2018. Some health policy analysts have recommended that Congress amend the Employee Retirement Income Security Act to make it clear that states have the authority to obtain claims data from self-insured employers. See Henry Aaron et al., "Letter to the Honorable Lamar Alexander on Slowing the Rate of Increase of Health Care Costs," Brookings Institution, March 1, 2019, https://www.brookings.edu/wp-content/uploads/2019/03/AEI_Brookings_Letter_Attachment_Cost_Reducing_Health_Policies.pdf.

14. Chris Wheeler and Russ Taylor, "New Year, New CMS Price Transparency Rule for Hospitals," Health Affairs Forefront, January 19, 2021, https://www.healthaffairs.org/do/10.1377/hblog20210112.545531/full/.

15. Centers for Medicare & Medicaid Services, "10 Steps to Making Public Standard Charges for Shoppable Services," https://www.cms.gov/files/document/steps-making-public-standard-charges-shoppable-services.pdf.

16. Nisha Kurani et al., "Early Results from Federal Price Transparency Rule Show Difficulty in Estimating the Cost of Care," Peterson-KFF Health System Tracker, April 9, 2021, https://www.healthsystemtracker.org/brief/early-results-from-federal-price-transparency-rule-show-difficultly-in-estimating-the-cost-of-care/.

17. Wheeler and Taylor, "New Year, New CMS Price Transparency Rule for Hospitals."

18. Susan Morse, "Final Rule Ups Financial Penalties to Hospitals That Ignore Price Transparency Regulation," *Healthcare Finance*, November 3, 2021, https://www.healthcarefinancenews.com/news/final-rule-cms-ups-financial-penalties-hospitals-

ignore-price-transparency-regulation.

19. Centers for Medicare & Medicaid Services, "CMS Completes Historic Price Transparency Initiative," press release, October 29, 2020, https://www.cms.gov/newsroom/press-releases/cms-completes-historic-price-transparency-initiative.

20. Centers for Medicare & Medicaid Services, "Requirements Related to Surprise Billing; Part II Interim Final Rule with Comment Period," September 30, 2021, https://www.cms.gov/newsroom/fact-sheets/requirements-related-surprise-billing-part-ii-interim-final-rule-comment-period.

21. For an overview of the limited results of current efforts, see Ateev Mehrotra et al., "Promise and Reality of Price Transparency," *New England Journal of Medicine* 278 (April 2018): 1348–54, https://www.nejm.org/doi/full/10.1056/NEJMhpr1715229.

22. Mehrotra et al., "Americans Support Price Shopping for Health Care, but Few Actually Seek Out Price Information."

23. Sunita Desai et al., "Offering a Price Transparency Tool Did Not Reduce Overall Spending Among California Public Employees and Retirees," *Health Affairs* 36, no. 8 (August 2017), https://www.healthaffairs.org/doi/10.1377/hlthaff.2016.1636.

24. See Hannah L. Semigran et al., "Patient Views on Price Shopping and Price Transparency," *American Journal of Managed Care* 23, no. 6 (June 2017), https://www.ajmc.com/journals/issue/2017/2017-vol23-n6/patients-views-on-price-shopping-and-price-transparency.

25. These communities forgo health insurance because of the belief that it detracts from the responsibility of members of the community to care for each other. There is also a more general aversion to modern advances that are viewed by leaders as undermining the traditional lifestyle of the community. Kristin Rohrer and Lauren Dundes, "Sharing the Load: Amish Healthcare Financing," *Healthcare* 4, no. 4 (December 2016): 92, https://www.ncbi.nlm.nih.gov/pmc/articles/PMC5198134/.

26. Katherine Hempstead and Chapin White, "Plain Talk About Price Transparency," Health Affairs Forefront, March 2019, https://www.healthaffairs.org/do/10.1377/hblog20190319.99794/full/.

27. These religious communities have also built relationships with nontraditional sources of care, including a clinic in Mexico, which caters to their cash-paying approach and offers deep discounts relative to domestic practitioners. See Joel Millman, "How the Amish Drive Down Medical Costs," *Wall Street Journal*, February 21, 2006, https://www.wsj.com/articles/SB114048909124578710.

28. Harris Meyer, "Hospital Develops Package Prices to Lure Cash-Paying Patients," *Modern Healthcare*, February 2, 2019, https://www.modernhealthcare.com/article/20190202/TRANSFORMATION04/190129925/hospital-develops-package-prices-to-lure-cash-paying-patients.

29. The federal tax preference for employer-paid premiums increases costs in those plans by an average of 35 percent. See John F. Cogan, R. Glenn Hubbard, and Daniel P. Kessler, "The Effect of Tax Preferences on Health Spending" (working paper, National Bureau of Economic Research, Cambridge, MA, January 2008), https://www.nber.org/papers/w13767.pdf.

30. Consumers are highly sensitive to price differentials when the amounts involved are significant and the information is presented to them clearly. See James C. Robinson

and Timothy T. Brown, "Increases in Consumer Cost-Sharing Redirect Patient Volumes and Reduce Hospital Prices for Orthopedic Surgery," *Health Affairs* 32, no. 8 (September 2013): 1392–97, https://bcht.berkeley.edu/sites/default/files/reference-pricing-impact.pdf.

31. For a description of one of the federal initiatives, see Centers for Medicare & Medicaid Services, "Bundled Payments for Care Improvement Advanced: Frequently Asked Questions," https://innovation.cms.gov/Files/x/bpci-advanced-faqs.pdf.

32. Joanne Finnegan, "Orthopedic Practice Among the First to Pursue Bundled Payments with Private Payers," Fierce Healthcare, April 20, 2017, https://www.fiercehealthcare.com/practices/orthopedic-practice-among-first-private-groups-to-soon-offer-bundled-payments.

33. See Centers for Medicare & Medicaid Services, "Conditions of Coverage (CfCs) and Conditions of Participations (CoPs)," https://www.cms.gov/Regulations-and-Guidance/Legislation/CFCsAndCoPs/index.html?redirect=/cfcsandcops/.

34. Ateev Mehrotra et al. also recommend using reference-based pricing to bring consumer incentives into more high-cost care. See Mehrotra et al., "Promise and Reality of Price Transparency."

35. Robinson and Brown, "Increases in Consumer Cost-Sharing Redirect Patient Volumes and Reduce Hospital Prices for Orthopedic Surgery."

3

Medicare

Few facilities or practitioners can afford to opt out of Medicare. It is the nation's largest payer of medical claims, and its rules and payment systems drive business planning and operational decisions in all of the nation's major health systems and physician groups.

Because of Medicare's influence, Medicare reforms have effects beyond the program's immediate reach. When Congress changed how Medicare pays for inpatient hospital stays in 1983, by using a lengthy list of diagnoses to establish prospectively determined fees, commercial insurers followed suit, with lasting consequences for the entire industry. Many other Medicare rules have had similarly consequential effects on how care is delivered to all patients, not just those enrolled in the program.

Medicare's centrality means it will be crucial to the success or failure of market incentives as an organizing principle for reform. If market incentives are to become decisive in disciplining costs, Medicare must incorporate them more fully in its design.

While Medicare's influence is extensive, it is not absolute. Private insurers are free to pay more for services than Medicare does (and use any form of reimbursement they find suitable) and manage costs through many different mechanisms that the federal government does not deploy (such as through managed care protocols). Further, medical service providers are not entirely dependent on the government for their revenue and thus have a degree of autonomy that limits federal control.

In addition, not all changes to Medicare have promoted tighter price regulation. In 1982, the program allowed health maintenance organizations (HMOs) to offer Medicare-covered benefits for a fixed monthly payment from the government. That option has evolved into Medicare Advantage (MA), which accounts for 40 percent of program enrollment. In 2010, Congress authorized experimentation with various provider-driven managed care arrangements using payment models that differ from the traditional rules.

Advocates of government-run health care find Medicare's regulations dictating payment terms appealing but its incorporation of some private options less so. Their plan to expand Medicare enrollment into a universal program (Medicare for All) is predicated on using government-administered insurance more heavily than private options.

Market advocates can advance their cause rather substantially by building on existing Medicare provisions that open the program to private incentives and initiatives with strengthened competition and more effective consumer choice. As with previous significant amendments to Medicare, the results would have system-wide implications, with all US health care moving in a market-oriented direction.

Medicare's Multiple Parts: Outdated Insurance and Misleading Trust Funds

It is not necessary to examine and specify all of Medicare's many detailed features to grasp its essence, which is that it is a publicly run, community-rated insurance plan that is heavily subsidized by taxpayers for a population (retirees and the disabled) that would have great difficulty securing health coverage on its own.[1]

The program's basic architecture and the pathways by which it provides insurance coverage for enrollees' medical expenses are important. Advancing market reforms does not require upending this basic design; rather, it requires inserting into it stronger price competition and more effective consumer incentives.

At enactment, Medicare was modeled on the prevailing private-sector insurance plans of the day: not-for-profit Blue Cross Blue Shield coverage for hospitalizations and physician services. Congress also looked to Social Security, enacted three decades earlier, for important design characteristics. Among other things, Medicare was not set up as an insurance plan for the entire population; eligibility is limited to persons who are mostly out of the workforce (or close to retirement): those age 65 and older and the disabled (the same populations eligible for Social Security). It was assumed then, and remains so today, that working Americans and their families would secure insurance at their places of employment or by purchasing coverage in state-regulated markets for individual policies.

Medicare's covered benefits, which are defined in the law, are divided into segments: Part A for hospitalizations and other facility-based services and Part B for physician and ambulatory care. Prescription drug coverage (called Part D) was added in 2003 and is financed similarly to Part B.

The hospital insurance (HI) trust fund is used to track Part A receipts and spending and is constructed like Social Security, with payroll taxes collected from current workers and their employers paying benefits for current retirees (so-called pay-as-you-go financing). Workers "earn" their Part A coverage for themselves and their spouses by paying employment taxes for a specified number of years (usually 10).

When eligible persons enroll in Part A, typically at age 65, they also can enroll voluntarily in Parts B and D by agreeing to monthly premiums covering a portion of their total costs. The balance of Parts B and D expenses, which are tracked in the supplementary medical insurance (SMI) trust fund, is financed by transfers from the Treasury's general fund—that is, taxpayers. At enactment, premiums collected from enrolled beneficiaries were expected to cover 50 percent of total SMI expenses. However, as health inflation escalated in the program's first decade, Congress limited the rate of growth of beneficiary premiums below that of total expenses, which meant a higher burden on taxpayers. Eventually, a new benchmark was set, pegging aggregate beneficiary premiums to 25 percent of total costs, which remains the target today.

Medicare's benefit design, which may have made sense at enactment but now is outdated, leaves the program's enrollees exposed to substantial costs. In Part A, beneficiaries must pay a deductible before coverage begins for inpatient hospital stays ($1,556 in 2022), a co-payment per day ($389 in 2022) for stays between 61 and 90 days, and a higher co-payment per day ($778 in 2022) beyond 90 days. Further, there is a lifetime limit of 60 days for inpatient stays lasting beyond 90 days; when those have been exhausted, the beneficiary is responsible for the full cost of inpatient care. In Part B, the beneficiary must pay out of pocket for a deductible before coverage begins ($233 in 2022) and then 20 percent of the cost of each service received.[2]

Part D has a standard benefit with a $480 deductible in 2022 and a 25 percent beneficiary co-payment for all costs above $480 and below $10,690. Above $10,690, the beneficiary pays 5 percent of costs.[3] Prescription drug plans participating in Part D are authorized to alter the standard cost sharing so long as the total actuarial value of what they are offering is equivalent to the benefit defined by the law.

Medicare's trust funds attract considerable political attention, for understandable reasons. HI relies entirely on tax collections, not subsidies, to meet its obligations, which means it could run short of funds and thus force Congress to take up corrective legislation. In 2021, the Congressional Budget Office (CBO) projected that the HI trust fund would be depleted of reserves in 2026, after which it could not cover 100 percent of benefit claims.[4]

While the impending insolvency of HI can be a powerful motivator and, under the right circumstances, propel sensible reforms forward, it has not always worked that way. Congress's interest is in ensuring Medicare beneficiaries receive coverage of their medical expenses. The path of least political resistance might be to replenish the HI trust fund with changes that cause minimal controversy, even if that means ignoring the fundamental source of the program's financial challenges.

Figure 1 exposes HI's small part in a much larger story of fiscal imbalance. Because the SMI trust fund is financed mainly with transfers from the Treasury, it is perceived as perpetually solvent even though its burden on taxpayers is already immense and will become overwhelming in the coming decades. The 2021 report on the program's financial outlook estimates that these transfers will total $5.6 trillion from 2021 to 2030 alone. By 2050, the annual transfer will equal 2.9 percent of gross domestic product (GDP), up from 0.7 percent in 2000.[5]

The core problem is rapid growth of total Medicare spending, driven by an aging population and escalating costs for services, not an imbalance in HI-only income and outgo. In 1990, total program spending equaled 1.9 percent of GDP; three decades later, it had reached 4.0 percent of GDP. Medicare's trustees expect costs will exceed 5.0 percent of GDP in 2030 and 6.0 percent in 2050.[6]

Figure 1. Total Medicare Spending and Sources of Financing

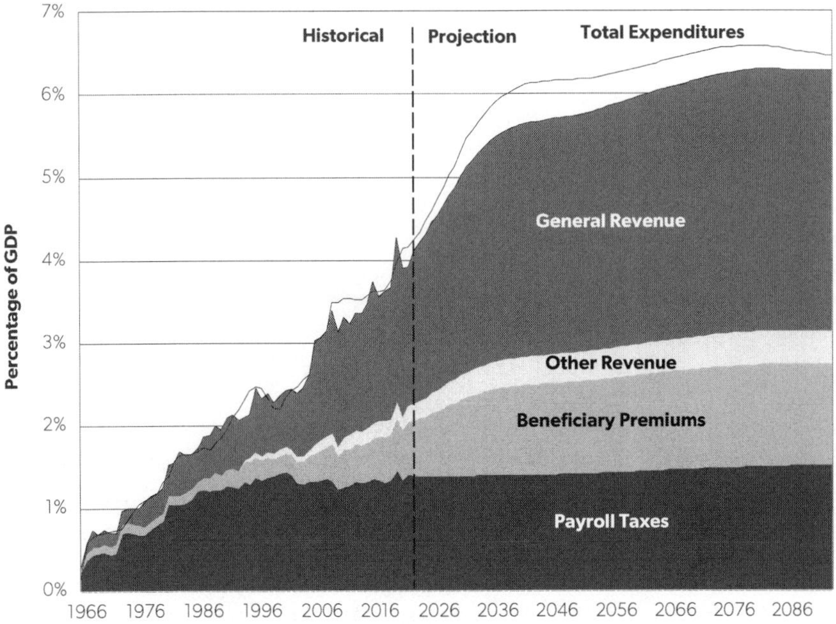

Source: Medicare Trustees, *The 2021 Annual Report of the Boards of Trustees of the Federal Hospital Insurance and Federal Supplementary Medical Insurance Trust Funds*, Centers for Medicare & Medicaid Services, August 2021, https://www.cms.gov/files/document/2021-medicare-trustees-report.pdf.

A Regulatory Colossus

To minimize opposition from powerful lobbies, Medicare was written at enactment to mimic the prevailing fee-for-service (FFS) plans being sold by private insurers in the marketplace. (As noted, these were mainly not-for-profit Blue Cross Blue Shield plans.) The government pledged to pay for services based on "reasonable cost," which in practice meant reimbursing providers for their self-reported expenses along with a standard additional margin.

This passive approach was never going to be sustainable because Medicare was never going to be an ordinary insurance plan. Overnight, it became the nation's largest single insurance plan, by enrollment, and its payments quickly became the most important source of revenue (and growth) for a majority of facilities and practitioners. With Medicare offering an open-ended (and tax-financed) source of funding, the initial payment system, with suppliers unilaterally determining their fees, was a recipe for rapid cost growth and inflationary pressures. Unsurprisingly, Medicare spending escalated far more quickly than the program's actuaries initially projected. From 1967 (the first full calendar year of Medicare coverage) to 1975, program spending grew at an average annual rate of 16.7 percent.[7]

While it did not take long for Congress to recognize it had a Medicare cost problem, its legislative response took several years to gather momentum and has been a continual (and incomplete) work in progress ever since. The intermittent nature of the effort should not be confused with an unclear overall direction. Both Congress and the Centers for Medicare & Medicaid Services (CMS), the agency responsible for administering the program, have pushed for ever more complex and onerous terms in every care setting as conditions for securing reimbursement from Medicare, and the payment amounts themselves are often set through opaque systems that are the subjects of controversy and disputes.

Two amendments stand out in the long transformation of Medicare into the undisputed regulator of all meaningful financial questions when paying for medical services. (See Table 1 for a longer list of significant amendments since 1980.)

First, in 1983, Congress created a new prospective payment system (PPS) for inpatient hospital services that phased out reimbursement based on each hospital's specific cost experiences. The Medicare PPS is built on a foundation of nearly 400 diagnostic-related groups, which are used to adjust a standard national payment for inpatient stays for the clinical complexity of individual cases. There are also adjustments for geographic differences in labor costs and many other factors.[8]

Running Medicare's inpatient PPS required hospitals to build complex billing systems conforming to the government's coding specifications. Over the years, the system has been updated and refined countless times. Because hospitals have invested so heavily in meeting Medicare's regulatory requirements, they are resistant to separate billing systems from other payers. Consequently, private insurers have had little choice but to conform to the terms Medicare has established, and, today, with

Table 1. Significant Medicare Amendments

Year	Reform
1982	Initiation of Medicare HMO Risk Contracting
1983	Hospital Inpatient PPS
1989	Revised Basis for Physician Fees
1990	Standardization of Medigap Insurance Plans
1997	Medicare+Choice Replaces HMO Risk Contracting
2003	Creation of Prescription Drug Benefit (Part D)
2003	Medicare Advantage Replaces Medicare+Choice
2010	Accountable Care Organizations
2015	Medicare Incentive Payment System (for Physician Fees) Replaces Sustainable Growth Rate

Source: Author.

few exceptions, the program's system of paying for inpatient stays is the basis for all such insurance claims. (Although, as noted, commercial plans typically pay a percentage add-on to Medicare's rates.)[9] It follows that when Medicare adjusts its rules, there are cascading effects throughout the entire health sector.

Medicare's regulation of physician fees followed a similar trajectory. In 1989, Congress authorized a new payment system using measures of the time and value of physician services to determine the fees they would be paid (along with geographic adjustments for differences in service-related costs).[10] As with inpatient care, Medicare's new requirements forced the nation's physicians to adopt billing systems that complied with the new, federally determined terms for payment. With this new system in place, private insurers fell into line and adopted Medicare's fee schedule as the starting point for their own claims processing systems.

The physician fee schedule also was tied to a budgeting construct intended to control aggregate spending. The sustainable growth rate

(SGR) was created in 1997 (to replace a predecessor system of spending discipline) and imposed an annual limit on the inflation rate for total fees paid by Medicare, tied to GDP growth. When aggregate spending on physician fees was expected to grow faster than the allowable rate, an automatic cut in per-services fees was supposed to eliminate the breach.

The SGR quickly collided with political reality. The aggregate spending cap was expected to be breached several times in the early 2000s and by large amounts, which would have triggered absolute reductions in per-service physician fees. Congress stepped in repeatedly to override the planned cuts, which made enforcement in subsequent years even more difficult (and politically unlikely). The inevitable abandonment of the discipline came in a 2015 law that stipulated low annual updates in physician fees as a condition of repeal of the device disciplining aggregate spending.[11]

As noted, the government's regulated payment systems are not mandatory for commercial insurers; they are free to set their own terms for financing care. In practice, however, their leverage in the market is usually not sufficient to introduce their own models. Medical care providers build their expensive and complex billing systems around Medicare's rules, and there is an expectation that private insurers will piggyback on this dominant model and not construct altogether different methodologies for paying for services. (This general rule has exceptions.) Mostly, providers negotiate with private payers over an appropriate percentage add-on to Medicare. The effect of this relationship between Medicare and private payers is to further amplify Medicare's already significant influence over the operational characteristics of entities providing medical services.

While the new payment systems for hospital and physician care have had the most far-reaching effects, Medicare's regulatory reach goes well beyond them. CMS has issued a stream of payment rules affecting payments for physician-administered drugs, ambulance services, skilled nursing care (after a hospital stay), outpatient services, laboratory tests, durable medical equipment, and much else. In most instances, Congress and the Medicare bureaucracy have labored to identify relevant data sources to set payments often without the benefit of being able to reference reliable market prices (which are hard to come by in a sector so dominated by insurance payments, subsidies, and regulations).

Once in place, Medicare's payment regulations have become all-important reference points for the sectors they affect and thus targets for interest group pressure campaigns and lobbying in Congress.

Plan Options in the Current Program

Medicare enrollees have coverage options. Presenting them more comprehensively, and with the different premium and cost implications front and center, is central to injecting stronger market incentives into the program.

FFS with and Without Medigap Supplemental Insurance. At enactment, Medicare was designed to be a publicly administered, FFS insurance plan. Generally, providers are paid for each service they render to Medicare patients. CMS operates as the insurance company and has systems in place to process the flood of medical claims submitted by the hospitals, physicians, and others providing services to the enrolled population. (CMS employs contractors to administer these payments.) Medicare FFS is the default option for providing coverage to the program's beneficiaries, and it remains dominant, both in its share of total enrollment and the effect it has on the larger health system. It is mainly through FFS's payment regulations that Medicare exerts influence system-wide.

From the beginning, many Medicare participants found the cost-sharing requirements of FFS unattractive and sought ways to avoid paying out of pocket when using services. Employers stepped in and provided wraparound plans for millions of retired workers. In addition, private insurance plans began selling Medigap policies directly to individuals.

Today, it is more the exception than the rule for Medicare beneficiaries to pay out of pocket for cost sharing. As shown in Figure 2, only 11 percent of Medicare enrollees do not have additional insurance beyond Medicare. Medigap plans cover 22 percent of enrollees, and employer plans cover an additional 18 percent. The private insurance option in Medicare—MA (discussed below)—covers 39 percent of enrollees, and these plans provide, at a minimum, a catastrophic limit on annual expenses and often much lower cost sharing across the board.[12]

Figure 2. Sources of Supplemental Coverage Beyond Medicare's Statutory Benefits for the Noninstitutionalized Population, 2018

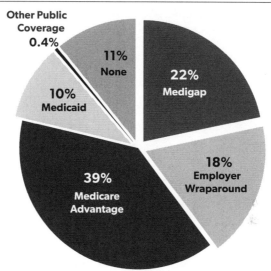

Source: Medicare Payment Advisory Commission, *Health Care Spending and the Medicare Program: A Data Book*, July 2021, https://www.medpac.gov/wp-content/uploads/import_data/scrape_files/docs/default-source/data-book/july2021_medpac_databook_sec.pdf.

In addition to private coverage, 10 percent of Medicare beneficiaries have incomes and assets low enough to qualify for Medicaid, which, in many cases, pays for all expenses not covered by Medicare (along with long-term services and supports).

Supplemental coverage is problematic in an FFS environment. FFS is unmanaged care; if a licensed provider renders a service to a patient, the presumption is that Medicare will pay for it, with minimal review of the clinical value of the intervention. Cost sharing is supposed to ensure the enrollees are cost sensitive so that they self-police their use of services. When Medigap or other insurance fills in what Medicare does not cover, beneficiaries become insensitive to the cost of using more services. One study has estimated Medigap coverage adds more than 20 percent to an individual's expected costs.[13]

Figure 3. MA Enrollment as a Percentage of Total Medicare Enrollment

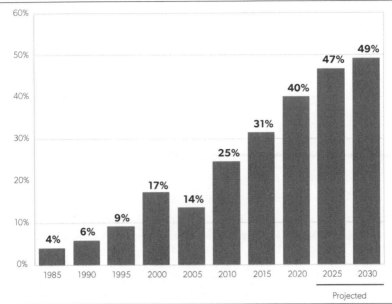

Note: Index of Spending by Year Relative to 2006 = 100
Source: Medicare Trustees, *The 2021 Annual Report of the Boards of Trustees of the Federal Hospital Insurance and Federal Supplementary Medical Insurance Trust Funds,* Centers for Medicare & Medicaid Services, August 2021, https://www.cms.gov/files/document/2021-medicare-trustees-report.pdf.

Medicare Advantage. MA is the private insurance option in Medicare. During the open enrollment season each fall, program beneficiaries can elect to get their Medicare-covered services through these commercial plans instead of through the government-run FFS option. As shown in Figure 3, enrollment in MA has grown steadily over the past 15 years, with commercial insurance now administering Medicare coverage for 40 percent of the program's total census (up from 14 percent in 2005). Current projections show continued strong demand for MA plans in future years, with a forecast that nearly half of all program beneficiaries will be enrolled in these private options by 2030.[14]

MA plans are paid a fixed monthly rate per enrollee (sometimes called "capitation") and are allowed to charge Medicare beneficiaries an additional monthly premium. Many MA plans offer benefits beyond Medicare coverage at no charge to the beneficiaries as incentives for enrollment.

The MA option has its origins in a modest amendment to Medicare in 1982, which introduced "risk contracting" for HMOs. The contention was that paying HMOs' monthly capitated rates, instead of fees for every service rendered, would shift insurance risk from the federal government to private plans and thus improve incentives for cost control. The plans were, and are, required to cover all medically necessary care within the aggregate amount of monthly payments they receive from the federal government and the beneficiaries, which means they have an incentive to eliminate unnecessary expenses and keep their enrollees as healthy as possible.

The risk contracting program has undergone many revisions since 1982, but the basic argument for its inclusion in Medicare has not really changed. It is expected that some privately administered managed care plans will provide coverage more efficiently than FFS will. Thus, they can offer benefits beyond what Medicare covers at little or no extra cost to the beneficiaries and reduce overall government expenses too. Program experience backs up the expectation that MA plans are more efficient than FFS. MA is popular because many Medicare participants can get lower cost sharing and broader coverage without paying the high premiums required by many Medigap insurance plans.

Critics of MA contend it has never reduced the government's costs, and they have a point; for many years, Medicare's payments to MA plans, which are set based on a combination of bids submitted from the plans and administratively determined benchmarks, have exceeded 100 percent of what Medicare would have spent to cover the same beneficiaries directly through FFS. The MA bids reflect what the private plans estimate it would cost to provide benefits defined in Medicare law. For bids below the benchmarks, the MA plans are required to return the excess to their enrollees as reduced cost sharing, premium rebates, or coverage of non-Medicare benefits. MA plans with bids above the benchmarks, which are rare, receive payments from the government equal to the benchmarks and must charge the beneficiaries premiums to cover their additional costs.

Further, there is strong evidence that MA plans receive risk-adjusted payments in excess of the relative risk of their enrollees compared to FFS. The risk-adjustment system is based on assigning diagnoses to patients, which gives the MA plans strong incentives to carefully assess each enrollee for relevant conditions. This incentive is weaker in FFS because payments

Table 2. MA Benchmarks, Bids, and Payments Relative to FFS (Percentage)

	Benchmarks	Bids	Payments
All MA Plans	108	87	101
MA HMOs	108	86	100

Source: Medicare Payment Advisory Commission, *Health Care Spending and the Medicare Program: A Data Book*, July 2021, https://www.medpac.gov/wp-content/uploads/import_data/scrape_files/docs/default-source/data-book/july2021_medpac_databook_sec.pdf.

are not adjusted for risk. The result is an imbalance that overcompensates MA plans.[15]

Congress has been reluctant to implement MA changes that could deliver program savings. For instance, during previous debates, there has been resistance to establishing a neutral competition between MA and FFS by tying payments for both to a competitive bidding model. Doing so might mean enrollment in FFS is more expensive than it is under current law for some beneficiaries (especially those living in high-cost markets), which makes it politically controversial. Consequently, Congress has maintained the policy that the monthly premium for enrollment in FFS will be uniform nationally (and is equal to the premium for enrollment in Part B), which complicates constructing a fair alternative system for paying MA plans.[16]

Even so, program data show that, on average, MA plans are less expensive than FFS is, as shown in Table 2. When measured on providing Medicare-covered services (and not additional benefits), MA plans submitted bids indicating they can do so for just 87 percent of the cost of FFS, and HMO bids suggest they can reduce costs by 14 percent relative to FFS. The actual payments to the MA plans are higher, with the plans required to use the rebates they receive (calculated as a percentage difference between their bids and the relevant benchmarks) as additional coverage and benefits for their enrollees. On a net basis, program payments to MA plans (including the rebates) are above the costs of FFS. Thus, MA is not reducing overall Medicare spending.[17]

One reason MA plans are price competitive with FFS is a little-known provision in current law that diminishes hospitals' leverage to extract pricing concessions. In the case of commercial insurance, medical service providers can require their patients to cover the cost difference between the prices they charge and what insurers pay for out-of-network care. In Medicare, hospitals that refuse to join an MA plan's network can only charge patients the amount that would have been allowed if the person had remained in FFS. In other words, there is no financial advantage to remaining outside of MA plan networks. The provision limiting "balance billing" in this context is intended to protect Medicare beneficiaries, but an additional effect is to substantially increase the ability of MA plans to pay rates for hospital care that track closely with FFS's regulated payments.[18]

Accountable Care Organizations. In the Affordable Care Act, Congress established a third option for receiving Medicare-covered services, through provider-driven managed care plans—labeled accountable care organizations (ACOs).

ACOs were not created to compete with MA or FFS; rather, the objective was to establish a new payment model within FFS that would emphasize high-value care rather than providing more revenue-generating services. Providers affiliated with ACOs continue to be paid based on Medicare FFS's complex rules, but they also can qualify for yearly bonuses if they hold costs below specified benchmarks while meeting quality standards.

The traditional conception of managed care is that it involves providing beneficial care within fixed amounts for an enrolled population, with per capita monthly payments establishing the total budget from which to finance all necessary and medically effective care.

ACOs are different in that they are managed care entities operating in an FFS environment, often without precise data on which patients they are expected to manage. In most cases, there is no enrollment of beneficiaries into the ACOs. Instead, CMS assigns beneficiaries to them based on physician claims data; if the doctor a beneficiary sees most often is affiliated with an ACO, then the beneficiary is automatically assigned to it too. The ACO is then held accountable for the full cost and quality of the care the beneficiary receives.

ACOs have delivered modest savings but generally disappointing overall results. The hope was that they would become catalysts for moving the provision of medical care in the US away from the still-dominant FFS model, which Medicare's size and influence (as the largest single payer of FFS claims) has done much to perpetuate. Instead, providers have joined ACOs in large numbers, but only on the condition that doing so entails little risk and minimal changes in their business plans.

The Prescription Drug Benefit

The 2003 law creating the prescription drug benefit—in a new Medicare Part D—did not conform to the government-administered model that had guided decision-making since 1965. Unlike Parts A and B, coverage for prescription drugs was to be provided entirely by private insurance, not a federally run plan; the law authorized the government to sponsor a fallback option only in markets with insufficient participation by commercial offerings. Further, the government was to have no role in setting drug prices. Instead, premium competition among the private plans was expected to hold down costs.

As it happens, the fallback was an unnecessary backstop. From the start of the benefit in 2006, Medicare beneficiaries have had access to scores of private drug plan offerings in every region of the country.

Like Part B, enrollment in Part D is voluntary; beneficiaries electing the coverage are required to pay a monthly premium for enrollment. Low-income enrollees get additional help from a special assistance provision, and many beneficiaries have access to drug coverage through their former employers or MA plans. Overall, in 2018, 88 percent of Medicare beneficiaries have insurance coverage for their prescription drug expenses, and some portion of those who remain uninsured likely have access to discounted prescriptions through the Department of Veterans Affairs or other public programs.[19]

Part D was designed to inject consumer choice and market discipline into Medicare using a reform framework often called "premium support." Instead of providing coverage directly, the government pays insurers a fixed monthly amount based on submitted bids from the participating plans in each market area. Beneficiaries select from among the offerings during an annual open enrollment season each fall. Importantly, the government's contribution does not increase when Medicare

Figure 4. Part D Average Monthly Premiums, 2006 to 2021

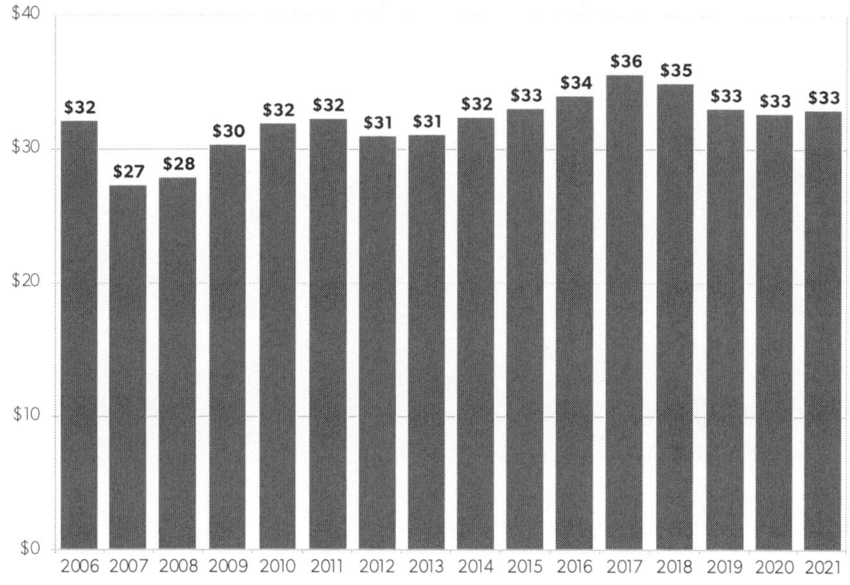

Source: Congressional Research Service, "Medicare Part D Prescription Drug Benefit," December 18, 2020, https://sgp.fas.org/crs/misc/R40611.pdf.

beneficiaries select more expensive plans. Consequently, Part D enrollees have strong incentives to choose low-premium options to minimize their out-of-pocket costs.

The program's focus on controlling premiums through competitive pressure has worked as planned, as shown in Figure 4. Beneficiaries enrolled in Part D paid, on average, roughly the same nominal monthly premium in 2021 ($33) that they did in 2006 ($32).[20]

While impressive, premium restraint does not tell the whole story because some Part D costs do not fall within the premium structure (as discussed in Chapter 7). To encourage plan participation, the benefit was designed to limit the risk for private insurers when a beneficiary's prescription expenses exceed a specified annual amount, set at $10,690 in 2021.[21] Above this threshold, the federal government pays for 80 percent of all costs, with the plans covering 15 percent and the beneficiaries the remaining 5 percent.

Figure 5. Cumulative Nominal Growth of Parts A and B Compared to Part D (2006 to 2020)

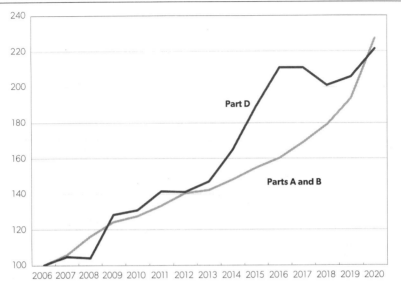

Note: Index of spending by year relative to 2006 = 100.
Source: Medicare Trustees, *The 2021 Annual Report of the Boards of Trustees of the Federal Hospital Insurance and Federal Supplementary Medical Insurance Trust Funds,* Centers for Medicare & Medicaid Services, August 2021, https://www.cms.gov/files/document/2021-medicare-trustees-report.pdf.

This off-loading of insurance risk onto the government has encouraged the Part D plans to negotiate price discounts as large rebates rather than lower list prices because higher pricing pushes more expenses above the catastrophic threshold. In 2020, the share of the government's total per capita spending associated with covering catastrophic expenses was over 80 percent, up from 35 percent in 2010.[22]

Shifting more expenses into the catastrophic range of the benefit undermines the program's overall cost discipline, as the plans are cost sensitive mainly about drug spending they must cover from within the amounts they collect in premiums. Figure 5 shows that overall Part D costs, measured nominally, were 121 percent higher in 2020 compared to 2006, while combined spending on Parts A and B was up 127 percent.[23]

The Absence of Transparent, Market-Driven Pricing and Consumer Incentives

As discussed more fully in Chapter 2, US health care has long been hampered by opaque and irrational pricing, which has made it all but impossible for consumers to play an active role in shopping for lower-cost care.

Medicare suffers from its own unique version of this general problem. While pricing for individual services is available, it is established in federal regulations using administrative data that may bear no relation to the pricing that would occur in a functioning market. Further, even with visibility into the regulated rates, it is still difficult for Medicare enrollees to know in advance of getting care what the all-in price will be for the services they will receive. That is because providers are not required to roll up their charges into pricing bundles covering full episodes of care.

A related problem is the lack of an incentive among program enrollees to price shop, which is a consequence, partially, of explicit federal policies. In the program's early years, beneficiaries' exposure to unexpected bills was a cause of great political controversy. In response, Congress took a series of steps that have insulated most beneficiaries from pricing considerations. Hospitals and physicians that agree to participate in Medicare must accept as payment in full the federal government's regulated rates, which minimizes the cost sharing the beneficiaries owe. Further, whatever expenses patients do face are usually paid by non-Medicare coverage, such as Medigap plans or Medicaid.

Providers are not required to participate in Medicare to receive payment; they can remain "out of network," so to speak. However, if they do, they are also limited in the amounts they can bill to their patients ("balance billing") above what Medicare pays for their services.[24] This requirement further diminishes the incentive for the program's enrollees to consider pricing before accessing services.

The Pivotal Reforms

It will be difficult to inject stronger market discipline into the provision of medical services in the US if Medicare does not lead the way, but the political challenge of reorienting the program away from price regulation toward competition and consumer choice should not be underestimated. Market reforms have been debated frequently over the past three decades, with disappointing results. (An important exception was the adoption of the premium support model for delivering the Part D benefit.) The primary impediment has been a Congress wary of asking Medicare beneficiaries to play a more active role in cost control.

To minimize opposition, reform must be seen as improving the financial status of most beneficiaries, not harming it. That can be done, even as reform lowers the government's overall costs, by sharing a generous portion of the savings from more efficient provision of care with program enrollees.

An effective reform plan will include a number of important changes, falling into four basic categories.[25]

Rationalizing Benefits, Coverage Options, and the Enrollment Process. Medicare has become a confusing and illogical set of benefits, organized into insurance components with separate cost-sharing requirements. Modern insurance plans are not designed with similarly fragmented benefit designs or multiple cost-sharing schemes for enrollees.

Further, the current structure is a counterproductive mix of mandatory (for Part A) and voluntary enrollment (for Parts B and D), with further options to enroll in privately administered MA or Medigap plans. In addition, some beneficiaries are placed into ACOs without their knowledge.

Adding to the complexity is the lack of a system of enrollment across these components that clearly presents the premium consequences of various coverage combinations, which adds to the confusion. Under current processes, it is not a simple matter for beneficiaries to compare the all-in financial implications of the various choices available to them.

Reform should begin with modernization and simplification of the benefit structure and enrollment process. Beneficiaries should be presented with the full range of their benefit options through one government-administered enrollment portal. Through it, they should be able to compare competing approaches for delivering covered services on an apples-to-apples basis and across the three main benefit components, as shown in Table 3.

Table 3. Restructured Choices for Medicare Beneficiaries

Required Medicare-Covered Services	Prescription Drug Coverage	Supplemental Coverage
Traditional FFS	Stand-Alone Part D Plans	Reformed Medigap Options
ACOs	Stand-Alone Part D Plans	ACO-Affiliated Medigap
MA Plans	MA-Affiliated Part D Coverage (MA-PD)	MA-Sponsored Optional Supplements

Source: Author.

Parts A and B should be combined into a single insurance plan, with one deductible and cost-sharing structure designed to encourage cost-effective use of care. There should be no coinsurance for inpatient hospital stays, and the cost sharing should be adjusted to give all beneficiaries protection against high, annual out-of-pocket costs (a "catastrophic cap").

The actuarial value of this redesigned benefit should equal what is required for covered benefits in current Medicare law. (This ensures no increase in federal costs.) Enforcing this neutrality requirement will necessarily mean the upfront, unified deductible will rise to levels that may seem unattractive to the program's enrollees. Nonetheless, the distributional effects of the redesign would be positive, with the sickest beneficiaries getting relief from elimination of coinsurance for hospital stays and limits on their annual out-of-pocket expenses.

Because of its unique design, Part D should remain a separate benefit initially and be integrated gradually into the combined Medicare insurance plan as premium support, as discussed below, is implemented for Parts A and B. One option would be to include Part D in standard coverage on a prospective basis, for new enrollees.

There should be three basic options for getting benefits covered under Parts A and B.

FFS, as administered by the federal government, would remain an enrollment option for all beneficiaries in all regions of the country.

ACOs would become provider-driven managed care plans competing with traditional FFS and MA plans. They would offer the full range of

Medicare-covered services for a fixed monthly premium. Providers participating in the various ACO demonstration models now being tested by CMS should be given time to transition into entities capable of taking on insurance risk and providing organized care to an enrolled patient population. They could contract with other insurance plans to perform functions outside their core competencies. They could pay their affiliated providers on any basis they determine is effective, but, at their discretion, they would be free to continue using Medicare's FFS payment rules.

MA plans would be required to offer all enrollees a package of benefits actuarially equivalent to coverage under Parts A and B, without supplemental benefits (which would be offered separately).

The next component of the benefit scheme would be for prescription drugs. Here, the Part D program would operate much as it does today, with private plans competing for enrollment (and no government-administered option). The Part D benefit package should be updated to lessen the incentive for using rebates for price discounts by requiring the plans to cover more of the expenses above the catastrophic threshold. Beneficiaries opting for enrollment into FFS or an ACO would choose from stand-alone Part D plans, while MA enrollees could accept their MA plan's drug coverage option (which the MA plans would be required to offer) or decline enrollment into Part D.

Finally, Medicare beneficiaries should be allowed to buy supplemental benefits that they self-finance with premium payments, although the available plans should be regulated to prevent private wraparound coverage from driving up public expenses.

For enrollees in FFS, they should be allowed to purchase Medigap coverage—but only in a modified form to make sense in the context of unmanaged care. With FFS insurance, cost sharing at the point of care is an important tool for moderating use of services. As noted, Medigap insurance that fills in all cost sharing drives up FFS costs. Thus, Medigap plans sold to FFS enrollees should not be allowed to fully eliminate cost sharing when patients are using more discretionary services in ambulatory settings. A minimum 10 percent coinsurance payment would provide a financial disincentive for overuse of services.

ACO enrollees should be allowed to purchase Medigap coverage, too, but the ACOs would be required to work with private Medigap plans to provide coverage that works with the managed care practices of the plan. In particular, ACO-affiliated Medigap plans should provide preferential cost sharing only to "in-network" providers, which would create more price sensitivity for out-of-network care.

MA plans attract enrollment today by offering supplemental coverage beyond the benefits required under current Medicare law. With these reforms, they could continue to offer these benefits, but they would be separated from statutorily required Medicare benefits and financed from beneficiary premiums. On a net basis, the effect likely will be similar to what occurs today, with MA plans achieving premium savings relative to FFS for benefits under Parts A and B, thus freeing up resources for providing expanded benefits without increasing overall costs for the beneficiaries. However, separating supplemental benefits from what is required by Medicare law is crucial for ensuring clear and vigorous premium competition because it will allow the beneficiaries to readily see price differences that have nothing to do with covered services.

This reformed structure of benefit components and competing sources of coverage, through a streamlined enrollment portal, would allow Medicare beneficiaries to see their options much more clearly than they do today. They could compare the premiums charged by FFS, ACOs, and MA plans when deciding how to secure their benefits under Parts A and B. They also could see what their premiums would be when combining options for Parts A and B coverage with those for Part D and supplemental benefits.

Ensuring Fair Premium Competition Among the Coverage Options. The crucial second piece of an effective reform is implementation of strong price competition among the various coverage options. As noted, the Part D benefit was designed to promote such competition, through a premium support design. Modest premium growth in the program has validated the model.

The next step is to implement premium support in Parts A and B. MA plans already submit competitive bids under current law, but those bids are considered in relationship to benchmarks that are determined through administrative formulas. Further, FFS does not participate in the bidding process, so the competition is unbalanced.

Figure 6. Premium Support Effects on Total Program and Enrollee Costs in 2024 Relative to Current Law (Percentage Change)

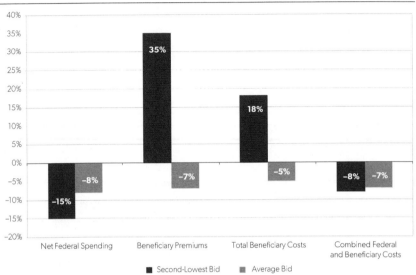

Source: Congressional Budget Office, "A Premium Support System for Medicare: Updated Analysis of Illustrative Options," Congressional Budget Office, October 2017, https://www.cbo.gov/system/files/115th-congress-2017-2018/reports/53077-premiumsupport.pdf.

Fair competition requires submission of bids from FFS, ACOs, and MA plans for the same set of actuarially equivalent benefits, as defined in Parts A and B of current Medicare law. FFS's bid would be a calculation by the government of the per-beneficiary costs in each market. The government should continue to refine its risk-adjustment methodology to ensure the competition is based on efficient care delivery and not differences in the underlying health status of the enrollees in the available coverage options.

The government's contribution toward coverage (its "premium support") should be based on the submitted bids. One option for setting the government's payment would be to tie it to the second-lowest bid in every market area (as defined in law or regulation). An alternative would be the average bid (weighted by enrollment) in each market.

The CBO has analyzed the budgetary effects of both approaches, as shown in Figure 6. (The government contribution would be a net payment, which removes the base beneficiary premium, set at what is required for enrollment into Part B under current law.)

With the second-lowest bid, overall costs for the federal government would fall by 15 percent, but net beneficiary expenses would rise by 18 percent, partly because FFS enrollees in high-cost markets would pay significantly higher premiums. Using the average bid to set the government's contribution would still lower the federal government's costs (by 8 percent), and it would leave beneficiaries (as a group) better off, with a 5 percent drop in their out-of-pocket expenses (including premiums).

The CBO's assessment of premium support confirms that competition would lower costs by encouraging migration into more efficient coverage options. It also suggests that the competition likely would slow cost growth in future years by encouraging development and adoption of cost-reducing technologies that improve the efficiency of care delivery.[26]

As noted previously, MA plans today benefit from the prohibition on balance billing for services provided out of their networks, which makes it unprofitable for hospitals to opt out of contract negotiations. To improve the functioning of the marketplace, this requirement should be repealed, especially as premium support would increase the pressure for cost reductions (and thus likely mitigate the potential for high costs). Relaxing this rule would force the MA plans to become more active managers of the care they provide.

The savings from more intensive premium competition among the coverage options can be shared with Medicare enrollees to make the reform more attractive politically. One approach would be to expand Medicare-covered benefits and increase the government's contribution toward the coverage. For instance, expanding Medicare benefits to include an annual out-of-pocket cost limit (so-called catastrophic protection) might be done as an add-on (rather than in an actuarially neutral manner). Medicare might also cover some benefits outside of what is provided in current law today (such as some dental services). These added benefits would lessen the initial savings from premium support but might diminish the political opposition that has made advancing reform legislation so difficult in the past.[27]

Competition and Price Shopping in FFS. Premium support is not the only means by which stronger market discipline can be introduced into Medicare. Enrollees in FFS can be encouraged to directly select low-cost and high-quality service providers too.

Medicare should become a leader in using standardized pricing to foster strong competition among service providers. Hospitals and physicians today have weak incentives to post clear pricing for their services, and the complexity of medical care makes price comparisons difficult for patients when multiple line items are billed for a full episode of care. Commercial insurance plans have tested the value of several service-focused competitive payment systems in recent years that could inform Medicare reform. For instance, employers have tested reference-pricing schemes, tiered cost-sharing arrangements, and favorable contract terms for centers of excellence to reduce costs for themselves and their workers.

CMS would promote strong price competition by building on these models and requiring participating providers to disclose pricing for standardized services covering common procedures. The key is to ensure a coordinated, all-in price from all the practitioners and facilities involved in delivering care to a patient. For instance, the government could require all providers involved in common surgeries to provide a combined all-in price for the services.

An important next step is to incentivize the Medicare enrollees to shop for lower-priced options. Medicare could do this by calculating benchmarks in every market (based on prevailing FFS rates) for the list of standardized interventions. Beneficiaries opting for providers that post prices below the benchmarks should keep some of the savings (perhaps 50 percent). In some cases, for expensive care (such as common surgeries), the payments to the Medicare beneficiaries could be substantial, which would create strong incentives for the providers to price their services more aggressively and for the beneficiaries to migrate to lower-priced options. There is strong evidence that this version of reference-based pricing (which is discussed more generally in Chapter 2) would deliver substantial savings for Medicare and the program's enrollees.[28]

Modernizing the Trust Fund Structure. Medicare's trust funds need updating to mirror the changes recommended for the program's benefit design, with Parts A and B combined into one offering. With the benefits combined, the trust funds should be merged, too (into a singular Medicare trust fund), with all receipts and expenses of the existing HI and SMI trust funds redirected to the combined account.

A crucial additional reform is recalibration of the basis for general fund support of the program's spending obligations. It should not be unlimited, as it is today for Parts B and D. Trust funds work only if their receipts are limited in some way and are defined to ensure affordability over time. That is distinctly not the case currently, with the government's contribution to Medicare expected to rise to levels that are unaffordable for taxpayers.

One option would be to tie the government's contribution to the new Medicare trust fund to what was paid in a reference year for Parts B and D coverage and then index that amount for subsequent years to the rate of growth in the national economy. This adjustment would ensure that current and future taxpayers contribute the same amount of their combined incomes each year toward ensuring adequate health services for the nation's elderly and disabled citizens.

Changing the basis of general fund support for Medicare will not by itself ensure an appropriate political response when trust fund depletion becomes imminent, as it would in time if the Treasury's annual contributions were tied to GDP growth. Congress can always override a previous law and could do so in this case by allowing general fund support to flow more freely. A reformed trust fund, in this sense, would be an imperfect mechanism for ensuring greater cost discipline.

Nonetheless, this reform would be an improvement over the status quo, which encourages an unhealthy and misguided focus on HI solvency, even as SMI spending becomes an ever-larger burden on taxpayers. A reformed trust fund mechanism might change the tenor of the public conversation around Medicare solvency, which might then help spur Congress to consider effective remedies.

As Medicare Goes

In the long-running debate over better health care cost control in the US, there is one important point of agreement: Medicare will be pivotal to whatever policy direction is chosen. In general, as Medicare goes, so does the nation's entire medical care system.

The Medicare agenda for proponents of stronger government control is clear enough. They want to cement Medicare's role as the nation's unchallenged regulator of provider pricing, adjust existing rules with selective tests of alterative payment models, and force commercial insurance to lower its rates to Medicare's levels.

Market advocates must advance an alternative vision if they are serious about using market incentives rather than regulations to discipline expenses and improve quality. Fortunately, they are not starting from scratch. At crucial points in Medicare's history, Congress inserted private options and consumer choice into the program's overall design, albeit with restrictive conditions that have limited the rigor of the competition and thus their effects. Market advocates can build on these existing features by strengthening price competition and making it easier, and more rewarding, for beneficiaries to select options that reduce their costs while improving the care and quality of the services they receive.

While securing such reforms will be challenging politically, the payoff would be substantial. Medicare would become more efficient and sustainable, and its wide influence would encourage take-up of similar reforms in other segments of the nation's health system.

Notes

1. For a more detailed description of Medicare's insurance value to enrollees, see James C. Capretta, "Rethinking Medicare," *National Affairs*, Spring 2018, https://www.nationalaffairs.com/publications/detail/rethinking-medicare.

2. Centers for Medicare & Medicaid Services, "Medicare Costs at a Glance," 2022, https://www.medicare.gov/your-medicare-costs/medicare-costs-at-a-glance.

3. Kaiser Family Foundation, "An Overview of the Medicare Part D Prescription Drug Benefit," October 13, 2021, https://www.kff.org/medicare/fact-sheet/an-overview-of-the-medicare-part-d-prescription-drug-benefit/.

4. Congressional Budget Office, "10-Year Trust Fund Projections," February 2021, https://www.cbo.gov/data/budget-economic-data#5.

5. Medicare Trustees, *The 2021 Annual Report of the Boards of Trustees of the Federal Hospital Insurance and Federal Supplementary Medical Insurance Trust Funds*, Centers for Medicare & Medicaid Services, August 2021, https://www.cms.gov/files/document/2021-medicare-trustees-report.pdf.

6. Medicare Trustees, *The 2021 Annual Report of the Boards of Trustees of the Federal Hospital Insurance and Federal Supplementary Medical Insurance Trust Funds*.

7. Medicare Trustees, *The 2021 Annual Report of the Boards of Trustees of the Federal Hospital Insurance and Federal Supplementary Medical Insurance Trust Funds*.

8. Medicare Payment Advisory Commission, "Hospital Acute Inpatient Services Payment System," November 2021, https://www.medpac.gov/wp-content/uploads/2021/11/medpac_payment_basics_21_hospital_final_sec.pdf.

9. There has been a long-running debate in the US over the relationship of Medicare pricing to fees paid by private insurers. Some analysts and industry representatives argue that lower Medicare fees lead to higher private insurance payments, which is referred to as "cost shifting." The balance of empirical evidence and standard economic theory suggest otherwise, with lower Medicare payments leading to lower private insurance fees too. For useful descriptions of the interplay of the level of payment seen in commercial insurance versus Medicare, see Roger Feldman, Bryan Dowd, and Robert Coulam, "Medicare's Role in Determining Prices Throughout the Health Care System," George Mason University, Mercatus Center, October 2015, https://www.mercatus.org/system/files/Feldman-Medicare-Role-Prices-oct.pdf; and Jeffery Clemens and Joshua D. Gottlieb, "In the Shadow of a Giant: Medicare's Influence on Private Physician Payments," *Journal of Political Economy* 125, no. 1 (February): 1–39, https://www.journals.uchicago.edu/doi/pdfplus/10.1086/689772.

10. Medicare Payment Advisory Commission, "Physician and Other Health Professional Payment System," November 2021, https://www.medpac.gov/wp-content/uploads/2021/11/medpac_payment_basics_21_physician_final_sec.pdf.

11. Jim Hahn and Kristin B. Blom, "The Medicare Access and CHIP Reauthorization Act of 2015," Congressional Research Service, November 10, 2015, https://sgp.fas.org/crs/misc/R43962.pdf.

12. Medicare Payment Advisory Commission, *Health Care Spending and the Medicare Program: A Data Book*, July 2021, https://www.medpac.gov/wp-content/uploads/import_data/scrape_files/docs/default-source/data-book/july2021_medpac_databook_sec.pdf.

13. Marika Cabral and Neale Mahoney, "Externalities and Taxation of Supplemental Insurance: A Study of Medicare and Medigap" (working paper, National Bureau of Economic Research, Cambridge, MA, October 2017), https://www.nber.org/system/files/working_papers/w19787/w19787.pdf.

14. Medicare Trustees, *The 2021 Annual Report of the Boards of Trustees of the Federal Hospital Insurance and Federal Supplementary Medical Insurance Trust Funds*.

15. Richard Kronick, "Why Medicare Advantage Plans Are Overpaid by $200 Billion and What to Do About It," Health Affairs Forefront, January 29, 2020, https://www.healthaffairs.org/do/10.1377/forefront.20200127.293799/full/.

16. For an overview of the Medicare Advantage (MA) payment system, see Medicare Payment Advisory Commission, "Medicare Advantage Program Payment System," November 2021, https://www.medpac.gov/wp-content/uploads/2021/11/medpac_payment_basics_21_ma_final_sec.pdf.

17. The Medicare Payment Advisory Commission has estimated that, when the risk profile of MA enrollees versus those in fee-for-service (FFS) is accurately assessed, the program overpays for MA coverage by 4 percent relative to what it would cost to care for the same beneficiaries in FFS. The agency also estimates that MA has never reduced costs for the Medicare program. See Medicare Payment Advisory Commission, "Medicare Payment Policy," March 2021, http://medpac.gov/docs/default-source/reports/mar21_medpac_report_to_the_congress_sec.pdf.

18. Robert A. Berenson et al., "Why Medicare Advantage Plans Pay Hospitals Traditional Medicare Prices," *Health Affairs* 34, no. 8 (August 2015): 1289–95, https://www.healthaffairs.org/doi/full/10.1377/hlthaff.2014.1427.

19. Medicare Payment Advisory Commission, *Health Care Spending and the Medicare Program*.

20. Congressional Research Service, "Medicare Part D Prescription Drug Benefit," December 18, 2020, https://sgp.fas.org/crs/misc/R40611.pdf.

21. Kaiser Family Foundation, "An Overview of the Medicare Part D Prescription Drug Benefit."

22. Medicare Trustees, *The 2021 Annual Report of the Boards of Trustees of the Federal Hospital Insurance and Federal Supplementary Medical Insurance Trust Funds.*

23. Medicare Trustees, *The 2021 Annual Report of the Boards of Trustees of the Federal Hospital Insurance and Federal Supplementary Medical Insurance Trust Funds.*

24. Cristina Boccuti, "Paying a Visit to the Doctor: Current Protections for Medicare Patients When Receiving Physician Services," Kaiser Family Foundation, November 30, 2016, https://www.kff.org/medicare/issue-brief/paying-a-visit-to-the-doctor-current-financial-protections-for-medicare-patients-when-receiving-physician-services/.

25. Medicare's financial challenges are so severe that reforms beyond those mentioned here are likely necessary. A more far-reaching restructuring of the program is presented in Capretta, "Rethinking Medicare."

26. Congressional Budget Office, "A Premium Support System for Medicare: Updated Analysis of Illustrative Options," October 2017, https://www.cbo.gov/publication/53077.

27. Robert Coulam, Roger Feldman, and Bryan Dowd, "Time to Save Money on Medicare Advantage: The Case for Competitive Bidding" (working paper, University of Minnesota, Minneapolis, MN, 2021).

28. James C. Robinson, Timothy T. Brown, and Christopher Whaley, "Reference Pricing Changes the 'Choice Architecture' of Health Care for Consumers," *Health Affairs* 36, no. 3 (March 2017): 524–30, https://www.healthaffairs.org/doi/pdf/10.1377/hlthaff.2016.1256.

4

Medicaid and the Children's Health Insurance Program

Medicaid is the largest public insurance program in the US by total enrollment, which would surprise many of the people who voted it into existence in 1965. In part, that is because it was overshadowed from its inception by Medicare, which was created in the same law as a health insurance addition to the popular Social Security program.

It may seem obvious now that Medicaid would grow rapidly, given the gaps left by the nation's other insurance systems, but in the mid-1960s, the future evolution of US health care was not yet clear. The US could have adopted a nationalized system that would have made a program focused exclusively on the poor a less relevant feature in the overall design. However, over time, the dominance of the nation's job-based insurance system for working Americans and their families came to be seen as an entrenched reality. A robust safety net became essential to sustaining private insurance as the first option for working Americans because employer plans are often not available to, or affordable for, lower-wage workers.

Medicaid also grew because of the social service needs of households caring for permanently disabled individuals, many of whom are categorically eligible for Medicaid because of their entitlement to cash support for the disabled poor. Further, other rich countries also provide publicly subsidized long-term care for the frail elderly, who require assistance beyond traditional medical care. Medicaid has become the default solution to this problem in the US, even for families that earned middle-class wages (or more) during their working years.

Medicaid has taken on these and other roles because it has been easier for Congress to enlarge its mission than to create new programs. Further, Medicaid's design facilitates growth. The federal share of its expenditures has never been limited, and because the states pay, on average, for less than half the cost of liberalizations, the usual budgetary concerns among state officials that might otherwise have slowed expansion have been less pronounced.

It has now been more than a half century since Medicaid was enacted, and the US health system looks different today than it did in 1965. It is a complex public-private system that leans heavily on Medicaid to provide a secure safety net for the nation's lowest-income households. That role can be strengthened even as the program is modified to be more consistent with vigorous price competition, which will make health care more efficient and affordable for all consumers and taxpayers.

Origins

The 1965 law placed Medicaid right behind Medicare in the sequence of titles in the Social Security Act. (Medicare is Title XVIII, and Medicaid is Title XIX.) Medicare understandably commanded more attention during the congressional debate and after enactment, because it serves the entire elderly population, so its constituency covers persons of varying means. Medicaid's target population is lower-income Americans and, at enactment, especially those who were out of the workforce because of disabilities or the need to care for dependent children.

Medicare also quickly became consequential in business decisions affecting the broader health system because of its leading role in writing payment rules for hospitals, physicians, and other service providers, which have become industry-wide standards. By comparison, Medicaid is administered by the states and thus involves scores of actors and agencies in its administrative decisions. This dispersion of authority lessens the program's national influence.

Medicaid was written to resemble, and expand on, predecessor programs. Beginning in the 1950s, Congress sought to improve medical access for poor Americans who were eligible for cash welfare by encouraging states to support the facilities and practitioners providing "indigent" care with "vendor" payments.[1]

In 1960, these state assistance plans were converted into the Kerr-Mills program, which introduced the concept of a federal matching system for state-administered medical coverage. With Kerr-Mills, the federal government used a measure of per capita state income to determine how much assistance states would receive when providing care to persons who could not afford medical care. Eligible beneficiaries included cash welfare recipients and elderly residents with incomes too low to fully cover their medical expenses (the so-called medically indigent). The states had substantial discretion over the eligibility criteria.[2]

The authors of Kerr-Mills hoped it would become a major expansion of the federal government's role in supporting access to medical care, and yet, by 1965, it was already clear that its reach would be modest. Only a few states implemented it aggressively (California, Massachusetts, and New York), and they were known as activist outliers with bureaucracies robust enough to take on a major expansion of their responsibilities.[3]

Although Kerr-Mills fell short of its original vision, it became the model for Medicaid, with its emphasis on the federal government providing matching funds for state-initiated expenditures, state administration and discretion over certain program rules, and a nexus to cash welfare support and the elderly needing nursing home care.

At enactment in 1965 and still today, Medicaid is optional; states are not required to participate. (Arizona held out until 1982.) But the law specifies a series of requirements for states that do choose to participate, centered around categories of eligible beneficiaries and required benefits.

Program Overview and Evolution

Medicaid was written to provide states with options in program design so long as they comply with minimum standards ("mandates") covering both eligibility groups and benefits. Table 1 provides an overview of the rules.

Medicaid's original focus was on providing access to medical services to persons eligible for cash payments pursuant to the various titles of the Social Security Act. In particular, mothers with dependent children who were eligible for income support under the old Aid to Families with Dependent Children (AFDC) program were automatically eligible for Medicaid. When Congress enacted welfare reform and replaced AFDC with a block grant to states, the mandate for coverage was transferred into an equivalent requirement that states maintain eligibility for Medicaid for families based on the old AFDC criteria. Medicaid also is provided to the disabled and elderly poor receiving assistance through the Supplemental Security Income (SSI) program, although states may impose somewhat more restrictive financial eligibility criteria.

Beginning in the 1980s, Congress enacted a series of program expansions that started as options and migrated into full or partial requirements. The focus was on providing access to health coverage for pregnant women and children who might not qualify for AFDC because of earned income. Currently, states are required to cover pregnant women with incomes below 133 percent of the federal poverty line (FPL) and children (under age 19) with incomes up to the same level. States may choose to establish higher income thresholds (up to 185 percent of the FPL) for pregnant women and infant children. Further, states must pay premiums and cost sharing for certain Medicare beneficiaries.[4]

Federal Medicaid law also includes a lengthy list of required and optional benefits, which are summarized in Table 1. Among the mandatory services are inpatient hospital stays, physician and nursing home care, and, for children, early and periodic screening, diagnostic, and treatment services (EPSDT), which cover preventive services for many common childhood ailments. States are permitted to provide prescription drugs, dental services, chiropractic care, eyeglasses, hospice services, and many other benefits, with wide variation in take-up among these categories. For instance, all states provide prescription drug coverage, while only 28 provide preventive dental care.[5]

The Medicaid statute has rules to ensure states provide these services equitably. States have discretion to establish boundaries for covered benefits—so-called amount, duration, and scope provisions. However, whatever rules are implemented must apply to all participants to prevent discrimination. Further, whatever benefits a state opts to provide must apply uniformly in all geographic areas ("statewideness"). Some exceptions to these rules are allowed for managed care contracts (which can be concentrated in certain localities) and home- and community-based services.[6]

The needs of the diverse population groups served by Medicaid vary widely and so, too, do their average annual expenses. Generally, Medicaid serves as a typical health insurance program for nondisabled adults

Table 1. Overview of Medicaid Mandates and Options

	Mandatory	Optional
Eligibility	• Parents and their children meeting financial requirements of the old AFDC program • Pregnant women with incomes less than 133 percent of the FPL • Children with family incomes less than 133 percent of the FPL • Persons qualifying for SSI • Foster care children and youth • Certain low-income Medicare beneficiaries • Certain permanent legal residents	• Pregnant women with incomes less than 185 percent of the FPL • Infants in families with incomes less than 185 percent of the FPL • Medically needy individuals with higher incomes but also high expenses • Non-elderly childless adults with incomes less than 138 percent of the FPL (ACA expansion)
Benefits	• Inpatient hospital stays • EPSDT • Services provided at federally qualified health centers • Family planning services • Medical transportation • Pregnancy-related services • Nursing home care • Physician services • Home health care	• Clinic services • Prescription drugs • Physical, occupational, and speech therapy • Dental services for adults • Personal care • Eyeglasses • Hospice services • Private-duty nursing • Optometry

Source: Medicaid and CHIP Payment and Access Commission, "Federal Requirements and State Options: Benefits," March 2017, https://www.macpac.gov/wp-content/uploads/2017/03/Federal-Requirements-and-State-Options-Benefits.pdf; and Medicaid and CHIP Payment and Access Commission, "Federal Requirement and State Options: Eligibility," March 2017, https://www.macpac.gov/wp-content/uploads/2017/03/Federal-Requirements-and-State-Options-Eligibility.pdf.

and their children. They need the coverage for the same reasons other working-age Americans need workplace health insurance: to provide access to care in the case of an unexpected emergency and to secure preventive care so they can remain healthy.

Figure 1. Medicaid Eligibility and Spending by Category, 2017

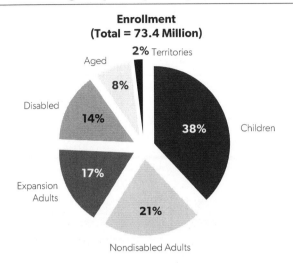

Enrollment
(Total = 73.4 Million)

2% Territories
Aged
8%
Disabled
14%
38% Children
17%
Expansion
Adults
21%
Nondisabled Adults

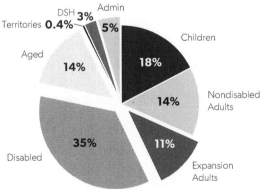

Spending
(Total = $607 Billion*)

DSH 3%   Admin
Territories 0.4%   5%
Aged   18% Children
14%
Nondisabled Adults 14%
Disabled 35%   11%
Expansion Adults

Note: * Total net spending in 2017 was $600 billion. Miscellaneous collections of $7 billion are not reflected in the figure.
Source: Centers for Medicare & Medicaid Services, *2018 Actuarial Report on the Financial Outlook for Medicaid*, April 2020, https://www.cms.gov/files/document/2018-report.pdf.

In contrast, the non-elderly disabled and the frail elderly require much more expensive care. Both groups often need social services in addition to intensive medical attention. Originally, it was expected that states would provide those nonmedical services exclusively through nursing homes, but that started to change in the 1980s with the emergence of more widespread home- and community-based options.

Figure 1 provides an overview of Medicaid enrollment by the various types of eligibility, along with the share of aggregate spending associated with each group. As shown, children and nondisabled adults are the largest categories of program participants, accounting for nearly 60 percent of total enrollment, while the non-elderly disabled and the aged represent just 22 percent of all participants. In terms of total spending, however, the disabled and aged account for nearly half of all spending, while about one-third of all spending is for children and nondisabled adults.[7]

As shown in Figure 2, the concentration of spending on the disabled and elderly is striking. In 2017, combined federal and state spending per non-elderly disabled person was $20,359, more than five times the level of spending per child ($3,836). The average spending per elderly participant was $15,059.

Congress has amended the Medicaid law regularly since its enactment more than a half century ago, as summarized in Table 2, but the changes have been primarily focused on incremental expansions of eligibility without changing the program's basic structure.

The Reagan administration ushered in a period of more frequent legislative amendments to the program than had occurred in the years immediately after enactment. In 1981, Congress agreed with the administration's push to give the states more flexibility in setting rates for hospital services separate from the methodology employed by Medicare (which, at that time, was tied to cost reports from the facilities). In return for this latitude, however, states were required to provide special payments to facilities serving disproportionately large numbers of uninsured patients and those with public coverage (discussed in more detail below).

Beginning in 1986, advocates for reducing the ranks of the uninsured began to use Medicaid as a primary tool for incremental eligibility expansions. The first step was to allow states to cover pregnant women and their infant children if the mothers' incomes were below 100 percent of the FPL. That was quickly followed, in 1987, with an amendment making this coverage a requirement for the states. In a series of additional measures stretching through the early 1990s, Congress expanded coverage to

Figure 2. Average Medicaid Spending per Enrollee, 2017

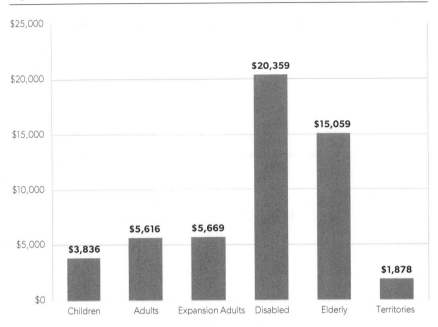

Source: Centers for Medicare & Medicaid Services, *2018 Actuarial Report on the Financial Outlook for Medicaid*, April 2020, https://www.cms.gov/files/document/2018-report.pdf.

pregnant women with higher incomes and to children up to age 18 living in families with incomes above traditional Medicaid eligibility levels.

These expansions accelerated the program's evolution and vastly increased its enrollment among groups that were left out of its original mandate. The political impulse that led to these expansions remained strong during this period and led in time to both the Children's Health Insurance Program (CHIP) and the Affordable Care Act (ACA).

The Federal Medical Assistance Percentage

State Medicaid decisions are heavily influenced by how the program is financed. Set at enactment, the formula for dividing costs between the

Table 2. Selective Legislative Changes to Medicaid

1981	Authorization of Waivers for Managed Care and Home- and Community-Based Services; Decoupling Medicaid's Hospital Payments from Medicare; Required Financial Support for DSH
1986	Optional Coverage of Pregnant Women and Infants up to Age 1 with Incomes Below 100 Percent of the FPL
1987	Mandatory Coverage of Pregnant Women and Infants
1988	Mandatory Financial Protection of Spouses of Nursing Home Residents and Coverage of Premiums and Cost Sharing for Low-Income Medicare Beneficiaries
1989	Mandatory Coverage of Children up to Age 6 with Family Incomes Below 133 Percent of the FPL
1990	Mandatory Coverage of Children Age 6 to 18 with Household Incomes Below 100 Percent of the FPL and Creation of the Prescription Drug Rebate Program
1991	DSH Spending Controls
1996	Welfare Reform/Elimination of Categorical Eligibility for AFDC Cash Welfare
1997	CHIP Created
2010	ACA Optional Coverage for Single Adults with Incomes Below 138 Percent of the FPL

Source: Centers for Medicare & Medicaid Services, "Medicare and Medicaid Milestones: 1937 to 2015," July 2015, https://www.cms.gov/About-CMS/Agency-Information/History/Downloads/Medicare-and-Medicaid-Milestones-1937-2015.pdf.

federal government and the states is based on the Federal Medical Assistance Percentage (FMAP). The FMAP is multiplied by the relevant category of Medicaid spending to determine the federal share of costs (with some exceptions). Expenditures not covered by the federal government are the state's obligation, or the "state match."[8]

State-specific FMAPs are calculated according to a formula set in law when Medicaid was enacted, as follows:

$$FMAP = 1 - [(Per\ Capita\ Income\ of\ a\ State)^2/$$
$$(Per\ Capita\ Income\ National\ Average)^2 * 0.45]$$

The formula was devised to provide more federal funding in states with lower per capita incomes. A state with a per capita income equal to the national average would have a FMAP of 55 percent, which means the state would be responsible for 45 percent of total Medicaid costs. Comparing the ratio of the squares of the state's per capita income and the national average amplifies the spread and thus increases support for lower-income states.

Medicaid law put a floor on the FMAP at 50 percent to ensure higher-income states would pay no more than 50 percent of Medicaid's costs. The law also specifies the FMAPs for US territories.

As shown in Figure 3, the states with the highest FMAPs in 2022 are Mississippi, West Virginia, New Mexico, and Kentucky. Twelve states have FMAPs set at the 50 percent floor.

Some Medicaid spending is covered by special financing rules, often expressed as adjustments to the standard FMAP. For instance, the FMAP for all states that elected to expand Medicaid pursuant to the ACA was initially 100 percent for the costs associated with those new enrollees and then phased down to 90 percent in 2020. Thus, for persons newly eligible for Medicaid under the terms of the ACA, the federal government is covering a much higher share of the costs than it is for beneficiaries who have long been eligible for enrollment (and often have lower incomes). As Table 3 shows, there are also FMAP exceptions for certain administrative expenses and services rendered by specific categories of providers (such as community health centers).[9] Overall, the federal government paid for 64 percent of total Medicaid spending in 2019.[10]

The Medicaid FMAP encourages states to expand their Medicaid programs. On average, every additional dollar of program spending is covered mainly by the federal government, not the states, which lessens the political resistance to more liberalized rules. Similarly, states are reluctant to take the initiative in trimming Medicaid costs because they do not reap the full benefit from retrenchment. (Most of the savings are returned to the federal Treasury.) Elected officials often perceive such cuts as not worth the trouble, as the political turbulence from implementing them exceeds the financial benefits for state budgets.

Figure 3. State-Specific FMAPs, 2022

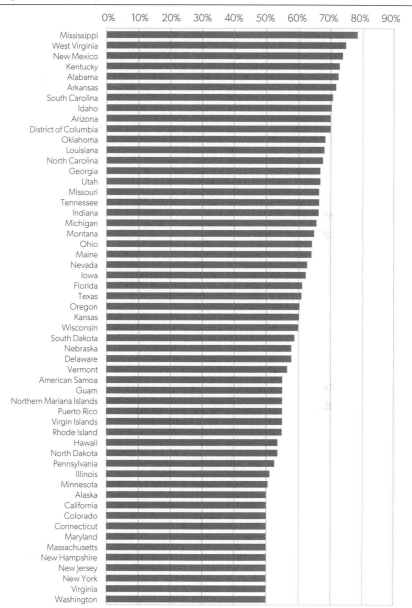

Source: Medicaid and CHIP Payment and Access Commission, *MACSTATS: Medicaid and CHIP Date Book*, December 2021, https://www.macpac.gov/wp-content/uploads/2021/12/MACStats-Medicaid-and-CHIP-Data-Book-December-2021.pdf.

Table 3. Selected Exceptions to Standard FMAP Rates

Territories (American Samoa, Guam, the Northern Mariana Islands, Puerto Rico, and the Virgin Islands)	55%
District of Columbia	70%
ACA Expansion Population*	90%
ACA Expansion Population for Holdout States (for Two Years)	95%
Premiums for Certain Low-Income Medicare Beneficiaries	100%
Indian Health Service Facilities	100%
Family Planning Services	100%
Costs During COVID-19 Emergency	Regular FMAP + 6.2 Percentage Points
Regular Administrative Activities	50%
Certain High-Priority Administrative Activities (Quality Reviews, Fraud Prevention, and Others)	75% / 90%

Note: * The FMAP began at 100 percent in 2014 and was phased down to 90 percent for 2020 and thereafter.
Source: Medicaid and CHIP Payment and Access Commission, "Federal Match Rate Exceptions," 2021, https://www.macpac.gov/federal-match-rate-exceptions/; and Medicaid and CHIP Payment and Access Commission, "Federal Match Rates for Medicaid Administrative Activities," 2021, https://www.macpac.gov/federal-match-rates-formedicaid-administrative-activities/.

The FMAP also has been an engine for creative state initiatives designed to maximize federal support without overburdening state taxpayers. Among other tactics, states have worked to include under the Medicaid umbrella state health expenditures that used to be financed entirely with state funds, such as school clinic resources and transportation costs for children requiring services.

Further, the federal government and the states have been engaged in a long struggle over the terms of appropriate state sources of funding for Medicaid. As discussed below in the context of disproportionate share hospitals, states discovered in the early 1990s that imposing taxes on medical service providers—so-called provider-specific taxes—would allow them to generate revenue for state matching funds without imposing any real economic burden on state taxpayers. This practice, and others like it, can distort the actual distribution of the Medicaid cost burden and make it appear that states are shouldering a larger burden than is really the case.

Medicaid and CHIP

In 1997, Republicans controlled Congress, and Democrat Bill Clinton was president. Despite the split political control of the elected branches, there was interest in furthering insurance coverage beyond what had occurred with previous Medicaid liberalizations. Led by Sens. Ted Kennedy (D-MA) and Orrin Hatch (R-UT), Congress debated and approved the creation of CHIP as part of a larger budget agreement.

CHIP is both an extension of Medicaid and a separate program with rules that differ in some instances from those that apply in Medicaid. CHIP's target population is children in households with incomes too high to qualify for Medicaid but still too low to reliably secure job-based coverage (through working parents). Its authorizing law includes the following notable provisions.

Financing. Republicans wanted CHIP to be financed from fixed federal allotments, with no individual entitlement to benefits, instead of open-ended matching payments, as is the case with Medicaid. Democrats wanted to retain a matching system that would encourage wide take-up by states. The compromise was to combine the two ideas.

Like Medicaid, CHIP is financed by a federal matching rate formula. The enhanced FMAP, or E-FMAP, is the same as it is for Medicaid (with exceptions in place for certain years) but is modified by reducing the state share by 30 percent. This adjustment increases the federal share of CHIP funding above what applies in Medicaid, with an allowable range of 65 to 85 percent.[11]

Total federal funding is limited by a fixed CHIP appropriation, which could restrict total state CHIP spending. (There is no individual entitlement to benefits in CHIP compelling more federal funds.) In theory,

Figure 4. Enrollment of Children in CHIP and Medicaid (Millions)

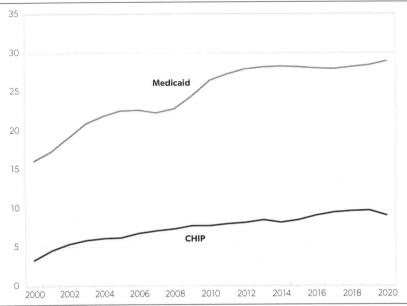

Source: Kaiser Family Foundation, "State Health Facts: Total Number of Children Ever Enrolled in CHIP Annually," November 1, 2021, https://www.kff.org/other/state-indicator/annual-chip-enrollment/; and Centers for Medicare & Medicaid Services, *2018 Actuarial Report on the Financial Outlook for Medicaid*, April 2020, https://www.cms.gov/files/document/2018-report.pdf.

states could be forced to implement pro rata reductions in coverage. In practice, however, federal funding has not been a limiting factor for CHIP obligations.

Annual state CHIP allotments are established differently in even and odd number years. In even years, states receive the allotment from the prior year increased by growth in national health spending and changes in the total population of children in the state. In odd years, states receive their actual spending from the prior year increased by the same indexing factors.[12]

Type of Program. States have the option to use their CHIP funds to expand Medicaid, create a separate program, or combine the two options into a hybrid scheme. As of 2017, the vast majority (40 states) ran hybrid programs, while eight states had implemented Medicaid-only expansions and two opted for a CHIP-specific program design.[13]

Benefits. States that opt to use their CHIP funding to expand Medicaid must provide the full Medicaid package of coverage to CHIP beneficiaries. Those implementing a CHIP-specific program can provide coverage that is tied to certain benchmark plans or apply for approval from the secretary of the US Department of Health and Human Services (HHS).[14]

States running CHIP-specific coverage options are permitted to charge premium and cost sharing in excess of what is allowed under Medicaid.

Eligibility. States have wide discretion in establishing income limits for CHIP-funded coverage. In general, CHIP is intended to subsidize coverage for children living in households with incomes too high for Medicaid but too low to secure reliable private insurance. Figure 4 shows total CHIP enrollment relative to the number of children covered under Medicaid (excluding Medicaid enrollment that is a consequence of CHIP). Most states provide CHIP to families above their Medicaid limits and up to about 200 to 300 percent of the FPL, with New York going as high as 400 percent of the FPL and Oregon as low as 185 percent.[15]

The ACA and Medicaid

The desire to cover the uninsured, which led to the incremental expansion of Medicaid in the 1980s and 1990s and to CHIP in 1997, was a principal motivation for enacting the ACA in 2010. The law took Medicaid enrollment to a much higher level than had occurred previously by bringing into its coverage the last remaining category of the uninsured that had not been targeted by the program—single, low-income adults (often men) without dependent children.

The architects of the ACA intended for its extension of coverage to this population to be mandatory, by inserting into the statute a penalty of full withdrawal of federal Medicaid funds from states that refused to comply. The Supreme Court ruled that this sanction was too extreme for a program that is supposed to allow for some state discretion. Consequently, the ACA expansion is an entirely voluntary option for the states.

Most states have taken it up even without fear of a penalty because the federal government has committed to paying for 90 percent of all added expenses (after initially providing for 100 percent). As of January 2022, 38 states plus the District of Columbia offered coverage to all persons with incomes below 138 percent of the FPL, as the ACA stipulates.[16]

As shown in Figure 5, the ACA expansion has dramatically affected program enrollment, with current estimates showing it increased the number of Medicaid participants by 12.3 million in 2020, which is about 16 percent of the total number of beneficiaries.

The Rise of Medicaid Managed Care Organizations

Over the past quarter century, state Medicaid program directors have shifted their administrative focus from fee-for-service (FFS) to privately administered managed care organizations (MCOs). Medicaid is now so dominated by capitated, risk-based payments to MCOs that most new program initiatives are built to be run through MCOs instead of FFS.

The migration to MCOs has been rapid. In 1999, just 15 percent of total Medicaid spending was channeled through MCOs. By 2012, it had risen to 37 percent. Further, in 2012, a remarkable 89 percent of full-benefit Medicaid enrollees (which excludes Medicare beneficiaries eligible only for premium or cost-sharing assistance) were receiving their services from providers under contract with MCOs as opposed to FFS care.[17]

The shift to MCOs has occurred more rapidly in some states than others, but it has been a widely dispersed trend, with 39 states plus the District of Columbia using MCOs for at least some of the services provided to beneficiaries as of 2019. The share of beneficiaries receiving their care through MCOs reached 69 percent in 2018, and spending on MCOs accounted for 46 percent of total program expenditures in 2019.[18]

The discrepancy between enrollment in MCOs and the share of total spending that goes through them is due to the ongoing practice in many states of carving out certain services from the risk-based capitated rates paid to the managed care plans, most especially for long-term services and supports for disabled and frail elderly beneficiaries. As of 2019, most states reported using MCOs for less than 75 percent of their disabled and frail elderly population, although the trend is toward more use of managed care for the services they require, not less.[19]

Figure 5. Medicaid Enrollment Increase from the ACA Expansion (Millions)

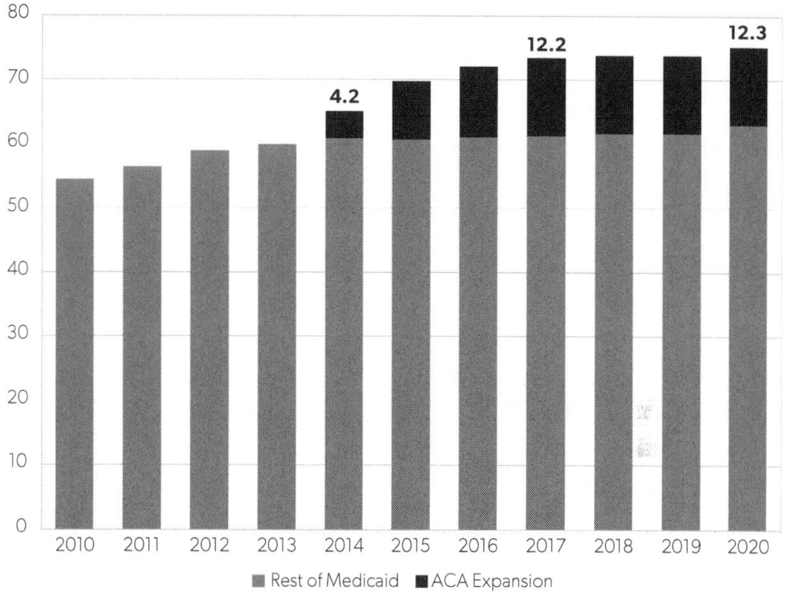

Source: Medicaid and CHIP Payment and Access Commission, *MACSTATS: Medicaid and CHIP Date Book*, December 2021, https://www.macpac.gov/wp-content/uploads/2021/12/MACStats-Medicaid-and-CHIP-Data-Book-December-2021.pdf; and Assistant Secretary for Planning and Evaluation, "Health Coverage Under the Affordable Care Act: Enrollment Trends and State Estimates," US Department of Health and Human Services, June 5, 2021, https://aspe.hhs.gov/sites/default/files/private/pdf/265671/ASPE%2520Issue%2520Brief-ACA-Related%2520Coverage%2520by%2520State.pdf.

Federal rules restrict some state MCO contracting. The capitated rates must meet national standards for actuarial soundness. In other words, they cannot be so low that beneficiaries will have trouble getting access to care. Further, the networks of participating providers cannot be so narrow as to make it difficult for the beneficiaries to find physicians willing to serve them.

Disproportionate Share Hospitals

In 1981, the Reagan administration pushed for more state flexibility to manage Medicaid expenses, in part by ending the federal requirement that Medicaid hospital payments must track those paid under Medicare's cost-plus

Figure 6. DSH Expenditures as a Percentage of Total Medicaid Spending

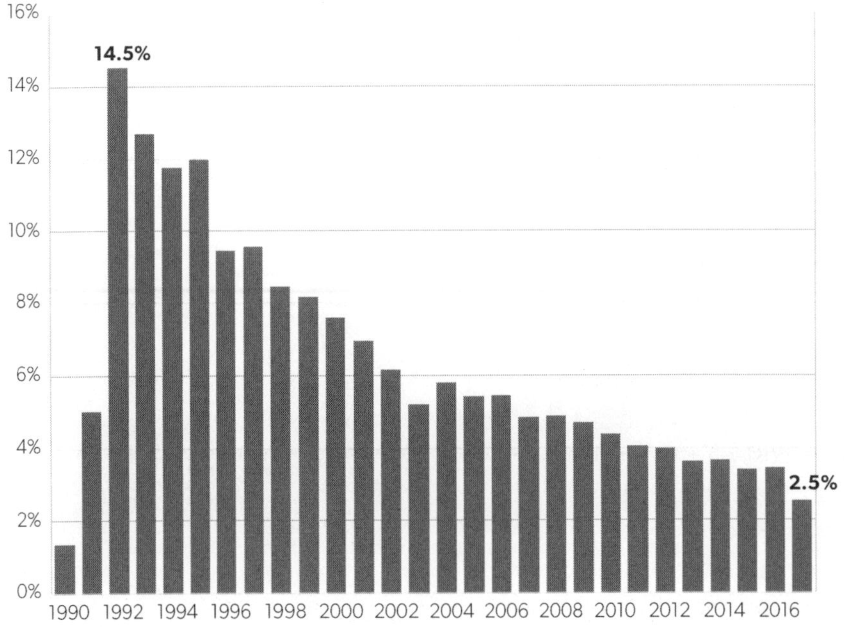

Source: Jean Hearne, "Medicaid Disproportionate Share Payments," Congressional Research Service, January 15, 2004, https://www.everycrsreport.com/files/20040115_97-483_3826ec3e30d033f80df 3042be7fa15adefd3b443.pdf; Medicaid and CHIP Payment and Access Commission, *MACSTATS: Medicaid and CHIP Date Book*, December 2021, https://www.macpac.gov/wp-content/uploads/2021/12/ MACStats-Medicaid-and-CHIP-Data-Book-December-2021.pdf; and Centers for Medicare & Medicaid Services, *2018 Actuarial Report on the Financial Outlook for Medicaid*, April 2020, https://www.cms. gov/files/document/2018-report.pdf.

reimbursement system. This change alarmed the hospital industry, which pushed for a companion provision requiring the states to provide separate financial support to facilities serving large numbers of uninsured and Medicaid patients—so-called disproportionate share hospitals (DSH) payments.

The Medicaid DSH requirement was initially a nonfactor in program spending, but that changed in the early 1990s when some states discovered it could facilitate access to additional federal support. By targeting the health sector with revenue-raising provisions, states found they could generate federal Medicaid funds that would be sufficient to fully reimburse the taxpaying facilities and provide them with additional financial support—all without burdening other state taxpayers with higher costs.

Not surprisingly, this practice proved popular in state capitals and spread rapidly. Federal Medicaid costs soared. As shown in Figure 6, Medicaid DSH costs reached their peak as a percentage of total program spending in 1993, at 14.6 percent.

The federal government responded by imposing limits on DSH and the use of provider-specific taxes, which prevented the explosive spending growth from continuing and gradually reduced its effect on total costs. The rules curtailing these practices locked in place existing practices, which worked to the disadvantage of states that did not adopt them.

Dual Eligibles

The cost-effective delivery of services in Medicaid becomes more complex than usual when the beneficiaries are also eligible for Medicare—the so-called dual eligibles, or "duals." In these instances, Medicare is the primary payer for acute care services, with Medicaid covering some or most expenses not paid for by Medicare.

According to the Medicaid and CHIP Payment and Access Commission (MACPAC), there were 12.5 million duals (of all types) in 2019, or 15 percent of all Medicaid participants.

Some duals are entitled to only modest Medicaid coverage. These "partial duals"—3.5 million people in 2019, or 28 percent of all duals—have incomes low enough to qualify for Medicaid coverage for certain cost sharing required by Medicare, or for their Medicare premiums, but they do not qualify for full Medicaid benefits. Medicare beneficiaries with incomes below 100 percent of the FPL and less than three times the assets allowable for enrollment into the SSI program—the so-called qualified Medicare beneficiaries—can have Medicaid cover their Medicare premiums and cost-sharing requirements. Beneficiaries with incomes above 100 percent of the FPL but below 120 percent—Specified Low-Income Medicare Beneficiaries—are entitled to have Medicaid pay their Medicare premiums but not their cost sharing.[20]

The more pressing financial concern for both Medicare and Medicaid is the cost of caring for the full duals, of whom there were nine million in 2019.[21]

Full duals incur much higher expenses than do those who are eligible for just Medicare or Medicaid. The Congressional Budget Office (CBO), in a report from 2013, estimated that full duals incurred combined Medicare and Medicaid expenses of $33,400 in 2009, which was more than four times the average spending of $8,300 for a nondual Medicare enrollee in the same year.[22]

There are numerous routes to becoming eligible for both programs. Two-thirds of full duals were eligible for Medicare first and then Medicaid. Twenty-seven percent were eligible for Medicaid first and then Medicare. Just under 5 percent of full duals became eligible for both programs simultaneously. Of those who followed the Medicare-then-Medicaid pathway, 68 percent were age 65 and older when they became eligible for Medicaid, and 60 percent were eligible for Medicare because of their age and work history. Most of those who qualified for Medicaid first were disabled and below age 65.[23]

The states and the federal government, and providers of medical and long-term services and supports (LTSS), do not always share the same financial incentives when caring for dual eligibles. For instance, under Medicare's rules, a patient requiring a hospital stay is eligible for spending a limited number of days in a skilled nursing facility to recover before being sent home. As Medicare's payments for these days in institutional care are higher than Medicaid's in most instances, the nursing homes have incentives to ensure that the patients who come under their care exhaust their Medicare eligibility before Medicaid coverage begins. States share this incentive, too, as Medicaid spending for nursing home care is delayed when Medicare pays for the first days of a stay.[24]

Similarly, when better coordination of care occurs in Medicaid, the federal government sees a reduction in its share of program spending, which is more than half the total. The states, of course, also benefit from the lower costs in Medicaid from better coordination. However, when integrated delivery reduces expenses in Medicare, perhaps by lessening the need for some expensive services, only the federal government benefits, as states do not pay for direct services under Medicare. (Although they do, through Medicaid, pay for some cost sharing owed by both partial and full duals.)

Over the past two decades, Congress and the Centers for Medicare & Medicaid Services (CMS) have attempted to improve the coordination between Medicare and Medicaid for dual eligibles, in part by making sure both levels of government will benefit financially from avoiding unnecessary expenses. While some progress has occurred, most duals receive services through fully independent FFS payment systems operated by both programs, with all that entails for fragmented and expensive care.

The primary integration strategies now being pursued, which are likely to serve as the starting point for further reforms, are as follows.

D-SNPs and FIDE-SNPs. In 2003, Medicare law was amended to create a new category of managed care plan, dubbed Dual Eligible Special Needs Plans (D-SNPs) because enrollment is only open to beneficiaries who are entitled to benefits from both programs. D-SNPs are a subcategory of Medicare Advantage (MA), which is the option within Medicare that allows beneficiaries to receive their Medicare-covered services through privately administered managed care plans.[25] MA plans receive a monthly capitated payment, which must cover the full cost of the program's statutory benefits, plus whatever supplemental benefits the plans offer.

D-SNPs could serve as a primary platform for better integration of care for dual eligibles because they must have a minimum capacity for managing care within a budget. However, given the large expenses associated with nursing home stays, many D-SNPs are reluctant to accept full risk for these costs. As of 2020, over 550 D-SNPs were operating nationwide, with enrollment of roughly one-quarter of the entire dually eligible population.[26]

In 2008, and then in 2010, Congress amended the D-SNP law to require the plans to have contracts with the state Medicaid agencies where they operate. These contracts give the states leverage over the D-SNP program because only state-approved plans are eligible to enroll beneficiaries. States use this leverage to ensure the D-SNPs meet minimum levels of care coordination for Medicaid-covered services, although fully capitated payments are not a requirement.

Fully Integrated Dual Eligible SNPs (FIDE-SNPs) take the next step and manage Medicaid-covered LTSS in addition to Medicare benefits. In theory, FIDE-SNPs are the integration answer to the dual eligibles challenge. To date, though, they have relatively low enrollment and a small overall footprint. As of early 2020, they accounted for only 11 percent of D-SNP enrollment and just 2 to 3 percent of the overall dual eligibles population.[27]

Financial Alignment Initiative. The ACA, enacted in 2010, created two new offices in CMS—the Center for Medicare and Medicaid Innovation and the Medicare-Medicaid Coordination Office—that have jointly sponsored demonstrations of new state-run models of care for dually eligible beneficiaries, under the banner of the Financial Alignment Initiative (FAI).

The CMS offices have worked with numerous states to test two models: capitation and managed FFS. Under capitation, the federal government and the state sign a three-way contract with a managed care plan. The plan accepts capitation from the federal government for Medicare-covered services and from the state for the benefits covered by Medicaid. The contracts are written to ensure both levels of government experience a reduction in total expenses. Ten states opted for a test of capitation.

The other option, managed FFS, involves a state-led effort using a third-party contractor, which may or may not be a managed care entity, to more carefully monitor the use of services by dually eligible beneficiaries. States that successfully reduce federal costs under these programs are eligible to share in the savings. Service providers are paid on a FFS basis, and the beneficiaries have no restrictions when selecting their caregivers. However, the contracted entities work with the beneficiaries to steer them toward services that are cost-effective and that might prevent the need for more expensive services later. Two states are conducting demonstrations of this model.

The results from the FAI have been disappointing so far. Most states are not participating in the demonstration program, and those that are participating have enrolled only a small percentage of their overall duals populations. Further, independent evaluations of the capitated model have yet to show reliable savings, although Washington state has lowered overall costs through its managed FFS test.

Waivers and Budget Neutrality

Medicaid and, after its enactment, CHIP have been heavily influenced by the federal government's approach to state-requested "waivers" of statutory rules and other requirements. Like so much else with these programs, the current centrality of state waivers to ongoing policy development in

Medicaid and CHIP was not the intent when the authorities for the demonstrations were enacted.

The origins of today's waiver-heavy policy debates can be found in the political philosophy of President Franklin D. Roosevelt. He urged ongoing experimentation in his administration in social welfare policy to foster a culture of evidence-driven program improvement. In 1962, the Kennedy administration took that spirit one step further by agreeing to a robust statutory authority aimed at state-initiated reforms—Section 1115 of the Social Security Act. After originally conceiving Section 1115 as permission for state experimentation in cash welfare assistance, Congress expanded the section's authority to cover Medicaid in 1965 and then CHIP in 1997.

Section 1115 specifically allows states to request permission from the federal government to run "demonstrations" that test alternatives to Medicaid's and CHIP's standard rules. Initially, the authority was used to pursue relatively modest program adjustments. That began to change during Ronald Reagan's presidency, and the focus on waivers accelerated in the 1990s.

Before 1982, Arizona refused to implement Medicaid, preferring instead to retain a county-based "indigent care" system that was the norm across the country before 1965. As the financial strain from health costs began crippling local governments in the state, Arizona's statewide officeholders came under pressure to drop their opposition to the adoption of a Medicaid program. They did so only after the federal government agreed to allow the state to operate it entirely under a Section 1115 waiver requiring mandatory managed care for all program participants. The waiver agreement struck between the federal government and the state in 1982—modified nearly continuously in the intervening four decades—continues to govern the state's Medicaid policies.

The other major development around that time was the application of neutrality to the federal budget as a major consideration in state-initiated waiver requests.

Section 1115 does not include the budgetary effects of submitted waiver requests as a required consideration for approval. That focus was advanced by Reagan administration officials who believed HHS was approving state waiver applications and federally sponsored Medicare and Medicaid experiments that would lead to higher federal outlays in future years. As part of a budget negotiation in 1983, these officials secured agreement from HHS to have the Office of Management and Budget review all future waiver and research demonstrations projects before they could be approved, including state-initiated requests under Section 1115, and to apply a policy of budget neutrality to all waiver applications.[28]

These developments, along with expansive state experiments in AFDC, changed perceptions among state officials of what might be possible through the waiver process.

Somewhat counterintuitively, the emergence of budget neutrality became a spur, rather than a deterrent, to state waiver activity in the 1990s, due mainly to the subjectivity of the estimation process. The federal actuaries who forecast Medicaid outlays do so based on national trends, which tend to include offsetting factors that even out across regions or states. For the national government, identifying the right average trend is sufficient for an accurate spending projection. For waivers, however, it is state-specific considerations that are crucial and difficult to identify from afar.

Consequently, discussions between federal and state officials over waiver submissions inevitably become negotiations over what should, or should not, be considered when building a state-specific Medicaid spending baseline. CMS has attempted to create some universal guidelines for these reviews to lessen the ambiguity and improve fairness, but these rules are not in law or regulation and are not so airtight as to discourage states from trying to maximize federal support.[29]

The heightened focus on budget neutrality also spurred state creativity. For instance, states could increase special payments to hospitals to cover the costs of uninsured patients (and use dubious methods when covering the state's share of these costs) and then use the elevated federal outlays to secure agreement for more liberalized eligibility rules under a waiver program while committing to cutbacks to the elevated level of special hospital payments.

These factors transformed the waiver process from a mechanism for testing limited experiments into a major pathway for implementing permanent, statewide reform plans during the 1990s and the first decade of the 2000s.

That began to change with the enactment of the ACA and its substantial Medicaid expansion and premium subsidy programs. With the federal government covering most of the enrollment premium for uninsured

Americans, the states have had less of a need in recent years for large waiver programs that feature incremental eligibility liberalizations.

Instead, the focus is now on policy innovations for goals beyond coverage expansion. During the Trump administration, several states, with the encouragement of federal officials, pursued work requirement rules for Medicaid (a focus that the Biden administration has now closed off). States are also pursuing waivers to improve behavioral health services, implement delivery system reforms, and integrate social determinants of health into program funding.[30]

While the era of sweeping Section 1115 waivers for program expansion is now likely over, the waivers that were agreed to during those years have taken on a life of their own, in part because they involve specific budget neutrality deals that states have come to rely on and want preserved. According to a tracking database maintained by the Kaiser Family Foundation, 44 states have 57 active Section 1115 waivers in place (as of October 2020), with another 26 applications (submitted by 21 states) still pending at CMS.[31]

Growth and Fiscal Pressure

The financial pressure created by Medicaid's rapid growth is, by itself, an important factor when considering how to reform it.

Medicaid's enrollment growth has been substantial for four decades. As noted, Congress approved a series of liberalizations starting in the 1980s, culminating in the large expansion included in the ACA. This growth was probably inevitable as the country turned to Medicaid as its safety-net insurance plan for persons not well served by job-based coverage. Even so, the program's size is now remarkable relative to how it was originally conceived. As shown in Figure 7, in 1970, just 6.8 percent of the total US population was enrolled in Medicaid. By 2020, more than one-quarter of all Americans were enrolled in either Medicaid or CHIP.

Medicaid is now so large that it plays a dominant role in certain aspects of US health care. Among other things, Medicaid pays for more than 40 percent of all births, and the program finances 30 percent of all nursing home care and nearly 60 percent of home health visits.[32]

Figure 7. Medicaid and CHIP Enrollment as a Percentage of the Total US Population

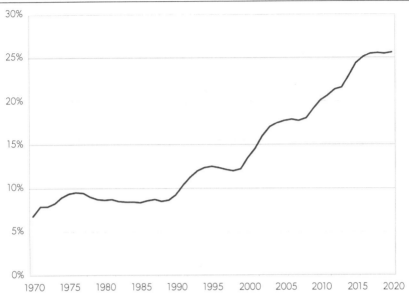

Source: Medicaid and CHIP Payment and Access Commission, *MACSTATS: Medicaid and CHIP Date Book*, December 2021, https://www.macpac.gov/wp-content/uploads/2021/12/MACStats-Medicaid-and-CHIP-Data-Book-December-2021.pdf; Kaiser Family Foundation, "State Health Facts: Total Number of Children Ever Enrolled in CHIP Annually," November 1, 2021, https://www.kff.org/other/state-indicator/annual-chip-enrollment/; and Federal Reserve Economic Data, website, https://fred.stlouisfed.org.

The growth of combined federal and state Medicaid spending has been commensurate with enrollment and escalating medical expenses. As shown in Figure 8, in 1970, the program's total cost was equal to less than 0.5 percent of gross domestic product (GDP). By 2020, it had risen to 3.3 percent of GDP.

The large share of Medicaid spending covered by federal payments eases the burden on states, but it does not eliminate it altogether. As shown in Figure 9, the state share of Medicaid, measured as a percentage of total state budgets (not counting federal support), has grown steadily too. In 1993, states had to set aside, on average, just under 11 percent of available funds for the program. By 2019, Medicaid consumed nearly 16 percent of available state-only revenue.

Figure 8. Total Federal and State Medicaid Spending as a Percentage of GDP

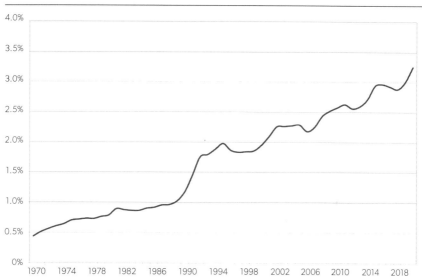

Source: Medicaid and CHIP Payment and Access Commission, *MACSTATS: Medicaid and CHIP Date Book*, December 2021, https://www.macpac.gov/wp-content/uploads/2021/12/MACStats-Medicaid-and-CHIP-Data-Book-December-2021.pdf; and Federal Reserve Economic Data, website, https://fred.stlouisfed.org.

At the federal level, Medicaid is one of the three entitlement programs, along with Social Security and Medicare, that has come to dominate the budget outlook. In 1970, the combined federal spending on these three programs was 3.7 percent of GDP. In 2020, it was 11.7 percent, and CBO projects it will be 17.1 percent of GDP in 2050 (when CHIP and ACA subsidies are included).[33]

A Reform Outline

While significant Medicaid and CHIP reform has been discussed intermittently by elected officials for many years, changes to the program's basic financing and benefit rules have never passed. Instead, Congress has adopted a series of incremental expansions that built on its original design.

Figure 9. State Medicaid Spending as a Percentage of Total State Budgets

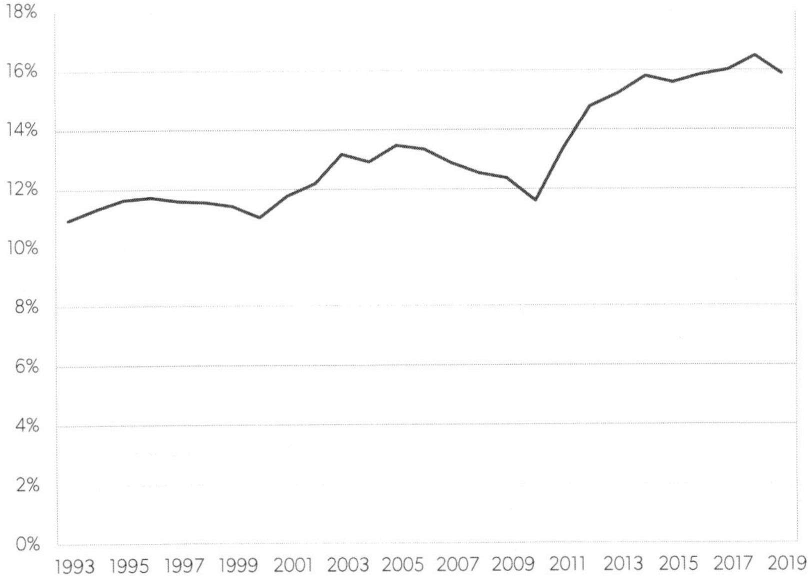

Source: Medicaid and CHIP Payment and Access Commission, *MACSTATS: Medicaid and CHIP Data Book*, December 2021, https://www.macpac.gov/wp-content/uploads/2021/12/MACStats-Medicaid-and-CHIP-Data-Book-December-2021.pdf.

An impediment to deeper change is Medicaid and CHIP's shared federal-state administration, which creates many interested parties with divergent agendas. States have their own visions for program evolution, and their plans might be disrupted if national leaders act on different objectives.

Despite the challenges, however, federal reform is important, particularly for advocates of market incentives. Medicaid and CHIP help shape the larger health system, and their growing costs are contributing to fiscal pressures. Medicare and job-based insurance are more important factors influencing the business practices of hospitals and physician groups, but the nation's safety-net programs can either reinforce or impede what market reforms aim to achieve.

Market advocates must be realistic, however, about how far they can go. The majority of voters value programs that prevent vulnerable individuals from going without beneficial medical services. Reform should further strengthen the protection these programs confer while making them more efficient and cost-effective.

The following is an outline of such an agenda.

Recognize Medicaid's Two Basic and Separable Functions. Medicaid, from its beginning, had two distinct roles in the nation's health system: providing traditional health insurance to low-income households and financing long-term care for the disabled and elderly. They are housed in one statute because Congress wanted to supplement cash support for low-income mothers with children (who require health insurance) and low-income elderly (who frequently need nursing home care). This latter function involves substantially higher federal and state costs per enrolled beneficiary.

Federal legislation should establish two parts in Medicaid to improve how these diverging roles interact with the broader systems in which they operate.

Medicaid and CHIP offer health coverage to individuals who do not have access to job-based insurance and have incomes too low to qualify for ACA assistance. To eliminate breaks in coverage and prevent expensive duplication, these platforms should work in coordination with each other to achieve population-wide enrollment (as discussed further below). Establishing a separate part of Medicaid devoted strictly to health insurance for nondisabled individuals would make it easier to adjust processes for better integration with the other insurance systems.

Similarly, Medicaid support for long-term services and support works with Medicare's home health and skilled nursing benefits, private long-term care insurance, and out-of-pocket spending by consumers and their families. Separating Medicaid's role in this broader system of long-term care from its role as a health insurance program for younger and healthier beneficiaries will facilitate processes that are better suited to these functions.

Rationalize Program Financing. Medicaid and CHIP are now financed by a complex combination of fixed allotments for certain services and populations and federal matching payments, which vary substantially by how the spending is categorized. The result is not necessarily a fair or sensible distribution of government support. Among other things, the current funding formulas are intended to support lower-income states with more generous federal support, but the rich states attract the most federal funds. Further, during economic downturns, Congress will often provide a boost to the FMAP, which mostly rewards the states with high Medicaid spending instead of those experiencing the highest levels of unemployment. Current FMAP policies are underwriting spending per person in some states that is well above what might be justified by differences in input costs, along with federal spending on some beneficiaries (such as those made eligible by the ACA) that is above the level for beneficiaries with lower incomes. Finally, the FMAP reduces the incentive for states to economize on spending because most of the savings would accrue to the federal Treasury and not state coffers.

Previous efforts to rationalize program funding have foundered because of the entrenched interests that have built up around the current system. Even so, changing how the federal government supports Medicaid and CHIP remains important for equity and cost-effectiveness.

The first objective should be to gradually move away from the original FMAP formula, which undermines budget discipline by making the political pain of implementing reforms excessive relative to the benefits. Moreover, using state per capita incomes as the basis for establishing the federal share of costs complicates tying payments to a rational measure of efficient service delivery.

Reform should be gradual and blend today's formula with a second basis of program financing that eliminates distinctions among Medicaid, DSH allotments, and CHIP and instead pays the states a fixed amount per enrollee based on a measure of reasonable costs per person for distinct subpopulations. Federal funding would rise and fall with enrollment, and thus there would be no threat to needed coverage. Within the program's health insurance function, the federal payments could support family coverage or individual insurance (primarily for single adults without children). For LTSS and long-term care, payments could differentiate among seriously disabled children, disabled adults under age 65, and the frail elderly.

Introducing per capita payments would encourage states to view program spending through a defined contribution lens. The federal payment for health insurance would be seen as supporting premium payments for the eligible population. Similarly, for LTSS, a fixed federal payment per person would encourage the use of managed care plans to coordinate these services with regular medical care, especially for persons also enrolled in Medicare.

State Requirements and Options. The ongoing uncertainty over Medicaid expansion in some states, along with the increasingly politicized negotiations around Medicaid waivers, points to the need for better rules governing this relationship. Generally, there need to be clearer and more enforceable minimum expectations for the states, less need for waiver requests through the granting of greater flexibility, and even less room for politicization of whatever waiver opportunities would remain in place.

The ACA was supposed to create a new minimum level of coverage through Medicaid by forcing the states to enroll all persons with incomes below 138 percent of the FPL. The Supreme Court ruled that this degree of coercion violated the Constitution, which complicates finding a national solution to more uniform standards.

However, the 2012 ruling did not foreclose all incentives for state compliance with federal expectations. Rather, it was a reaction to the heavy-handed penalty in the ACA (the full withdrawal of all federal Medicaid funding) that effectively removed any state discretion.

An alternative would retain some level of state flexibility. One option would be to give the states the choice to provide coverage up to 100 percent of the FPL or to 138 percent as specified in the ACA. States agreeing to one or the other income threshold would then be granted greater flexibility to alter certain program parameters without the need for a federal waiver (such as over-covered benefits and a small amount of cost sharing for certain services).

States that refused to comply would lose only a portion of their federal support (perhaps 5 to 10 percent) and would be ineligible for federal waivers from other Medicaid requirements.[34]

Population-Wide Insurance Enrollment. As discussed in more detail in Chapter 6, every American should be enrolled in health insurance to ensure they have ready access to primary care and more intensive services in the event of a serious health setback. Going without insurance worsens health outcomes.

Medicaid is crucial to achieving population-wide enrollment, but some of its current rules impede progress. Most important, the program continues to rely on month-to-month income tests for enrolled beneficiaries, which adds to coverage churn and creates needless breaks in protection. Monthly eligibility assessments do not make sense in the context of health insurance, as stability in access to services is often crucial in restoring and protecting patient health.

Reform could promote continuous insurance coverage by establishing Medicaid eligibility on an annual basis. This assessment could be the same basis for determining a person's eligibility for ACA subsidies and thus could be built into the same administrative process (as detailed in Chapter 6). Among other things, for health insurance enrollment, the ACA's system of exchanges could become the default system for identifying and enrolling eligible households into either Medicaid or a private plan. Some of the current distinctions between the MCOs offered through Medicaid and the private coverage offered through the ACA might begin to fade, thus simplifying insurance enrollment for all households not covered by job-based plans.

The Dually Eligible. The most significant opportunity for cost reductions in Medicaid is to be found in better management of services for dually eligible beneficiaries. As noted in this chapter, Medicaid spending for this population is well above the average per-person spending for parents, children, and single adults who are enrolled in the program, and yet most dual eligibles receive both their Medicaid and Medicare benefits in unmanaged and uncoordinated settings. Providing full Medicaid and Medicare benefits through integrated managed care plans could delay or prevent some institutionalized care and lower the costs of treating many of the chronic conditions afflicting these patients.

Past reform efforts have produced only minor positive results. The ACA created an office within CMS for Medicare-Medicaid coordination, which has been testing new models for incentivizing better management of the combined medical and social service support offered by the two programs. Unfortunately, the take-up of these models has been modest and the savings minimal.

It is past time for a more forceful initiative.

One approach would be to require the managed care plans participating in one of the two programs to have in place the capacity to manage services provided by the program that is not their contractual client. Thus, all managed care plans participating in MA would be required to have sufficient reach to manage the social services covered by Medicaid in the event an MA enrollee becomes eligible for full Medicaid after first entering the Medicare program. Similarly, the MCOs participating in Medicaid would need to have in place the capacity to manage Medicare-covered benefits in the event a disabled Medicaid participant becomes eligible for Medicare after first getting Medicaid-covered services (perhaps at the point a person turns age 65). Both levels of government would need to approve the contracts for these plans before going into effect.

These parallel requirements would vastly expand the capacity for managing these services by forcing the plans participating in both programs to build effective provider networks through their contracts with facilities and practitioners.

Past calls for better coordination have stumbled in part because the federal and state governments have not agreed to a system for sharing savings from these initiatives. A requirement imposed on managed care plans in both programs should help settle the matter. The contracts that allow them to participate in one or the other program could be used to force an agreement between the relevant states and the federal government over the expected savings from the contract and the method for dividing it between them.

Market Discipline. Because Medicaid's role is to serve as a safety net for low-income households, there is resistance to conceiving of, and implementing, reforms to the program that would harness market principles to cut expenses based on the misperception that the beneficiaries would necessarily be exposed to additional costs. But market reforms can be designed to provide only savings to the beneficiaries and no additional costs, if that is what policymakers choose to do.

As discussed in Chapter 1, there are two general options for injecting market pressure into the health sector: forcing stronger competition among the health plans offering services or requiring more standardization and transparency on the prices charged by facilities and practitioners when offering services to patients. Both provide viable opportunities for cost reductions in Medicaid.

As noted, the program already relies heavily on full-service, privately administered MCOs to provide coverage to the vast majority of Medicaid participants. Many states currently allow their beneficiaries to participate in selecting the MCOs providing their coverage, but take-up of these options is generally weak. Instead, states usually assign their Medicaid beneficiaries to MCOs.

That approach could be modified to encourage the beneficiaries to participate in the selection process by allowing them to share in the savings when opting for plans with lower-than-average total premiums. The beneficiaries would never pay more when they choose more expensive options, but the state could provide them with a monthly cash payment reflecting some of the cost reduction from lower-priced plans.

A similar approach is possible for some high-volume services that can be scheduled in advance and thus are amenable to price shopping. The states could require their licensed clinicians and facilities to post pricing for standardized definitions of the most common services patients need (such as certain diagnostic tests, services related to childbirth, and some surgeries) and then allow the beneficiaries to keep some of the savings if they opt to receive care from a provider charging a below-average price. Again, there would never be a penalty for selecting higher-priced practitioners, but the opportunity for savings would be sufficient to encourage stronger price competition and thus would lower overall costs.

Market-Driven Health Care Needs a Safety Net

Some market advocates are uneasy with Medicaid's growth and ever-expanding role in US health care. Their focus is on strengthening price competition and consumer choice, and Medicaid is seen as running counter to their goals because it mostly exempts enrollees from weighing financial considerations when getting coverage or paying for services.

It's a shortsighted perspective, however. A market-driven system can catalyze more efficiency and innovation in medical care, but it will struggle to serve lower-income households without public subsidies and rules.

Voters understand this limitation and will be reluctant to embrace market reforms unless there is a strong safety net in place to protect vulnerable Americans. In other words, a strong safety net is not a hindrance to a market-driven health system but instead can facilitate it by making it more acceptable politically.

Medicaid also can reinforce market incentives. The program is already transitioning away from FFS care and toward a fully managed system, with an extensive role for private insurers. States can bring more market discipline to their contracting strategies by giving the program's participants more of a role in selecting coverage and perhaps allowing them to share in savings when opting for lower-priced coverage and service providers.

Support for a strong safety net is not an excuse to ignore Medicaid's role in the nation's fiscal challenges. Without reform, Medicaid spending, along with Social Security and Medicare, will overwhelm the federal government by pushing public debt up to levels that are well beyond what is sustainable. Fortunately, there are opportunities for cost savings that do not undermine the program's protections. In particular, better coordination of Medicaid with Medicare for the dually eligible can reduce costs by preventing unnecessary nursing home stays.

Implementation in the coming years of this and other reforms will be necessary to avoid the more abrupt and potentially damaging adjustments that might be required to ameliorate the effects of a fiscal crisis.

Notes

1. Judith D. Moore and David G. Smith, "Legislating Medicaid: Considering Medicaid and Its Origins," *Health Care Financing Review* 27, no. 2 (Winter 2005), https://www.ncbi.nlm.nih.gov/pmc/articles/PMC4194918/pdf/hcfr-27-2-045.pdf.

2. Moore and Smith, "Legislating Medicaid."

3. Moore and Smith, "Legislating Medicaid."

4. Medicaid and CHIP Payment and Access Commission, "Federal Requirement and State Options: Eligibility," March 2017, https://www.macpac.gov/wp-content/uploads/2017/03/Federal-Requirements-and-State-Options-Eligibility.pdf.

5. Medicaid and CHIP Payment and Access Commission, "Federal Requirement and State Options."

6. Medicaid and CHIP Payment and Access Commission, "Federal Requirement and State Options."

7. Centers for Medicare & Medicaid Services, 2018 *Actuarial Report on the Financial Outlook for Medicaid*, April 2020, https://www.cms.gov/files/document/2018-report.pdf.

8. Congressional Research Service, "Medicaid's Federal Medical Assistance Percentage (FMAP)," July 29, 2020, https://sgp.fas.org/crs/misc/R43847.pdf.

9. Congressional Research Service, "Medicaid's Federal Medical Assistance Percentage (FMAP)."

10. Robin Rudowitz et al., "Medicaid Financing: The Basics," Kaiser Family Foundation, May 7, 2021, https://www.kff.org/report-section/medicaid-financing-the-basics-issue-brief/.

11. Alison Mitchell, "Federal Financing for the State Children's Health Insurance Program (CHIP)," Congressional Research Service, May 23, 2018, https://sgp.fas.org/crs/misc/R43949.pdf.

12. Mitchell, "Federal Financing for the State Children's Health Insurance Program (CHIP)."

13. Medicaid and CHIP Payment and Access Commission, "State Children's Health Insurance Program (CHIP)," February 2018, https://www.macpac.gov/wp-content/uploads/2018/02/State-Children%E2%80%99s-Health-Insurance-Program-CHIP.pdf.

14. Medicaid and CHIP Payment and Access Commission, "State Children's Health Insurance Program (CHIP)."

15. Medicaid and CHIP Payment and Access Commission, "State Children's Health Insurance Program (CHIP)."

16. Medicaid and CHIP Payment and Access Commission, "State Children's Health Insurance Program (CHIP)."

17. Kaiser Family Foundation, "Status of State Medicaid Expansion Decisions: Interactive Map," February 24, 2022, https://www.kff.org/medicaid/issue-brief/status-of-state-medicaid-expansion-decisions-interactive-map/.

18. Congressional Budget Office, "Exploring the Growth of Medicaid Managed Care," August 2018, https://www.cbo.gov/system/files/2018-08/54235-MMC_chartbook.pdf.

19. Elizabeth Hinton and Lina Stoylar, "10 Things to Know about Medicaid Managed Care," Kaiser Family Foundation, February 23, 2022, https://www.kff.org/medicaid/issue-brief/10-things-to-know-about-medicaid-managed-care/.

20. Hinton and Stoylar, "10 Things to Know About Medicaid Managed Care."

21. Centers for Medicare & Medicaid Services, "Dually Eligible Beneficiaries Under Medicare and Medicaid," February 2020, https://www.cms.gov/Outreach-and-Education/Medicare-Learning-Network-MLN/MLNProducts/downloads/medicare_beneficiaries_dual_eligibles_at_a_glance.pdf.

22. Medicaid and CHIP Payment and Access Commission, *MACSTATS: Medicaid and CHIP Date Book*, December 2021, https://www.macpac.gov/wp-content/uploads/2021/12/MACStats-Medicaid-and-CHIP-Data-Book-December-2021.pdf.

23. Congressional Budget Office, "Dual-Eligible Beneficiaries of Medicare and Medicaid: Characteristics, Health Care Spending, and Evolving Policies," June 2013, https://www.cbo.gov/sites/default/files/113th-congress-2013-2014/reports/44308dualeligibles2.pdf.

24. Zhanlian Feng et al., *Analysis of Pathways to Dual Eligible Status*, US Department of Health and Human Services, May 2019, https://aspe.hhs.gov/sites/default/files/

migrated_legacy_files/189226/DualStatus.pdf.

25. Congressional Budget Office, "Dual-Eligible Beneficiaries of Medicare and Medicaid."

26. Nancy Archibald et al., *Integrating Care Through Dual Eligible Special Needs Plans (D-SNPs): Opportunities and Challenges*, US Department of Health and Human Services, April 2019, https://aspe.hhs.gov/sites/default/files/migrated_legacy_files/188071/MMI-DSNP.pdf.

27. Nick Johnson, Christopher S. Kunkel, and Annie Hallum, "Changing How Medicare and Medicaid Talk to Each Other," Milliman, March 2020, https://www.milliman.com/-/media/milliman/pdfs/articles/changing_how_medicare_and_medicaid_talk_to_each_other.ashx.

28. Johnson, Kunkel, and Hallum, "Changing How Medicare and Medicaid Talk to Each Other."

29. Cynthia Shirk, "Shaping Medicaid and SCHIP Through Waivers: The Fundamentals," *National Health Policy Forum*, no. 64 (July 22, 2008), https://hsrc.himmelfarb.gwu.edu/cgi/viewcontent.cgi?referer=&httpsredir=1&article=1199&context=sphhs_centers_nhpf.

30. Timothy B. Hill, "Letter to State Medicaid Director," August 22, 2018, https://www.medicaid.gov/federal-policy-guidance/downloads/smd18009.pdf.

31. Kaiser Family Foundation, "State Health Facts: Births Financed by Medicaid," 2020, https://www.kff.org/medicaid/state-indicator/births-financed-by-medicaid/.

32. Kaiser Family Foundation, "State Health Facts: Births Financed by Medicaid."

33. Kaiser Family Foundation, "State Health Facts: Total Number of Children Ever Enrolled in CHIP Annually," November 1, 2021, https://www.kff.org/other/state-indicator/annual-chip-enrollment/; and Medicaid and CHIP Payment and Access Commission, *MACSTATS*.

34. In *Dole v. South Dakota* (1987), the Supreme Court ruled that federal penalties of this size were permissible with highway funding to encourage state compliance with a national age standard on alcohol consumption. See Congressional Research Service, "Medicaid and Federal Grant Conditions After *NFIB v. Sebelius*: Constitutional Issues and Analysis," July 17, 2012, https://crsreports.congress.gov/product/pdf/R/R42367.

5

Employer-Sponsored Insurance

Employers have been an important source of health insurance in the US for the entirety of the postwar era and have popularized many health system innovations. Even so, the coverage they sponsor has shortcomings that lead to periodic calls for its elimination. Those efforts have all failed because tens of millions of workers value what their employers provide and are reluctant to trade it in for untested alternatives. Nonetheless, the flaws remain and are holding back the performance of US health care more generally.

Among other problems, employer-sponsored insurance (ESI) is not offered to millions of workers, which leaves them to find their coverage on their own in a less attractive remnant market. Further, ESI can be insecure even for covered employees if they are at risk of losing their jobs during a downturn. Even more troubling is the system's persistently rising costs, which often have exceeded the growth rate of workers' wages.

Many companies are aware of these problems and have attempted to address them through changes they have implemented in the offerings under their direct control. Some of these efforts have shown promise and broken new ground. Overall, however, they have been far too small in scale to influence the overall direction of the broader system, especially with respect to cost discipline.

ESI, like the health sector in which it operates, requires a structured market to work optimally. With the right changes, workers participating in these plans could become effective consumers, both when selecting their specific insurance plans and when deciding where and when to get certain services (the two pathways outlined in Chapter 1). The effect would be to amplify the system improvements that would come from similar changes in Medicare and other coverage.

The private sector plays an important role in improving ESI, but it cannot fix its problems on its own. Congress must change the laws that govern how the ESI market works to make the coverage more secure for

Figure 1. Health Insurance Coverage in the US, 2021

Population Under Age 65 (Millions)

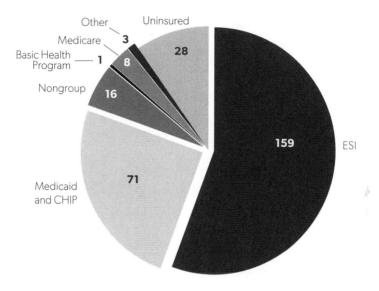

Source: Congressional Budget Office, "Federal Subsidies for Health Insurance Coverage for People Under Age 65: CBO and JCT's July 2021 Projections," July 2021, https://www.cbo.gov/system/files/2021-08/51298-2021-07-healthinsurance.pdf.

workers and their families and to allow market principles to govern how it functions.

Coverage Gaps

Health insurance coverage in the United States relies heavily on employer provision for the working-age population. As shown in Figure 1, the Congressional Budget Office (CBO) estimates that 155 million people under age 65—or nearly 57 percent of the non-elderly population—were enrolled in employer plans in 2021.[1] An additional 71 million people will be enrolled in Medicaid or the Children's Health Insurance Program. The CBO estimates 28 million people were uninsured, which is slightly more than in 2016 (27 million).[2] Nearly all Americans age 65 and older get their primary

Figure 2. Percentage of US Population Under Age 65 with ESI, 1998–2018

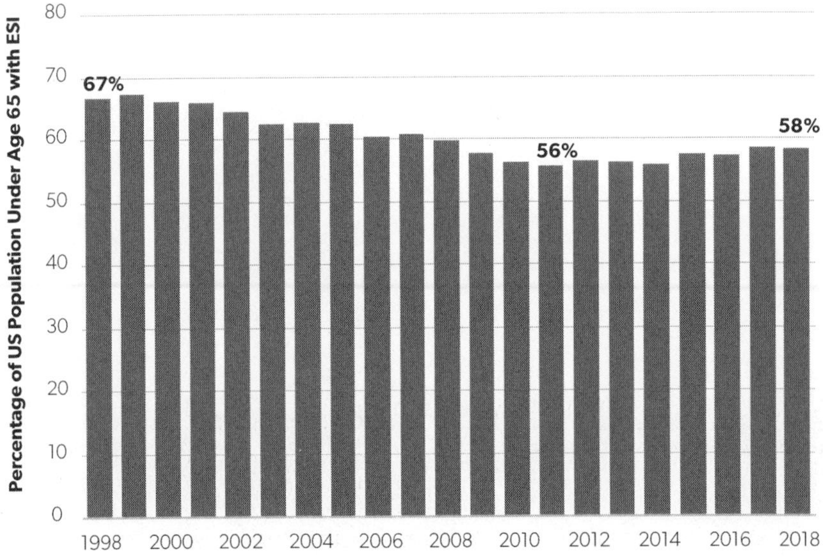

Source: Matthew Rae et al., "Long-Term Trends in Employer-Based Coverage," Peterson Foundation and Kaiser Family Foundation, April 3, 2020, https://www.healthsystemtracker.org/brief/long-term-trends-in-employer-based-coverage/.

coverage through Medicare; for those under age 65, eight million are enrolled in the program. (These are persons who are eligible based on a permanent disability.)

While ESI remains the dominant form of coverage for the non-elderly, enrollment in job-based insurance has been declining as a percentage of the overall population in this age group, as shown in Figure 2. In 1998, 67 percent of the non-elderly US population was enrolled in ESI. By 2018, the percentage fell to 58 percent. The CBO expects it to continue to fall over the next decade, to around 54 percent in 2031.[3]

ESI is not a guaranteed option for all American workers. The Affordable Care Act (ACA) requires most firms to offer their employees some form of health coverage, but this provision does not apply to many smaller businesses. (See the first sidebar for a description of the ACA provisions.) As shown in Figure 3, among low-income households, workers with ESI offers are the exception, not the rule. In 1998, among workers with incomes

Figure 3. Percentage of Workers Offered ESI, by Income and Year

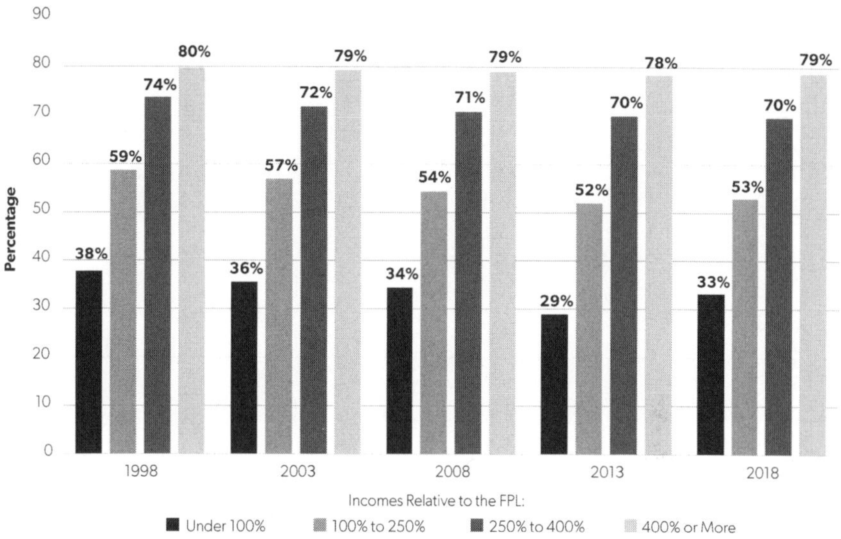

Source: Matthew Rae et al., "Long-Term Trends in Employer-Based Coverage," Peterson Foundation and Kaiser Family Foundation, April 3, 2020, https://www.healthsystemtracker.org/brief/long-term-trends-in-employer-based-coverage/.

below the federal poverty line (FPL), only 38 percent had an offer of ESI, and by 2018, that share fell to 33 percent. In contrast, among workers with incomes above 400 percent of the FPL, 79 percent had an offer of ESI in 2018, down slightly from 80 percent in 1998.

Workers, Not Firms, Pay for ESI

The financial burden of job-based insurance on workers is obscured by premium payments coming mainly from firms, not employees. According to the Kaiser Family Foundation's annual survey of employer plans, in 2021 firms paid about 73 percent, or $16,250, of the $22,220 average annual premium for family coverage, with workers paying the remainder of the costs.[4]

This division of the premium burden creates the impression that workers are shielded from rising costs. In reality, workers in competitive

Figure 4. ESI Premiums vs. Wages, Cumulative Growth, 2000 to 2019

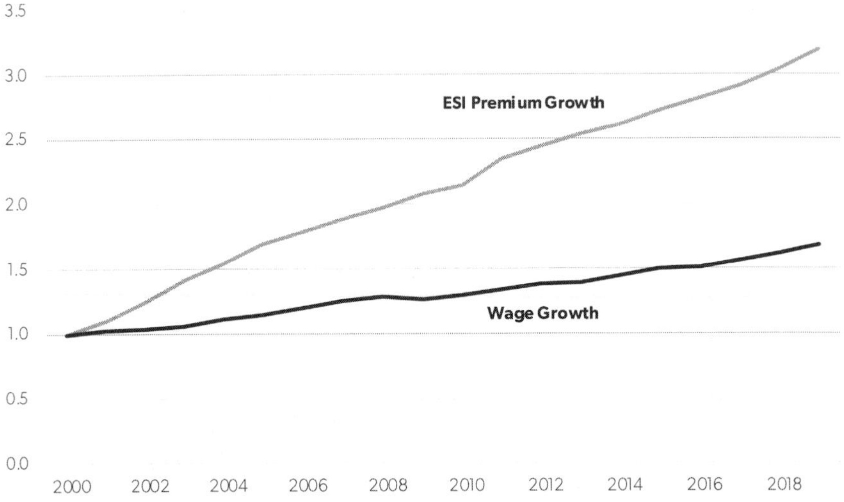

Note: Index of spending by year relative to 2000 = 1.0.
Source: Kaiser Family Foundation, "Employer Health Benefits: 2020 Annual Survey," 2020, http://files.kff.org/attachment/ReportEmployer-Health-Benefits-2020-Annual-Survey.pdf; and Social Security Administration, "Average Wage Index Series," 2019, https://www.ssa.gov/oact/cola/AWI.html#Series.

industries absorb most, if not all, of the premiums for ESI because their employers pay them lower wages to make room for the premium payments that appear to come out of the firms' accounts. Employers target the total cost of compensation, not just wages and salaries; when ESI premiums rise rapidly, there is less room for growth in cash compensation.

The pressure that rising health costs have imposed on wages has persisted for many years. From 2009 to 2018, for instance, total compensation for middle-income households grew at an average annual rate of 2.6 percent, yet wages grew by less than 1 percent each year over the same period. Rapidly rising health benefit costs led firms to limit their pay raises for their workers.[5]

Figure 4 illustrates the gap that has accumulated over time between the costs of health benefits and the wages that workers receive to pay for the other expenses they incur. In 2019, health benefit costs for employers were 220 percent higher than they were in 2000. By contrast, wages in 2019 were only 68 percent above what they were in 2000.

The Affordable Care Act's Employer Offer Requirement

The Affordable Care Act (ACA) requires firms with at least 50 full-time employees (as defined by the law) to offer qualified health coverage to their workers and family members. A formula translates part-time workers into full-time-equivalent employees to determine whether the requirement applies.

Insurers offering group coverage to employer clients must comply with the ACA's essential health benefits (EHB) rules. Firms offering self-insured coverage are exempt from the EHB requirements except that they cannot impose annual or lifetime limits on any services covered by their plans that overlap with coverage required in the EHB rules.

An employer offer of coverage must meet minimum financial standards to qualify as ACA compliant. The insurance must have an actuarial value of at least 60 percent, which means cost sharing for the enrollees can account for no more than 40 percent of the costs of covered benefits. Further, the employee share of the premium cannot exceed a specified threshold of annual income; these thresholds are lower for lower-income households and are adjusted each year based on growth in premiums for ACA-compliant plans. Beginning in 2022, the maximum an employee with income of at least 300 percent of the federal poverty line is allowed to pay for ACA-compliant employer-sponsored insurance (ESI) is 9.61 percent of his or her annual income.[6]

Employers failing to comply with the ACA's coverage offer requirement are subject to penalties. Firms that offer coverage to at least 95 percent of their full-time employees pay the lesser of a penalty based on the number of their workers receiving subsidized coverage through the ACA or a penalty applied based on total employment. For firms that offer coverage to less than 95 percent of their full-time employees, their penalty is tied to their total employment regardless of the share enrolled in ESI.[7]

A Collective Action Problem

Employers offer insurance to their workers as part of their compensation packages. Firms want to attract good employees, so they have an incentive to offer high-quality health benefits. Federal tax law encourages firms to be generous with their health benefits by exempting employer-paid premiums from workers' payroll and income tax obligations. Because cash wages are fully taxable, firms and workers have an incentive to emphasize generosity in health coverage when deciding how to adjust compensation levels.

Expansive employer coverage contributes to system-wide cost escalation. Hospitals and physician groups organize their operations in part to appeal to workers covered by generous job-based insurance. When that coverage lacks meaningful cost discipline, the entire system becomes more expensive.

Over the years, many large firms have recognized that their health offerings lack cost discipline and have tried to implement corrective measures. There have been modest successes. But a single company cannot, on its own, fix the problems that afflict ESI because it is too small to make a big difference—and it has to compete for labor with other employers. If prospective employees perceive that one firm's health benefits are lacking relative to an industry norm, that will hurt that firm's ability to recruit a high-quality workforce.

The solution is a change in federal tax law that forces all employers to grapple with controlling costs. The ACA attempted to do this with the Cadillac tax. Job-based coverage remained tax-free for workers, but companies with high-cost plans were scheduled to pay an excise tax on premiums above specified thresholds, beginning in 2018.

The business community, along with labor unions, strongly opposed the Cadillac tax during the initial debate on the ACA and after the law was enacted. Congress reacted to this pressure by delaying it twice before finally repealing it altogether in 2019.

A Framework for More Cost-Effective and Stable ESI

While ESI needs reform, it should not be abandoned altogether because it has strengths worth preserving.[8] ESI makes private insurance readily available and affordable to the vast majority of working-age Americans and their families. This insurance is, in general, high quality; it provides enrollees with ready access to large networks of physicians and hospitals with acceptable levels of cost sharing. And because the coverage is sponsored mainly by private firms, it is adaptable to changing industry circumstances and needs.

Without ESI, the US could become even more heavily dependent on public insurance enrollment, which would also mean increased pressure for government regulation of health care prices. Congress should improve the value of ESI by implementing reforms that strengthen its security, portability, and cost-effectiveness.

A Firm-Level Tax Credit for Compliant ESI Coverage. The ACA's Cadillac tax would have imposed a new cost on running high-premium job-based plans. The idea was to encourage firms to lower the costs of their plans to avoid paying the tax. It likely would have worked; few firms were expected to pay the penalty, which means employers were expected to adjust what they were offering—by using more managed care, for instance—to reduce the premiums they would owe for the coverage. Even so, employers and employees saw the Cadillac tax as an overly blunt and indiscriminate instrument that would have shifted more costs onto them instead of lowering them for all involved.

To avoid repeating the Cadillac tax saga, the next attempt at changing the tax treatment of ESI needs to emphasize incentives for reform rather than penalties. One option would be to offer tax credits directly to firms that voluntarily comply with new ESI coverage standards.

The CBO estimates that the aggregate value of the current law tax subsidy for ESI was $313 billion in 2021, or $1,970 per person enrolled in the coverage.[9] Redirecting a portion of this subsidy to firms without imposing any additional costs on workers should be possible. As a condition of receiving the credit, firms would be required to lower the amount of their contribution toward ESI premiums (to avoid adding to the overall federal tax subsidy) and implement reforms in ESI that maximize the value of that coverage for their employees. The objective of this plan would be to lower net costs for workers, when accounting for the premiums they must pay for their coverage and the wages they receive from their employers.

For example, as shown in Figure 5, under current law, the average 2021 ESI premium for family coverage was about $22,220, with workers paying just over one-quarter of the premium, or $5,970.[10] The balance of the premium—$16,250—was paid by firms (although, as noted, health coverage is part of a total compensation package paid to workers, and, in competitive labor markets, higher premiums for this coverage tend to crowd out funds available for cash wages). Employees enjoy a tax break with ESI because the employer share of the premium is not counted as wages for payroll or income tax purposes. The implicit tax subsidy is worth about $4,800 annually for workers in the 22 percent tax bracket.[11]

The tax treatment of ESI could be altered to give firms a credit for each worker enrolled in coverage. For instance, firms could get $500 annually for workers selecting individual coverage and $1,000 for those selecting family policies. Firms would be required to apply these credits to the premiums workers owe for ESI enrollment. Further, firms receiving the credits would be required to lower the amount of their pre-reform premium contributions by roughly three times the value of the credit, or $1,500 for individuals and $3,000 for families. These reductions would apply to the amounts contributed in the year preceding the first year in which the tax credit was payable to firms and would ensure that the aggregate federal subsidy for ESI insurance did not increase with the initiation of the federal premium credits for ESI plans.[12]

After one year of receiving the new federal premium credit, firms should be allowed to increase their defined contribution payments for worker coverage but only by affordable amounts when considering total compensation growth. For instance, the rise in the allowable levels of defined contribution ESI support could be tied to a measure of national wage inflation. For firms that have never offered ESI, the law should specify a maximum allowable contribution level tied to the average amount paid by employers providing support below the tax-preferred limit. Over time, disparities among firms in the allowable levels of tax-preferred defined contribution ESI support could be phased out and transitioned to a uniform national standard.

Figure 5. Moving to Firm-Level Tax Credits for ESI

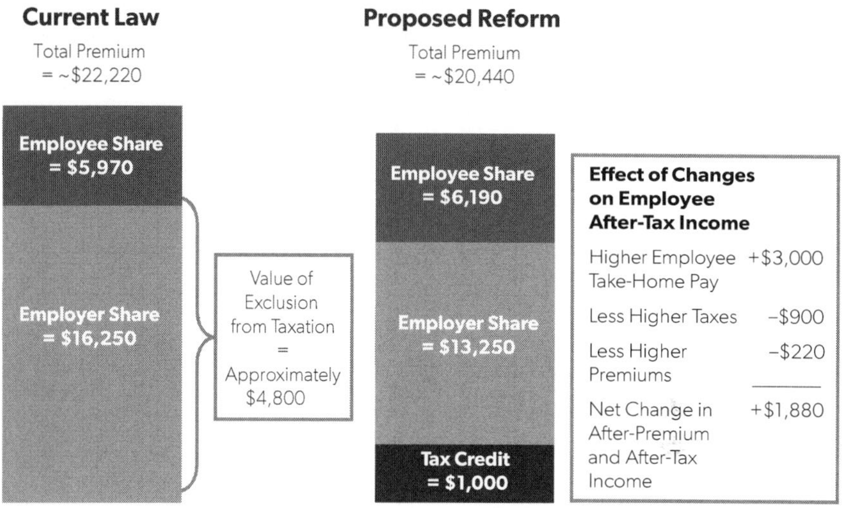

Current Law

Total Premium
= ~$22,220

Proposed Reform

Total Premium
= ~$20,440

Employee Share
= $5,970

Employer Share
= $16,250

Value of
Exclusion
from Taxation
=
Approximately
$4,800

Employee Share
= $6,190

Employer Share
= $13,250

Tax Credit
= $1,000

Effect of Changes on Employee After-Tax Income

Higher Employee Take-Home Pay	+$3,000
Less Higher Taxes	−$900
Less Higher Premiums	−$220
Net Change in After-Premium and After-Tax Income	+$1,880

Source: Author.

Further, employers would be required to hold harmless their employees by passing through the $1,500 or $3,000 reduction in premium contributions in the form of higher cash wages. Firms in competitive industries will move in this direction even without a federal requirement because of the need to offer compensation that attracts prospective employees. However, a requirement to pass through to workers the amounts previously made as premium payments is likely to lessen workers' fears that the reform would worsen their overall financial position. Employers could lower their contributions for ESI by more than the minimum specified in federal law if they pass through the reduction to workers in the form of higher cash wages and salaries.

For this reform to have maximum reach, it would need to encourage both for-profit and not-for-profit firms to embrace it. Thus, the tax credit should be applicable to both income and employment taxes owed by firms. Firms would be required to pass it through to workers as a credit toward ESI coverage, with the costs covered by applying the credit to the amounts otherwise owed in federal income or payroll tax payments.

Defined Contribution Payments, Standardized Coverage, and Plan Choice by Workers. ESI reform can improve workers' financial position if the cost of coverage falls relative to what it would be under current law. Less expensive ESI plans would make room for higher cash wages. As shown in Figure 5, workers with family coverage that costs 8 percent less after the reform would come out $1,880 ahead from the tax credit proposal. They would pay more in taxes and premiums, but their higher pay would more than make up for these added costs.

A substantial drop in ESI premiums is not an unrealistic expectation if the reform is designed properly. The CBO has estimated that a similar plan—premium support in Medicare—would reduce overall costs in Medicare by 8 percent after a transition period.[13] The reform proposed here for ESI coverage is based on the same construct, with workers having strong incentives to select low-premium plans because doing so will lower their out-of-pocket premium expenses. Putting cost-conscious consumers in charge of choosing their coverage will increase the pressure on insurers to cut their costs and offer lower premium options.

Intensifying premium competition in ESI requires employer compliance with three related reforms.

First, employers accepting the federal premium credit must agree to convert their premium payments into defined contribution payments that their workers control. Most importantly, the level of support an employer provides has to be fixed (with two levels allowed, for individual and family coverage) and cannot increase or decrease based on plan selections by workers. Converting all employer ESI support into defined contribution payments ensures workers must consider the full cost differences of the plans from which they are choosing their coverage. For instance, if an employer provides $15,000 in defined contribution support for family coverage and two plans are available with premiums of $18,000 and $19,000, respectively, workers choosing the more expensive plan would pay the extra $1,000 in annual premium out of their own resources.

Second, the benefits covered by competing ESI plans must be standardized as far as possible. The goal is to force intensive competition at the level of premiums charged for the insurance and not to allow insurers to confuse the choice by altering what benefits are covered. With standardized offerings, insurers would be forced to compete on how effectively they can control the hospital, physician, and other costs that are directly related to caring for patients. Small adjustments in benefits (such as lowering the cost sharing required for vision care) confuses the choices available to consumers and makes it impossible to identify the insurers most adept at eliminating waste and inefficiency in the provision of care, which is where the focus must be to slow overall cost growth.

Third, firms participating in this voluntary reform must give their employees meaningful coverage options. The benefits must be standardized, but workers should have a say in how strict their plans manage care on their behalf, and, as discussed below, the federal government should ensure at least one of their options has a proven record of cost control while delivering high-quality care.

ESI would remain a flexible platform for offering health coverage, even with this reform. Employers could experiment with on-site clinics, primary care services, and prevention programs for diabetes and other chronic diseases. The change required by this reform is a commitment to coupling those design features with offerings that foster competition and lower premiums for their workers.

An Updated Dual-Choice Requirement. In the early 1970s, as health costs soared in the aftermath of implementation of Medicare and Medicaid, the Nixon administration was looking for ways to bring more discipline to the health sector. It eventually turned to an emerging form of insurance coverage—the health maintenance organization (HMO)—as a potential solution. (See the second sidebar for a description of the 1973 HMO Act.)

HMOs were not invented in the 1970s. In the postwar years, Kaiser Permanente and other managed care plans pioneered combining insurance with organized systems of care delivery to control costs more effectively than fee-for-service insurance. However, in these early years, these health plans were prominent only in certain parts of western states and had little overall effect on national health expenditures. The Nixon administration wanted them to become the norm throughout American health care rather than the exception, which is what led it to push Congress to pass legislation to promote HMO enrollment.

The Health Maintenance Organization Act of 1973

In the early 1970s, in the aftermath of implementation of Medicare and Medicaid, one of the architects of the "managed competition" school of health reform, Paul Ellwood, pressed the Nixon administration to embrace health maintenance organizations (HMOs) as part of a nationwide solution to rising costs. He found a receptive audience. In 1973, the administration worked with Congress to pass the HMO Act of 1973, which marked the beginning of a long period of growth of managed care plans in American health care.[14] HMOs existed before 1973—Kaiser Permanente began operating a publicly available plan in 1945—but the new law spurred the expansion of HMOs to parts of the country where they had minimal enrollment or were nonexistent.

The 1973 law had five main provisions.

Federal Definition. The law defined HMOs as health plans that accept prepayment for health services (instead of fee-for-service) and have tight relationships with the facilities and practitioners providing care to patients. Some HMOs own hospitals and employ physicians directly, while others maintain contractual relationships with their affiliated providers that give them a higher level of institutional control than is the case in unmanaged plans.

Federal Certification. HMOs could apply for federal certification by the US Department of Health and Human Services. Certification was a condition for receipt of funding and preferential market access.

Federal Preemption. The federal law overrode state laws that inhibited the formation and licensure of HMOs as valid health insurance products.

Federal Funding. The law created new funding streams that directly supported the HMO industry's expansion and growth.

(*continued on the next page*)

(continued from the previous page)
The Dual-Choice Requirement. Employers subject to federal fair labor laws (generally firms with at least 25 employees) were required to include federally certified HMOs in their offerings to workers if HMOs operating in the relevant geographic areas requested to be included as plan options. Further, the employer contribution toward the HMO coverage had to be at least as generous as what employers provided for the non-HMO offerings. The dual-choice requirement was repealed in 1988.[15]

Among other things, the law required employers with more than 25 workers to include at least one HMO in their health plan offerings to workers if an HMO offered coverage in the geographic area populated by an employer's workforce. This so-called dual-choice requirement was to be enforced mainly by the HMOs themselves by petitioning employers to offer their plans. It proved to be an important mechanism for growing the industry in its early years.[16] In 1988 amendments, the dual-choice requirement was terminated, effective in 1995.[17]

Managed care plans are pervasive in US health care today, with a large presence in Medicare, Medicaid, and ESI. Yet health costs continue to rise rapidly, and there is strong evidence of widespread inefficiency in the delivery of care.[18] Whatever its merits, the managed care industry has yet to tame the forces in health care that lead to excessive use of some services, overpriced care, and wasted resources.

A new dual choice–type requirement should force employers to include in their offerings plans with demonstrated value, as measured by their ability to satisfy the following conditions.

Effective Management of Care. Certified plans should have demonstrated their capacity to deliver high-quality care at below-average costs. Aggregate data can identify the insurance plans that are most adept at delivering value for common procedures and interventions. Plans with unacceptably low levels of measured value could be excluded from federal certification, perhaps with a process for an expedited reapplication after implementing corrective measures.

Facilitation of Consumer Price Shopping. Insurers should be required to maintain effective consumer engagement programs that are proven to work in controlling costs. In particular, insurance seeking federal certification should operate reference-payment programs that reward consumers for using high-value and low-cost service providers. Reference-based payment schemes, as discussed in Chapter 2, provide fixed amounts of reimbursement to groups of providers for delivering the full spectrum of services required for common procedures (such as joint replacement surgery). Consumers have strong incentives to use low-priced providers because they must pay for any expenses in excess of the fixed payments from their insurance plans. The most effective model also allows consumers to share in savings from using providers with costs below the benchmark paid by an insurance plan.

Protection of Consumers from Surprise Medical Bills. A 2020 federal law attempts to eliminate surprise bills for in-network care, but it is not yet certain it will work as planned. Insurers receiving federal certification should be required to have in place controls and contracts that fully protect their enrollees from surprise bills when receiving care from their affiliated providers.

Like the dual-choice requirement of decades ago, a new federal certification process should confer benefits on the plans that can meet high standards for cost control. In particular, federally certified insurance should be given presumptive access to ESI markets by requiring employers to offer their workers at least one federally certified insurance plan. Requiring employers receiving the tax credit to use defined contribution payments would ensure these plans could compete on a level playing field with non-certified coverage.

Federally Certified Private Exchanges. ESI reform should make it easier for firms, including those with fewer than 50 employees, to offer coverage to their workers and improve their pricing leverage in the market. Both objectives would be served by jump-starting a system of private insurance exchanges serving the employer sector.

Under the ACA, state or federally run exchanges are used to organize the market for individuals buying coverage on their own. Exchanges efficiently organize a health insurance market because they aggregate tens of thousands of potential consumers into a large pool when making purchase decisions. Insurers establish uniform plan offerings and premiums for all participants in the same exchange pool.

An important benefit of using exchanges for insurance enrollment is improved portability of coverage. While imperfect, private exchanges would allow some workers leaving one firm for another to keep the same health insurance when switching jobs, in the cases when both firms use the same exchange to organize coverage offerings for their workers.

Private exchanges already exist in the employer sector, with several large benefit consulting companies sponsoring them for their clients, but enrollment has been well below what was expected when they launched in the years immediately after the ACA was enacted.[19]

A major barrier is the risk profiles of various industries and firms. Employers with relatively younger workers are reluctant to join pools with other firms out of fear that risk factors alone would drive up costs for their workers. Consequently, the exchanges have been unable to gain sufficient traction to make concerns about risk selection less salient.

The federal government could facilitate the emergence of a stronger private exchange system for employers by establishing a certification program for them as well. Employers offering coverage to their workers through these certified exchanges would automatically qualify for a slightly enhanced federal tax credit for coverage (perhaps $550 for individual coverage and $1,100 for families) and would be exempt from having to organize competing insurance offerings for their workers (because the exchanges would do it for them). (The added cost of this incentive could be offset by controlling the total amount of tax-exempt defined contribution payments from the participating employers.) Firms would need only to make defined contribution payments to the exchanges in support of their workers' enrollment choices.

The federal criteria for exchange certification should focus on fostering strong premium competition among insurers and balance the desire for scale with some competition among the exchanges.

Coverage offered through certified private exchanges should adhere to the same competitive framework guiding ESI more generally: defined contribution payments by employers, standardization of benefits to facilitate premium comparisons by consumers, and full control over plan choice in the hands of workers, not the firms employing them.

The federal government should divide the country into defined markets and allow a limited number of private exchanges to be certified in each area. The markets might follow the boundaries applicable to drug benefit offerings in Medicare. Further, only private exchanges that can achieve meaningful scale (after a transition period) should be allowed to retain federal certification.

Finally, an important objective of private exchange growth is easier access to ESI for workers in small firms. To be certified, private exchanges should be required to meet minimum thresholds of enrollment among workers in smaller firms (however that might be defined in the law).

While not a guarantee, federal certification of private exchanges would increase the chances that some private exchanges would reach sufficient scale to influence pricing in the market. Insurers would be forced to compete vigorously on cost control to reach their market-share goals.

Improving ESI to Preserve It

Job-based health insurance has played an important role in providing coverage to American workers and their families in the postwar era. Even without the ACA's requirement to offer insurance, most firms have gladly sponsored coverage because of its importance to the well-being of their employees. Employers also have developed important innovations by experimenting with various types of managed care arrangements and popularizing the use of employee-owned health savings accounts.

Yet despite the obvious value of ESI to workers, it is becoming increasingly clear that it, like Medicare and Medicaid, needs to be updated to promote stronger market discipline. Cost pressures are contributing to wage stagnation and income inequality, which are serious concerns beyond what they mean for accessing needed care. No amount of initiative or innovation by individual firms can solve this problem. It will require a systemic solution, enacted by Congress.

The starting point is to replace the now-repealed Cadillac tax with a tax credit that comes with conditions. Employers accepting the new tax credit would be expected to implement reforms that create competitive pressures for lower costs and lower premiums. Other changes would make it easier for firms to offer coverage and band together in large pools that will facilitate lower prices.

Some companies may resist new federal expectations for ESI. Policymakers have been hearing for decades from some companies that they want to solve the problem without the government getting involved. And yet, the promised solution never arrives.

That is not surprising given that employers operate in competitive labor markets, which makes it untenable for individual firms to get out of step with the standards of their industries.

The first move for improving ESI thus lies with policymakers. The public values ESI coverage and would like it to continue. The answer, then, is to enact changes in federal law that will strengthen this entire class of coverage, by creating new standards that will facilitate cost cutting and market discipline. The result will be better health care for workers—and higher wages too.

Notes

1. Congressional Budget Office, "Federal Subsidies for Health Insurance Coverage for People Under Age 65: CBO and JCT's July 2021 Projections," July 2021, https://www.cbo.gov/system/files/2021-08/51298-2021-07-healthinsurance.pdf.

2. Congressional Budget Office, "Federal Subsidies for Health Insurance Coverage for People Under Age 65: Tables from CBO's March 2016 Baseline," March 2016, https://www.cbo.gov/sites/default/files/recurringdata/51298-2016-03-healthinsurance.pdf.

3. Congressional Budget Office, "Federal Subsidies for Health Insurance Coverage for People Under Age 65: CBO and JCT's July 2021 Projections."

4. Gary Claxton et al., *Employer Health Benefits: 2021 Annual Survey*, Kaiser Family Foundation, November 3, 2021, https://files.kff.org/attachment/Report-Employer-Health-Benefits-2021-Annual-Survey.pdf.

5. Peter G. Peterson Foundation, "What Are the Trends Slowing Wage Growth and Fueling Income Inequality?," July 30, 2019, https://www.pgpf.org/blog/2019/07/what-are-the-trends-slowing-wage-growth-and-fueling-income-inequality.

6. Internal Revenue Service, "Internal Revenue Bulletin: 2021–35," August 30, 2021, https://www.irs.gov/irb/2021-35_IRB#REV-PROC-2021-36.

7. Ryan J. Rosso, "The Affordable Care Act's (ACA's) Employer Shared Responsibility Provisions (ESRP)," Congressional Research Service, January 9, 2019, https://fas.org/sgp/crs/misc/R45455.pdf.

8. The general form of the first two recommendations presented in this chapter were developed in conversations with an industry expert on employer-sponsored coverage. The specific formulations, however, are the sole responsibility of the author.

9. Congressional Budget Office, "Federal Subsidies for Health Insurance Coverage for People Under Age 65: CBO and JCT's July 2021 Projections."

10. Claxton et al., *Employer Health Benefits*.

11. This estimate is based on an effective tax rate of 29.7 percent (22 percent for income taxes and the employee share of the payroll tax).

12. A reduction by firms in employer-sponsored insurance (ESI) premium payments of three times the value of the credit is an approximation of the value of the tax break for not paying taxes on current ESI payments. The amount of the required ESI premium reduction could be calibrated to more exactly equal the previous value of the tax break on a firm-by-firm basis.

13. Congressional Budget Office, "A Premium Support System for Medicare: Updated Analysis of Illustrative Options," October 2017, https://www.cbo.gov/system/files/115th-congress-2017-2018/reports/53077-premiumsupport.pdf.

14. Esther Uyehara and Margaret Thomas, "Health Maintenance Organization and the HMO Act of 1973," RAND Corporation, December 1975, https://www.rand.org/content/dam/rand/pubs/papers/2009/P5554.pdf.

15. Beth C. Fuchs, "Managed Health Care: Federal and State Regulation," Congressional Research Service, October 8, 1997, https://www.everycrsreport.com/files/19971008_97-938EPW_046b2240a0226328c280576158960ddffa38d14e.pdf.

16. Peter D. Fox and Peter R. Kongstvedt, "A History of Managed Health Care and Health Insurance in the United States," in *Essentials of Managed Health Care*, 6th ed. (Burlington, MA: Jones & Bartlett Learning, 2013), https://samples.jbpub.com/9781284043259/Chapter1.pdf.

17. Fuchs, "Managed Health Care."

18. William H. Shrank, Teresa L. Rogstad, and Natasha Parekh, "Waste in the U.S. Health Care System: Estimated Costs and Potential for Savings," *Journal of the American Medical Association* 322, no. 15 (October 7, 2019), https://jamanetwork.com/journals/jama/article-abstract/2752664.

19. Bruce Japsen, "Private Exchange Growth Hits 8M, but Slows Among Large Employers," *Forbes*, January 20, 2016, https://www.forbes.com/sites/brucejapsen/2016/01/20/private-exchange-growth-hits-8m-but-slows-among-large-employers/.

6

Covering the Uninsured

The US has a higher percentage of citizens and residents going without health insurance than is the norm in other advanced economies. Decisively addressing this persistent shortcoming is central to building support for a market-based reform because voters will resist expansion of the consumer role if millions of Americans remain vulnerable to substantial financial and health risks.

The US has made progress toward reducing the number of persons going without coverage in recent years, but it has not fully eliminated breaks in protection. Some market advocates worry that making coverage for the remaining uninsured a priority will lead inevitably to more governmental control.

It is a regrettable misperception and likely the opposite of the truth. It is possible, and desirable, to combine market reforms with stable insurance coverage for all, but doing so requires policies that correct for the tendency toward breaks in protection that can occur when consumers must participate in frequent reenrollment requirements.[1]

The association of full, population-wide insurance enrollment—often called "universal coverage"—with public control is understandable given that single-payer advocates have worked to convince the public of this connection.[2] And it is certainly more straightforward to cover everyone in a single public insurance plan than through multiple commercial offerings. With single payer, insurance is conferred to the eligible population (citizens and legal residents) through processes that impose negligible administrative burdens on individuals. Typically, eligibility is automatic at birth, or when a person is permitted entry as a legal resident, and is maintained until death without the need for reenrollment at any time during the intervening years.

Multi-payer insurance schemes are a necessary feature of a market framework, but they also entail higher administrative costs. Coverage is a function of enrollment into a specific plan for a specific period; tracking who is in what plan, and when, adds complexity and costs. It is a predictable consequence of repetitive enrollment requirements that some individuals will drop out of coverage, and those breaks will increase their financial and health risks.

But the US can move much closer to population-wide protection and make spells without insurance more infrequent with policies that lessen the reenrollment burden on the populations susceptible to coverage breaks. Embracing these needed reforms should be a priority for market advocates, as they would reassure the public that the United States's public-private health system can incentivize innovation and high-quality care without sacrificing the security that reliable health insurance provides.

The Importance of Health Insurance

The value of health insurance has been debated for many years in part because convincing empirical evidence one way or the other has been hard to capture. Most consumers want to enroll in coverage for financial and health reasons, but even patients without insurance consume significant amounts of medical care. Isolating the effects of insurance has been difficult because other factors may influence patients' outcomes beyond their insurance status.

Despite the obstacles, however, evidence has been accumulating in recent years confirming what common sense would predict, which is that health insurance is valuable because it improves both mental and physical health.

Several years ago, Oregon authorized a small insurance expansion that facilitated a natural experiment testing the benefits of Medicaid coverage. The state made enrollment in the program available to a randomly selected subset of a target population that was required to pay a premium for the coverage; those not offered enrollment served as a control group. Researchers found that, after two years, the clinical benefits of Medicaid were detectable in enrollees' improved mental health but not in their physical well-being. One might surmise that the financial security that came from Medicaid enrollment lowered the enrollees' stress and anxiety compared to those who remained uninsured.[3]

The US Treasury Department conducted a different experiment by drawing a sample population from tax filers identified as uninsured in 2015. The taxpayers were sent letters in January 2017 notifying them of the federal tax penalty owed for going without insurance and advising them of the enrollment steps needed to avoid a similar penalty in 2017. (The penalty was repealed in legislation passed in December 2017, which went into effect in January 2019.) A subgroup of the sample was randomly selected to not receive the informational letter. Subsequent data revealed that those who received the letter were more likely to enroll in coverage in 2017 than those who did not receive the letter, and those age 45 to 64 experienced a 0.06 percentage point lower mortality rate in 2017 and 2018. This difference may appear negligible, but it translates into one fewer death for every 1,648 people.[4]

This latter study adds to a growing list showing enrollment in health insurance is important for readily accessing care. A 2017 review found 17 separate analyses documenting that enrollment in health insurance improved access to important medical services and provided greater financial security. Insurance enrollees had higher utilization rates of services associated with better clinical outcomes, including more rapid detection of treatable conditions, more timely surgical procedures, and greater adherence to prescription drug therapies.[5]

Skeptics often note that medical care, not insurance, can be lifesaving and improve well-being and that many services are consumed without insurance paying the bill. While that is true, important medical interventions are often expensive and thus well beyond the reach of an average American household's personal budget. A study of colorectal cancer treatment in Massachusetts found a statistically significant increase in expensive interventions (including tumor removals requiring hospital stays) among those who were made newly eligible for insurance by a reform passed in 2006.[6] Without insurance, access to health-improving care is likely to be impaired for some patients.

Figure 1. US Uninsured Population Under Age 65, 2010–20

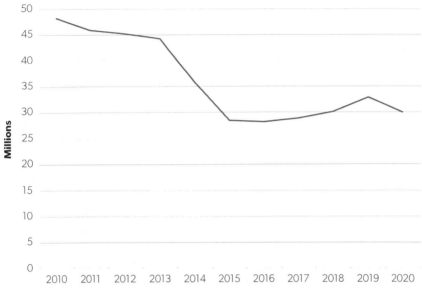

Source: US Department of Health and Human Services, "Trends in the US Uninsured Population: 2010 to 2020," February 11, 2021, https://aspe.hhs.gov/system/files/pdf/265041/trends-in-the-us-uninsured. pdf.

Who Are the Uninsured?

The Affordable Care Act (ACA), enacted in 2010, aimed to expand health insurance enrollment in the US. During the congressional debate, the law's authors frequently spoke of trying to align the US with other wealthy countries by ensuring all Americans, with few exceptions, would be enrolled in either public or private coverage.[7]

The law fell short of this goal but made progress. As shown in Figure 1, the US Department of Health and Human Services (HHS) estimates 30.0 million people under age 65 went without insurance in 2020, down from 48.2 million in 2010.[8] Congress's 2017 repeal of the ACA's tax penalty enforcing the individual requirement to secure coverage (the so-called individual mandate) makes it unlikely that the number will fall appreciably in coming years without new policies.

While the ACA did not fully eliminate breaks in insurance coverage, it created the conditions to close gaps even more than has occurred to date because many who remain uninsured are eligible but not enrolled in available plans. Recent legislation (described below) has further increased subsidization of coverage and made even more people who otherwise would be uninsured eligible for discounted premiums and, in some cases, free insurance altogether.

Those who remain uninsured (estimated at 28.9 million people in 2021, according to a Kaiser Family Foundation analysis that applied recently expanded subsidy rates to 2019 data) can be divided into six basic categories, as shown in Figure 2.

- With the passage of expanded ACA subsidies (running through 2022), 11.0 million of the uninsured are eligible for subsidized premiums in the exchanges.

- An additional 7.3 million of the uninsured are eligible for Medicaid.

- About 3.5 million have offers of affordable employer coverage.

- Some 2.2 million are in the Medicaid coverage gap. They reside in states that have not expanded Medicaid as authorized by the ACA and yet have incomes too low—below 100 percent of the federal poverty line (FPL)—to qualify for ACA premium subsidization.

- Another 1.1 million are eligible for ACA plans but have incomes that push their required premium payments above the full cost of the benchmark plan in their market area. Consequently, they are ineligible for premium subsidization. Generally, higher-income individuals are less likely to qualify for subsidization because their incomes make room for additional individual premium payments and thus make it more likely that they will be expected to pay the full premium themselves without any government subsidization.

- Finally, 3.9 million of the uninsured are ineligible for subsidized coverage because they reside in the US without the proper documentation for doing so.

Figure 2. Estimated Non-Elderly Uninsured in 2021

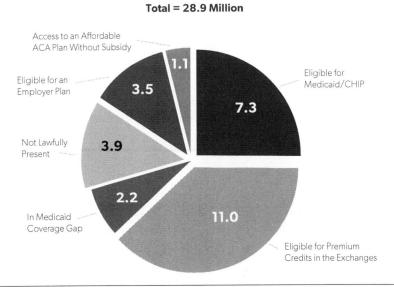

Total = 28.9 Million

Access to an Affordable ACA Plan Without Subsidy — 1.1

Eligible for an Employer Plan — 3.5

Not Lawfully Present — 3.9

In Medicaid Coverage Gap — 2.2

Eligible for Medicaid/CHIP — 7.3

Eligible for Premium Credits in the Exchanges — 11.0

Source: Matthew Rae et al., "How the American Rescue Plan Act Affects Subsidies for Marketplace Shoppers and People Who Are Uninsured," Kaiser Family Foundation, March 25, 2021, https://www.kff.org/health-reform/issue-brief/how-the-american-rescue-plan-act-affects-subsidies-for-marketplace-shoppers-and-people-who-are-uninsured/.

In a separate examination of the characteristics of the uninsured, the Congressional Budget Office (CBO) found the following, also based on 2019 data:[9]

- Low-income households go without coverage far more often than do those with higher incomes. Of those without coverage in 2019, 57 percent lived in households with incomes below 250 percent of the FPL.

- Most of the uninsured live in households with wage earners. In 2019, only 11 percent of the uninsured had no support from wage income, and 82 percent were working full-time or lived with someone who did.

- Short spells without coverage are common. Over recent two-year periods, about 25 percent of the population under age 65 experienced breaks in their insurance enrollment.

- At any given point in time, however, those who are uninsured will go without coverage for an extended period. In 2019, 11 percent of the uninsured went without coverage for one to five months, 9 percent for six to 11 months, and 80 percent for 12 months or longer.

- Complex eligibility rules impede coverage. Twenty-eight percent of uninsured households had members who were both eligible and ineligible for Medicaid or the Children's Health Insurance Program (CHIP).

- Another important impediment is perceived and actual costs. Among single persons who were uninsured in 2019, about half were eligible for a plan with a premium below 5 percent of their incomes and 64 percent for plans with premiums below 10 percent of their incomes. The legislation enacted in March 2021 (see below) has increased the subsidization of ACA plans and thus lowered costs further for more uninsured households.

The 2021 ACA and Medicaid Expansions

President Joe Biden campaigned on expanding the ACA to reduce the number of uninsured persons living in the country and lower premiums for many households, both insured and uninsured. Congress enacted provisions in 2021 consistent with the president's agenda, as part of a large COVID-19 response plan called the American Rescue Plan Act (ARPA).[10]

The law had several health coverage provisions (including subsidized premiums for unemployed persons eligible for enrollment in former employers' plans), but the focus here is on the expansions to the ACA, including the temporary subsidy increases for 2021 and 2022 that might be extended into the future.

ACA Premium Subsidy Increases. Before ARPA, the ACA established maximum premium amounts by household income tied to a benchmark plan in each market, with the maximum premium starting at 2.07 percent of income at 100 percent of the FPL and increasing to 9.83 percent at

400 percent of the FPL. Households with incomes above 400 percent of the FPL were ineligible for premium assistance.

ARPA increased subsidies at all income levels for 2021 and 2022.[11] For households with incomes between 100 and 150 percent of the FPL, there is no premium requirement for enrollment in benchmark plans. At 400 percent of the FPL and higher, the maximum premium is set at 8.5 percent of income, thus making many more higher-income households eligible for assistance. Between 150 and 400 percent of the FPL, the maximum premium amounts also are lower relative to what was required by pre-ARPA federal law.[12]

ARPA has increased both the numbers of Americans who are eligible for subsidized premiums for coverage and the subsidy amounts previously eligible households will receive. Matthew Rae et al. estimate 21.8 million people will be eligible for subsidized coverage in 2021, up from 18.1 million under pre-ARPA rules. The increases in monthly subsidies range from $33 for households with incomes below 150 percent of the FPL to $213 for households with incomes between 400 and 600 percent of the FPL.[13]

Incentives for States to Adopt the ACA Medicaid Expansion. ARPA includes a new and permanent financial incentive for states to adopt the Medicaid expansion authorized by the ACA. Under the ACA, all states were offered enhanced federal funding if they agreed to expand eligibility for program enrollment to persons with incomes below 138 percent of the FPL. The federal government paid for 100 percent of the cost of the expansion through 2016, which then was phased down to 90 percent beginning in 2020. In the new law, states that adopt the expansion can get a 5 percentage point bump in the federal matching rate for the cost of the expansion in eligibility for two years following implementation.[14]

As of January 2022, 12 states have not yet implemented the ACA's Medicaid expansion.[15] ARPA's financial incentives are aimed at encouraging these states to agree to the ACA's authorized expansion more rapidly.

ARPA's higher subsidies will modestly reduce the number of uninsured in the US in 2021 and 2022. Before ARPA was enacted, the CBO estimated there would be 31 million people not enrolled in health insurance in 2022; ARPA is expected to reduce that number by about 1.3 million people.[16]

An Automatic Enrollment Framework

The ACA's individual mandate was an attempt to ensure all Americans stayed continuously enrolled in health insurance. It proved too weak and unpopular to fulfill that objective. An alternative to compulsory coverage is reducing the enrollment burden for uninsured individuals. As noted, most of the uninsured are eligible for subsidized or even free plans; what is lacking is a mechanism for connecting them to protection with less time and effort on their part. A system of automatic enrollment into available coverage options would increase take-up by making it far easier for millions of people to sign up for heavily subsidized plans.

Automatic enrollment will require extensive changes in the administration of subsidized coverage and the rules governing the enrollment process.[17] These changes would lessen the need for individuals to navigate a complex process and place more of a burden on the federal government, states, and insurance plans to make staying continuously enrolled far easier for millions of the currently uninsured.

An effective reform will have several characteristics.

A Joint Federal-State Initiative. The federal government must create a national automatic enrollment framework, but it cannot, on its own, implement the needed changes. Most of the uninsured are eligible for Medicaid, CHIP, or an ACA-subsidized plan. The states play a key role in administering all of these coverage options. Therefore, the federal government should use its authority to establish a system of automatic enrollment that is facilitated by federal processes and data but which is ultimately implemented by states and private insurance plans. The federal government can encourage active state participation in automatic enrollment by making available grant funding for state expenses.

While automatic enrollment is different than the individual mandate, the precedent from the ACA's mandate of using federal tax forms to identify the uninsured is a useful starting point for improving insurance take-up (even as compulsory enrollment is set aside). The requested information is minimal and would be hard to collect systematically in any other way. Further, the benefits from higher insurance enrollment and the lower burden placed on individuals through other enrollment processes are well worth the administrative cost of continued inclusion of insurance enrollment data in annual federal tax filings.

Shifting the Open Enrollment Timeline and Moving Toward Full-Year, Aligned ACA and Medicaid Eligibility. Currently, open enrollment for ACA-subsidized insurance occurs in the late fall and early winter for coverage starting in January, and eligibility is estimated based on income from the calendar year preceding the year in which enrollment selections are being made. For instance, enrollment into 2021 coverage took place mainly in November and December 2020, based on 2019 incomes. Individuals also must pay back premium credits if their actual 2021 incomes turn out higher than the amounts used to estimate their discounts. Moreover, Medicaid eligibility remains a month-to-month matter in most circumstances, which creates substantial instability in coverage. Lower-income households are prone to fluctuations in monthly incomes because of job changes and household members moving into and out of the workforce.

To improve take-up, the ACA and Medicaid enrollment periods should be aligned to follow the tax filing season and thus allow the prior year's income to govern eligibility for a coverage year beginning partway through the calendar year. The change in timelines is summarized in Table 1.

As shown, ACA and Medicaid eligibility could start in July 2022 (and last until June 2023), based on 2021 income reported in tax filings in February through April 2022. Further, once eligibility is established based on 2021 income, an individual should remain eligible for coverage for the full 12-month period, irrespective of concurrent income fluctuations.

This revised enrollment timeline would allow income tax data to become the only verification requirement for enrollment and thus bring much-needed simplicity to the entire process. Further, it would improve program integrity by basing premium subsidization for coverage on income data that are already required to be collected by the federal government. There would be no need for a complex reconciliation process that leads to errors and impedes higher take-up.

There also is precedent for using prior-year tax data to determine eligibility for federal assistance. Federal student aid for higher education uses federal tax data as the basis for establishing eligibility for various sources

Table 1. Enrollment Process Timelines

	Current	Proposed
Insurance Year	January 2022–December 2022	July 2022–June 2023
Open Enrollment	November 2021–December 2021	April 2022–May 2022
Income Eligibility	Initial Estimate: 2021 Actual Eligibility: 2022	No Estimate Needed Actual Eligibility: 2021
Final Adjudication	Tax Filing for 2022 (April 2023)	Tax Filing for 2021 (April 2022)

Source: Author.

of support, and Medicare uses the income tax system for determining premium requirements for higher-income participants.

Federal Tax Filing Insurance Status and Coverage Opt In. To effectuate this shift, federal tax forms must be modified to identify who was uninsured in the prior calendar year and who remains uninsured at the time of the filing. Further, the forms should ask uninsured filers if they would like to have their insurance and income data shared with their states for insurance enrollment purposes and then whether they would like to be enrolled in insurance that requires no premium payment on their part. Tax and income data for individuals who accept this offer could then be shared with the states to match individuals with available insurance plans. Persons who are found eligible for Medicaid would be enrolled in that program, while others would get private plans offered through the ACA exchanges.

New Zero-Premium Plans (with Adjustable Deductibles). This new framework should make new coverage options available on the ACA exchanges to persons who would otherwise go without coverage. A recent analysis estimates that six million of the uninsured are already eligible for zero-premium coverage through the ACA exchanges.[18] More would be if ACA-compliant insurance plans were allowed to adjust their deductibles upward (and thus lower their premiums) for persons who agree to be automatically enrolled into zero-premium plans. This coverage would ensure these individuals have protection for high-cost medical events, which is the primary purpose of such coverage, without imposing any premium obligation.

Zero-premium plans could include a limited set of preventive services and drug coverage that would be available to enrollees even before they satisfied their annual deductibles. Including such a benefit would improve the attractiveness of signing up and thus improve take-up among the uninsured.

Retention of Consumer Choice. Automatic enrollment should not be seen as a softer version of the individual mandate. Individuals would not be required to stay enrolled in health insurance if they wish to go uninsured. Moreover, placement into default coverage would occur only after consumers were given the opportunity by the state to select an insurance plan on their own. Those who do not make a selection and are enrolled into coverage automatically by their states would be presented a second time with options for enrolling in other available products, including those requiring monthly premium payments. Persons placed into plans should be given a minimum of one month to select alternative coverage after being notified of their initial placements.

While the federal government should construct a national framework, with tax filings providing the essential data to make it work, states should have flexibility to modify the standard template. For instance, some states might wish to use their own income tax systems to supplement the federal tax data or provide a check against it (such as verifying whether filers remain uninsured). They could also use other administrative processes to identify who remains uninsured, such as applications for driver's licenses and local property tax registration forms when persons move into the state.

Establishing a new national system of automatic insurance enrollment for the uninsured will be complex, so allowing some states to serve as early test cases could be useful. For instance, the federal government could select 10 willing states to demonstrate the concept and then move to full nationwide implementation after three years based on an evaluation of the early adopters' experiences.

Employer-Sponsored Zero-Premium Options

A federal-state system of automatic insurance enrollment will not eliminate all coverage gaps. Workers declining offers of qualified coverage from their employers are ineligible for ACA premium subsidies in the marketplaces. As noted, 3.5 million of the uninsured fall into this category. Many could be enrolled in health insurance if their employers were given more flexibility to sign up otherwise uninsured workers for zero-premium plans.

Congress should authorize employers to supplement their normal insurance enrollment procedures with a follow-on option for workers who decline coverage during the initial round. Employees indicating they have no alternative sources of coverage to their employers' plans could be offered coverage with no premium requirement; the employer contribution would cover the full cost. To ensure employers incurred no higher expense for these workers compared to their other employees, the offered coverage could have a higher deductible compared to the standard insurance offering.

As with the federal-state automatic enrollment process, workers would be under no obligation to accept insurance they prefer to decline.

Closing the Medicaid Coverage Gap

The most compelling case for improved coverage options is for the uninsured who reside in the so-called Medicaid gap. They have incomes below 100 percent of the FPL but live in states that have not yet adopted the Medicaid expansion the ACA authorized. Consequently, their incomes are too low to qualify for premium subsidies on the ACA exchanges (which begin at 100 percent of the FPL) and yet too high to qualify for the often low eligibility standards of pre-ACA Medicaid. With limited discretionary incomes and no insurance, their access to needed medical services is likely impaired and probably limited to publicly funded health clinics.

ARPA upped the financial incentive for the 12 holdout states to adopt the ACA's expansion of Medicaid eligibility to 138 percent of the FPL, but it is unclear if this will be sufficient to induce a change in position for all of them. The opposition to the ACA Medicaid expansion in some states appears more ideological than financial.

As discussed in Chapter 4, states should be given more flexibility and a stronger incentive to comply with a minimum level of coverage of at least 100 percent of the FPL for persons who were ineligible for Medicaid in the pre-ACA era. States that complied with this expectation would get the favorable federal funding available under the ACA (until Congress passed a full revision of federal Medicaid payments to the states, as also recommended in Chapter 4). States failing to meet this standard would lose 5 to 10 percent of their federal support. Above 100 percent of the FPL, states could rely on the ACA marketplaces to cover other low-income households.

There is no guarantee that this would encourage the remaining holdouts to close the coverage gap, but it would be less expensive than having the federal government take on the full responsibility itself. Providing ACA plans to persons below 100 percent of the FPL would be more costly than a Medicaid expansion because payment rates for physician services are generally higher in commercial plans.[19]

The Difficult Problem of Undocumented Immigrants Who Are Uninsured

As noted previously, 13 percent of the uninsured, or 3.9 million people, reside in the US without proper legal authority to do so. Many undocumented immigrants arrived in the country with temporary visas that they then overstayed. Under the ACA, the uninsured who fall into this category are ineligible for premium subsidization and thus are vulnerable to becoming uninsured. Current Medicaid law also prohibits federal financing of their insurance coverage. However, six states and the District of Columbia are using state-only funds to provide Medicaid coverage to children living in undocumented households.[20]

Other high-income countries also prohibit full access to subsidized insurance for their undocumented immigrant populations. For instance, immigrants residing unlawfully in the UK are not eligible for full coverage through the National Health Service (NHS).[21] As a consequence, several hundred thousand persons in that country are uninsured (even as the NHS is often described as a universal coverage program). Canada applies similar screens for coverage under its provincial insurance plans.[22]

That other nations face the same dilemmas when considering options for their undocumented populations does not mean the US has adopted a satisfactory solution. Most of the immigrants to the US who are uninsured have low incomes and therefore are unlikely to have sufficient resources to pay the full premiums themselves for private coverage. (In contrast, some undocumented workers in the US with higher-paying jobs have coverage through their employers; there are no screens in force today preventing firms from offering these workers insurance.)

Sensible immigration reform is needed for many reasons, one of which is providing a better resolution of the health insurance status of undocumented persons. Even without comprehensive reform, some steps would help.

Most importantly, federal law should not punish immigrant children for their parents' actions. While worrying about the effect of subsidized health coverage on unlawful migration is understandable, humanitarian concerns should take precedence with children. A straightforward option would allow all children in undocumented households to qualify for coverage through CHIP, which operates within a fixed total of annual federal spending; consequently, this eligibility expansion should not lead to a substantial increase in required federal appropriations.

Many of the children gaining coverage through such a provision will remain in the US permanently, one way or another. It would be far better policy, even from a narrow cost perspective, to ensure they get adequate medical attention, as it would help them avoid preventable (and perhaps expensive) health problems later in their lives.

Prioritizing a Workable Solution

The US is an outlier among countries with advanced economies in not mandating enrollment in approved health insurance plans or organizing automatic public insurance coverage for all citizens and legal residents. Instead, Americans are enrolled in a mix of public and private insurance offerings that are not always well coordinated and that include frequent and repetitive enrollment requirements that can lead to breaks in protection.

Even with these challenges, however, the US has made progress toward reducing the ranks of the uninsured, and additional policies would close many of the remaining gaps. The starting point should be recognition that public policy has already made most of the uninsured eligible for subsidized coverage. Changes in enrollment procedures would ensure far more of them could get low-cost insurance protection.

That should be an important objective of all US policymakers, but most especially those who support using market incentives to improve quality and control costs. There is a perception today that market solutions are incompatible with secure insurance for the entire population and thus put at risk access to needed medical services, most especially for persons from lower-income households. That is not true, but market advocates need to show voters how population-wide insurance protection and market incentives can coexist. Doing so will substantially strengthen the case that the US should continue to follow its own unique course by combining a pluralistic and competitive system of insurance provision with a level of security that all its citizens and legal residents deserve.

Notes

1. The Netherlands and Switzerland have insurance arrangements that combine public regulation and private coverage, and both achieve near 100 percent population-wide enrollment. Mandatory enrollment requirements play a significant role in their high coverage numbers. For example, see Joost Wammes, Niek Stadhouders, and Gert Westert, "International Health Care System Profiles: Netherlands," Commonwealth Fund, June 5, 2020, https://www.commonwealthfund.org/international-health-policy-center/countries/netherlands; and Isabelle Sturny, "International Health Care System Profiles: Switzerland," Commonwealth Fund, June 5, 2020, https://www.commonwealthfund.org/international-health-policy-center/countries/switzerland.

2. The term "universal coverage" is avoided in this chapter because it implies coverage of most medical expenses for 100 percent of a nation's legal residents at all times. The US recently repealed the compulsory insurance enrollment provisions of the Affordable Care Act, which makes achieving full, uninterrupted coverage, with no exceptions, difficult to achieve and thus unlikely. To prevent confusion, the policies in this chapter are discussed in the context of moving toward an objective of full, population-wide enrollment in coverage without guaranteeing that some persons might still experience breaks in protection.

3. Katherine Baicker et al., "The Oregon Experiment—Effect of Medicaid on Clinical Outcomes," *New England Journal of Medicine* 368 (May 2, 2013): 1713–22, https://www.

nejm.org/doi/full/10.1056/NEJMsa1212321.

4. Jacob Goldin, Ithai Z. Lurie, and Janet McCubbin, "Health Insurance and Mortality: Experimental Evidence from Taxpayer Outreach" (working paper, National Bureau of Economic Research, Cambridge, MA, December 2019), https://www.nber.org/system/files/working_papers/w26533/w26533.pdf.

5. Benjamin D. Sommers, Atul A. Gawande, and Katherine Baicker, "Health Insurance Coverage and Health—What the Recent Evidence Tells Us," *New England Journal of Medicine* 377 (August 21, 2017): 586–93, https://www.nejm.org/doi/full/10.1056/NEJMsb1706645.

6. Andrew P. Loehrer et al., "Impact of Health Insurance Expansion on the Treatment of Colorectal Cancer," *Journal of Clinical Oncology* 34, no. 34 (December 1, 2016): 4110–15, https://www.ncbi.nlm.nih.gov/pmc/articles/PMC5477821/.

7. Barack Obama, "Remarks by the President to a Joint Session of Congress on Health Care," September 9, 2009, https://obamawhitehouse.archives.gov/the-press-office/remarks-president-a-joint-session-congress-health-care.

8. Kenneth Finegold et al., "Trends in the US Uninsured Population: 2010 to 2020," US Department of Health and Human Services, February 11, 2021, https://aspe.hhs.gov/sites/default/files/private/pdf/265041/trends-in-the-us-uninsured.pdf.

9. Congressional Budget Office, "Who Went Without Health Insurance in 2019, and Why?," September 2020, https://www.cbo.gov/system/files/2020-09/56504-Health-Insurance.pdf.

10. Congressional Research Service, "American Rescue Plan Act of 2021 (P.L. 117-2): Private Health Insurance, Medicaid, CHIP, and Medicare Provisions," April 27, 2021, https://crsreports.congress.gov/product/pdf/R/R46777.

11. President Joe Biden has proposed in the American Families Plan to permanently extend the higher levels of insurance subsidization provided in the American Rescue Plan Act for 2021 and 2022.

12. Congressional Research Service, "Health Insurance Premium Tax Credit and Cost-Sharing Reductions," February 3, 2022, https://crsreports.congress.gov/product/pdf/R/R44425.

13. Matthew Rae et al., "How the American Rescue Plan Act Affects Subsidies for Marketplace Shoppers and People Who Are Uninsured," Kaiser Family Foundation, March 25, 2021, https://www.kff.org/health-reform/issue-brief/how-the-american-rescue-plan-act-affects-subsidies-for-marketplace-shoppers-and-people-who-are-uninsured/.

14. MaryBeth Musumeci, "Medicaid Provisions in the American Rescue Plan Act," Kaiser Family Foundation, March 18, 2021, https://www.kff.org/medicaid/issue-brief/medicaid-provisions-in-the-american-rescue-plan-act/.

15. Kaiser Family Foundation, "Status of State Action on the Medicaid Expansion Decision," February 24, 2022, https://www.kff.org/health-reform/state-indicator/state-activity-around-expanding-medicaid-under-the-affordable-care-act/.

16. Congressional Budget Office, "Federal Subsidies for Health Insurance Coverage for People Under 65: 2020 to 2030," September 2020, https://www.cbo.gov/system/files/2020-09/56571-federal-health-subsidies.pdf; Congressional Budget Office, "Who Went Without Health Insurance in 2019, and Why?," September 2020,

https://www.cbo.gov/system/files/2020-09/56504-Health-Insurance.pdf; and Congressional Budget Office, "Reconciliation Recommendations of the House Committee on Ways and Means," February 17, 2021, https://www.cbo.gov/system/files/2021-02/hwaysandmeansreconciliation.pdf.

17. For a more detailed discussion of automatic enrollment considerations, see Christen Linke Young et al., "How to Boost Health Insurance Enrollment: Three Practical Steps That Merit Bipartisan Support," Health Affairs Forefront, August 17, 2020, https://www.healthaffairs.org/do/10.1377/hblog20200814.107187/full/.

18. Daniel McDermott and Cynthia Cox, "A Closer Look at the Uninsured Marketplace Population Following the American Rescue Plan Act," Kaiser Family Foundation, May 27, 2021, https://www.kff.org/private-insurance/issue-brief/a-closer-look-at-the-uninsured-marketplace-eligible-population-following-the-american-rescue-plan-act/.

19. Diane Alexander and Molly Schnell, "The Impacts of Physician Payments on Patient Access, Use, and Health" (working paper, National Bureau of Economic Research, Cambridge, MA, July 2019), https://www.nber.org/system/files/working_papers/w26095/w26095.pdf.

20. Samantha Artiga and Maria Diaz, "Health Coverage and Care of Undocumented Immigrants," Kaiser Family Foundation, July 15, 2019, https://www.kff.org/racial-equity-and-health-policy/issue-brief/health-coverage-and-care-of-undocumented-immigrants/.

21. Neal James Russell et al., "Charging Undocumented Migrant Children for NHS Healthcare: Implications for Child Health," *British Medical Journal* 104, no. 8 (August 2019), https://adc.bmj.com/content/archdischild/104/8/722.full.pdf.

22. Adrian Humphreys, "Illegal Immigrants Have No Right to Free Health Care: Court," *National Post*, July 8, 2011, https://nationalpost.com/news/canada/illegal-immigrants-have-no-right-to-free-health-care-court.

7

Prescription Drug Pricing

Prescription drugs play an outsize role in perceptions of US health care because consumers see those prices more readily and often than they see the prices of other medical services.[1] That US pricing for these products far exceeds what is paid in other advanced economies reinforces the view that something more should be done to better control their costs. A survey from 2017 found that 40 percent of respondents believed lowering prescription drug prices should be Congress's top priority.[2]

Addressing this concern has been easier said than done, however. Two major impediments are the complexity of current pricing policy and that two policy objectives for the pharmaceutical sector are in tension with each other. Policymakers want to ensure effective therapies are available to all consumers at the lowest possible cost to society. At the same time, they want to ensure drug companies have strong incentives to continually research and introduce improved treatments. Many other high-income countries lean heavily toward satisfying the first goal while hoping for the best with the second.

While challenging, improving the US drug pricing environment is possible if policymakers approach it with the proper expectations. As with the rest of health care, we need an improved structure for the market, with a focus on stimulating more intense competition among manufacturers and drug researchers.

Patents, the Food and Drug Administration, and Hatch-Waxman

Pharmaceutical development is a high-cost, high-risk venture that can take years of work with no guarantees of commercial success. The remedy that the US and other advanced economies use to rectify the mismatch between risk and societal reward is intellectual property protection. Companies that achieve breakthroughs get significant market power to set prices for a period without fear of copycat competition, which tends to push prices up but also encourages the development of therapies with potentially large benefits for patents. The policy challenge is to strike a sensible balance between affordable access and innovation.

The US Constitution established intellectual property protection as a core responsibility of government. Article I, Section 8 of the Constitution grants Congress the power "to promote the Progress of Science and useful Arts, by securing for limited Times to Authors and Inventors the exclusive Right to their respective Writings and Discoveries."[3] President George Washington signed the first patent law in 1790, and Thomas Jefferson, then secretary of state, sat on the original board vested with the authority to grant patents.[4]

The Constitution made patent protection temporary to ensure there would be incentives for continuous progress and to prevent inventions that would be broadly beneficial to society from being held back permanently from widespread use.[5]

Companies that develop new drugs or biologic products typically secure patents protecting the intellectual property associated with the potential therapies. Patents are granted by the Patent and Trademark Office to applicants who discover any new, useful, and novel "process, machine, manufacture, or composition of matter." Patents last for 20 years from the date of the application and prohibit competitors from making and selling products that infringe on the inventor's property rights.[6]

The Food and Drug Administration (FDA) regulates the sale and use of all pharmaceutical products, including those with patent protection. In 1962, amendments to the Federal Food, Drug, and Cosmetic Act codified the requirement that all new drugs must be deemed "safe and effective" to be marketed and used in treating patients. Safety and effectiveness are determined through clinical trials. Once trials are completed, the pharmaceutical company can seek approval to sell the drug in the US market by filing a new drug application with the FDA.

The Drug Price Competition and Patent Term Restoration Act of 1984—commonly referred to as the Hatch-Waxman Act after its chief sponsors, Sen. Orrin Hatch (R-UT) and Rep. Henry Waxman (D-CA)—provided protections for drug innovators while facilitating and strengthening incentives for introducing generic competitors to brand-name drugs. The new law was, in part, a reaction to federal court decisions in a patent infringement case, *Roche Products v. Bolar Pharmaceutical.* Bolar's effort to develop a generic version of a Roche product was determined to violate the patent even though the use was said to be experimental and noncommercial.

Hatch-Waxman struck a compromise intended to establish clearer rules for generic competitors entering into the market. The law permitted generic manufacturers to get a head start on their copycat products (before patents expire) so long as the work is related to meeting regulatory requirements. In exchange, it gave innovator companies longer patent protection periods in some cases and periods of data exclusivity that preclude generic applications from using the clinical data associated with approval of the innovator drug. Generic companies got an incentive to be first to the market with a copycat product, with 180 days of market exclusivity for the first generic entrant.

The Biologics Price Competition and Innovation Act, which was incorporated into the Affordable Care Act (ACA) of 2010, created an approval process for "biosimilar" products that is roughly parallel to the process for generic drugs.[7] Biologic products are large-molecule therapies, generally derived from living biological organisms or tissues. Although making exact generic copies of biologics is not possible, clinical data from innovator biologics can be used to produce products that are biosimilar and do not have clinically meaningful differences from the FDA-approved product. The 2010 law confers data exclusivity on innovator biologic products of 12 years, after which companies seeking to produce biosimilars can use the innovator's clinical data to begin the FDA approval process themselves.[8] The FDA has approved 33 biosimilar products since the 2010 law went into effect.[9]

The Market Environment

According to the Congressional Budget Office, consumers obtain about three-quarters of their prescription drugs from retail pharmacies and the remainder from nonretail providers.[10] Retail pharmacies include storefront operations (such as chain pharmacies and pharmacies in food stores) and mail-order pharmacies. Nonretail providers include hospitals, clinics, other health care providers, and federal facilities. Consumers typically pay

Figure 1. Illustration of the Typical Product and Payment Flows

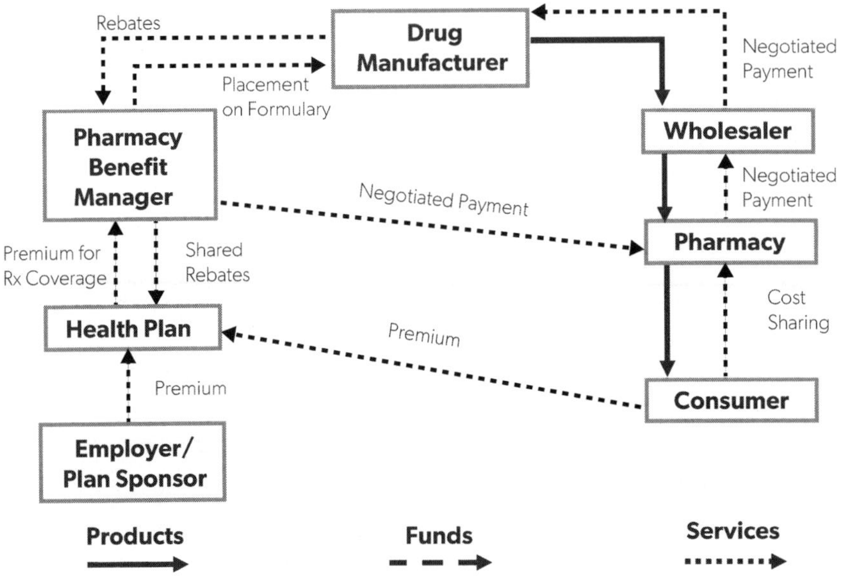

Source: Congressional Budget Office, "Prescription Drug Pricing in the Private Sector," January 2007, https://www.cbo.gov/sites/default/files/110th-congress-2007-2008/reports/01-03-prescriptiondrug.pdf.

part of the cost of prescriptions, with the rest covered by third-party payers (including private health plans, Medicaid, Medicare, and the Departments of Veterans Affairs and Defense). The price of the product depends on a complex set of rules, rebates, discounts, and other cross-subsidies that vary depending on whether the consumer is paying fully out of pocket or is purchasing the prescription through a third party.

Figure 1 illustrates the product and payment flows associated with the production and distribution of pharmaceutical drugs. Moving pharmaceutical products from manufacturers to patients is heavily influenced by the need to maintain product security throughout the supply chain. The FDA has long imposed chain of custody rules on the manufacturers and distributors of pharmaceutical products to ensure patients receive only authorized products that have been shipped and dispensed under proper conditions.

Pharmacy benefit managers (PBMs) do not purchase drugs from manufacturers or deliver them to pharmacies or other providers. They are hired by employers and health insurers to negotiate lower prices from manufacturers and retail pharmacy chains.

PBMs gain leverage in pricing negotiations with manufacturers mainly through using drug formularies. A formulary is a list of drugs available to enrollees in a health plan. Most formularies have tiers tied to how much the enrollees must pay out of pocket.

Generic drugs are typically in the lowest tier with the lowest cost sharing. Branded products may be in higher tiers requiring higher patient out-of-pocket spending. Placement on the formulary depends on the price negotiated with the manufacturer, the availability of rebates, the availability of therapeutic substitutes, and other factors.

Because they represent many potential customers enrolled in different health plans, PBMs have bargaining power to extract discounts from drug manufacturers, paid in the form of rebates. In return for agreeing to make these rebate payments, drug manufacturers secure the placement of their products on preferred formulary tiers that require lower cost sharing from patients. These incentives steer patients to a formulary's preferred drugs, which then leads to greater sales of products and higher rebates.

Relying on rebates rather than upfront price concessions is controversial, however. Manufacturers are willing to offer these discounts because they align with actual product sales. PBMs and health plans also have an incentive to prefer rebates over price discounts.

Rebates lower the net prices paid by insurers for prescription drugs, but they do not necessarily lower the cost sharing required from the consumer. Rebates are typically paid to PBMs after the drugs have been sold to patients, and a share of those rebates is passed on to the employer or health plan. That payment to the plan can be used to lower premiums, reducing the employer's cost of sponsoring health plans for its workers. Rebates might not be used by plans to lower the cost-sharing requirements of patients consuming the highest-cost drugs.

Commonly Used Pricing Terms

Several pricing concepts are frequently used as the starting points for determining the actual prices various purchasers pay in the pharmaceutical market. The following are some of the more important pricing terms commercial purchasers and public programs use.

Average Wholesale Price. The average wholesale price is a published list price for sales by wholesalers to retail pharmacies. It does not represent what pharmacies actually pay. Instead, it is sometimes used as the reference price for payments to pharmacies from payers such as Medicaid, pharmacy benefit managers (PBMs), and insurers.[11]

Wholesale Acquisition Cost. The wholesale acquisition cost (WAC) is a publicly available manufacturers' list price for sales of drugs to wholesalers. However, it is not the price wholesalers pay to acquire drugs from manufacturers. For single-source drugs (which are brand-name drugs still under patent protection), the WAC often reflects what retail pharmacies pay wholesalers.[12]

Average Manufacturer Price. The average manufacturer price (AMP) is the average price paid to manufacturers for drugs dispensed through retail pharmacies, after accounting for rebates and discounts paid to wholesalers or pharmacies. It does not include rebates paid to PBMs, Medicaid, or other insurers. Federal law requires drug manufacturers to disclose this information to the Centers for Medicare & Medicaid Services. The AMP is the reference price used to calculate rebates under the Medicaid program.[13]

Average Sales Price. Medicare Part B pays an amount equal to average sales price (ASP) plus 6 percent for Part B drugs and biologic products administered in physician offices and outpatient settings (described in more detail below). ASP was defined in law when Congress created

(continued on the next page)

(continued from the previous page)

the prescription drug benefit in 2003 to reflect the average sales price received by manufacturers from most purchasers, net of rebates and discounts. Sales to Medicaid, Medicare Part D plans, and federal or 340B-covered purchasers are excluded from the calculation.[14]

Best Price. Best price is the lowest manufacturer price (net of discounts and rebates) paid for a drug by any purchaser (excluding certain federal and state purchasers). Best price is used to calculate rebates from manufacturers to ensure that state Medicaid programs are, in fact, receiving the best price available in the market (other than sales to government purchasers, Medicare Part D plans, and entities purchasing under the 340B program).[15]

The Patient's Price. While many different pricing terms are used in the industry, the price beneficiaries pay at the retail pharmacy is most politically salient. That price is a function of many different factors and depends heavily on the patient's insurance coverage. For example, a patient needing a drug early in the year who has not yet paid the annual deductible may have to pay the full cost of the prescription. After that, the patient typically pays coinsurance or a fixed-dollar co-payment. The amount of the patient's liability depends on whether the prescription can be filled by a generic product, which formulary tier the drug is on, and other factors.

Federal Programs and Pricing Policies

The following are the major federal programs and policies that influence the pricing of prescription drugs, both in these programs and the larger marketplace.

The Medicaid Drug Rebate Program. All state Medicaid programs cover outpatient prescription drugs. Concern about the rising cost of drugs and the impact on Medicaid budgets led to the mandatory best-price rebate provision in the Omnibus Budget Reconciliation Act of 1990.

Best-price rebates are not tied to the actual prices the states pay to pharmacies. Instead, manufacturers pay states a rebate on brand-name drugs equal to 23.1 percent of the average manufacturer price (AMP) or the difference between the best price for the drug and AMP, whichever is greater.

Manufacturers of generic drugs must pay rebates of 13.1 percent of AMP. To discourage manufacturers from raising their prices to wholesalers, an additional rebate amount is required if the AMP for a drug rises more rapidly than general consumer inflation. The total amount of rebates cannot exceed 100 percent of AMP.[16]

The best-price requirement includes a strong enforcement mechanism. Only manufacturers that have entered into rebate agreements with the federal government are guaranteed that their drugs or biologic products will be covered by state Medicaid programs. Manufacturers that decline to participate risk having barriers, such as prior authorization rules, imposed on their products. (Prior authorization requires a physician to obtain payment approval from a health plan before prescribing a particular medication.)

The introduction of the Medicaid rebate program changed pricing incentives in the pharmaceutical market. Manufacturers must now include in their pricing decisions how offering steep discounts to certain purchasers will affect the rebate calculation in Medicaid. If a manufacturer offers a more heavily discounted price to a private purchaser, that new lower price must be extended to Medicaid. The resulting loss of revenue from Medicaid programs nationwide will almost always be larger than the revenue gain from expanded private sales.

The Medicaid rebate program has reduced the incentive for manufacturers to offer steep discounts to private purchasers and may have resulted in somewhat higher launch prices, particularly for drugs that are likely to have a significant market share in Medicaid.[17] The prices some private purchasers of brand-name drugs pay are probably higher than they would have been absent the rebate program.

The federally required best-price rebates are shared by the states and the federal government based on the Federal Medical Assistance Percentage used to determine the federal contribution to each state's Medicaid program. Many states have separately negotiated with manufacturers for supplemental rebates, which are not shared with the federal government. As of September 2021, 46 states plus the District of Columbia were collecting supplemental rebates from manufacturers through agreements of varying types.[18]

The 340B Program. Soon after the rebate program took effect, some of the discounts manufacturers had previously extended to purchasers serving lower-income populations were pulled back.[19] Congress responded to this development with Section 340B of the Public Health Service Act. The aim of 340B is to provide preferential pricing for safety-net facilities serving large numbers of lower-income households.

The 340B program does not require rebates. Instead, it places a ceiling on the prices that manufacturers can charge to "covered entities." The price ceiling is set at AMP less the Medicaid rebate: 23.1 percent of AMP for brand-name drugs and 13.1 percent for generics (with some exceptions based on inflation and for certain types of drugs). The 340B ceiling is often below the net price state Medicaid programs pay for the same products because state Medicaid programs usually pay an initial price (before rebates) that exceeds AMP.[20]

Manufacturers are not required to participate in 340B, but most do because Medicaid and Departments of Defense and Veterans Affairs prohibit payments to manufacturers that boycott it.[21]

Sixteen categories of "covered entities" are eligible to purchase drugs under the 340B price ceiling. The main categories of covered entities are hospitals and clinics meeting eligibility standards, including federally qualified health centers and other clinics receiving federal grants, such as those providing care to HIV-positive patients. Not-for-profit and publicly owned hospitals with substantial low-income patient loads (disproportionate share hospitals, or DSH) also qualify.

The ACA expanded the definition of covered entities to include facilities with special designations under the Medicare program, including critical access hospitals, sole community hospitals, rural referral centers, and cancer centers. About one-third of all hospitals are public or not-for-profit and have DSH percentages exceeding the 340B threshold.

Federal rules limit which patients receiving care from a covered entity are qualified to receive prescription drugs purchased at 340B discounted prices. In general, eligible patients must be receiving care from someone who has a clear and recognizable professional affiliation with the covered entity. As a practical matter, there is little restriction on the types of patients who can be prescribed drugs purchased under the program.

Participating facilities can purchase drugs using 340B pricing directly from manufacturers or wholesalers and then store the drugs themselves at their sites. Alternatively, covered entities can contract with participating pharmacies to dispense the drugs to their patients.

Covered entities are not restricted in the prices they charge insurers or patients for the drugs they purchase under 340B. Consequently, covered entities can buy prescription drugs at discounted prices under 340B and then receive reimbursements from insurers and patients based on prices that exceed the price ceiling. For instance, hospital outpatient departments can purchase oncology drugs under the 340B price ceiling and charge Medicare higher rates when treating elderly patients covered by Part B (discussed below).

In response to the attractive discounts under 340B pricing and the ACA's expanded list of covered entities, the number of covered entities participating in the program has exploded. Figure 2 shows that only 8,605 sites participated in the program in 2001. By 2017, the number had grown to nearly 38,400.

Medicare Part B Payments for Prescription Drugs. The Medicare program pays for prescription drugs administered in physician offices and hospital outpatient departments under Part B. These drugs generally require professional administration because they are injected or infused rather than consumed orally. Drugs that can be taken by the patient without professional assistance are usually covered under Part D (discussed below).

Providers (either physician offices or hospital outpatient departments) purchase Part B–covered drugs directly from wholesalers or manufacturers at prices that are negotiated privately and not tied to Medicare's payment. The Medicare reimbursement rate is the average sales price (ASP) plus 6 percent, which might exceed the price the provider pays.

Because providers keep the difference between the Part B payment and the price they actually pay, providers have a strong incentive to negotiate low prices for Part B drugs. The Medicare Payment Advisory Commission

Figure 2. Total Number of US Provider Entities Participating in the 340B Program

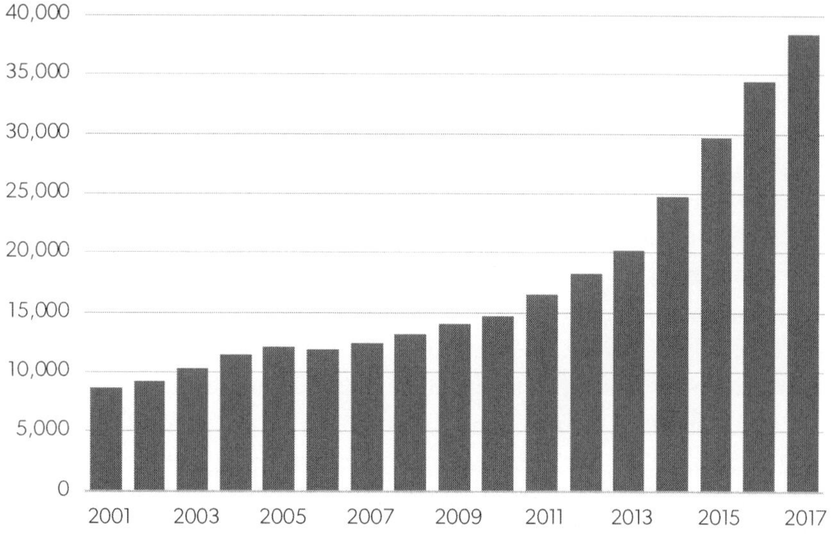

Note: The 2012 data are an approximation.
Source: Government Accountability Office, "Drug Pricing: Manufacturer Discounts in the 340B Program Offer Program Benefits, but Federal Oversight Needs Improvement," September 2011, https://www.hrsa.gov/sites/default/files/opa/programrequirements/reports/gaooversightneeded09232011.pdf; and Government Accountability Office, "Drug Discount Program: Update on Agency Efforts to Improve 340B Program Oversight," testimony before the Subcommittee on Oversight and Investigations, Committee on Energy and Commerce, US House of Representatives, July 2017, https://www.gao.gov/assets/690/685903.pdf.

(MedPAC) analyzed invoice prices for 34 high-expenditure drugs purchased by providers under Part B. In most cases, the providers were paying a price that was below 102 percent of ASP, while Medicare was paying 106 percent of ASP for the products.[22]

Further, because Medicare pays a 6 percent add-on to ASP, physicians and outpatient departments have an incentive to prescribe higher-priced products when lower-priced alternatives are available. A higher ASP creates a larger add-on payment from the Medicare program, giving suppliers more room to negotiate prices with purchasers.

Single-source drugs (for which there are no generics or biosimilars) are paid under their own unique billing code at ASP plus 6 percent. For multiple-source drugs, Medicare pays 106 percent of the weighted average

ASP for all the products in the category. Payment for biosimilar products is 100 percent of the weighted average ASP for all the biosimilars in the therapeutic category plus 6 percent of the ASP for the particular biosimilar being used.

The Medicare Part D Program. In 2003, Congress created a new prescription drug benefit in Medicare—Part D—which began offering coverage in 2006, well after many private health plans were covering the same products for working-age Americans and their families. Previously, Medicare beneficiaries obtained drug coverage through retiree plans sponsored by former employers, private supplemental insurance, or Medicaid. Like Part B, enrollment in Part D is voluntary and requires a monthly premium.

The design of the prescription drug benefit is unusual. First, it is an insurance benefit that covers only prescription drugs rather than a wider range of medical services. Second, it is offered only through private plans rather than through a government-administered insurance model, as is the case with the rest of Medicare. Third, the law establishing it prohibits the US Department of Health and Human Services (HHS) from directly negotiating drug prices. Unlike Medicare Parts A and B, which pay providers using detailed federally determined fee schedules, drug prices under Part D are set through private negotiations rather than public price controls.

Beneficiaries can choose their drug benefit coverage each year from among the available options in their market area. (The country is divided into 34 drug plan markets.) Those options include stand-alone prescription drug plans (PDPs) or Medicare Advantage (MA) plans that cover the full range of Medicare benefits plus drug coverage, known as MA-PD plans.

Medicare pays a fixed monthly contribution toward Part D coverage based on premiums submitted by the private plans in a bidding process. Beneficiaries pay the difference between the government's contribution and the plan's total premium. Consequently, beneficiaries have an incentive to select low-premium plans to minimize their monthly premium payments.

Private plan participation in the program has been robust from the benefit's introduction in 2006. Although the law provides for a federally administered "fallback" plan if fewer than two privately administered plans are in a region, that provision has never been invoked. In 2022,

Figure 3. Medicare Prescription Drug Benefit, 2022

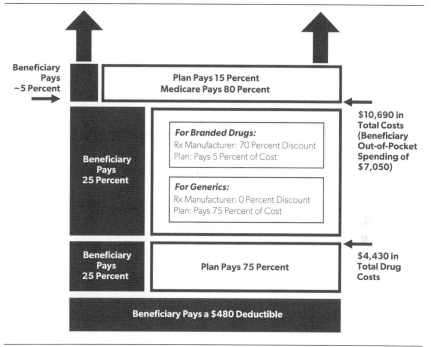

Source: Kaiser Family Foundation, "An Overview of the Medicare Part D Prescription Drug Benefit," October 13, 2021, https://www.kff.org/medicare/fact-sheet/an-overview-of-the-medicare-part-d-prescription-drug-benefit/.

776 stand-alone PDPs are competing for enrollment across the country, with the average beneficiary selecting from 23 PDPs and 31 MA-PD options.[23]

The Medicare drug benefit reflects Congress's desire to provide attractive coverage while limiting the program's overall cost. The standard benefit provides some upfront insurance protection (after an initial deductible) and catastrophic protection for high-expense cases. Although the law specifies a standard plan, entities offering PDPs and MA-PD plans are permitted to adjust the benefit parameters so long as the total value of what they offer is actuarially equivalent to the standard package.

As shown in Figure 3, in 2022, the initial deductible is $480, and beneficiaries pay a 25 percent coinsurance rate on drug purchases above the deductible and below $4,430 in total drug costs, with the PDP or MA-PD coverage paying the other 75 percent. Between $4,430 and $10,690, the beneficiary is still required to pay 25 percent coinsurance, but the plans cover only 5 percent of the cost. The balance is covered by required 70 percent discounts from drug manufacturers on the prices they charge for their products. Above $10,690 in total expenses, the beneficiaries pay 5 percent of the added cost, the plans pay for 15 percent, and the Medicare program pays for the remaining 80 percent.[24]

Part D plans or their PBMs have a strong incentive to seek rebates and other incentive payments from manufacturers and pharmacies. However, Part D plans have less incentive to bargain for lower net drug prices at the point of sale. That is because, as noted, the plan's liability for drug costs drops significantly—to just 15 percent—after the beneficiary has reached the annual catastrophic threshold. Medicare covers 80 percent of these costs (which are called "reinsurance" payments). Given a choice between a lower gross price and a larger rebate, Part D plans generally prefer the latter.

This incentive for large rebates has resulted in "a growing disparity between gross Part D costs, calculated based on cost of drugs at the point of sale, and net Part D drug costs," which account for what the Centers for Medicare & Medicaid Services terms direct and indirect remuneration.[25]

Plans offering lower premiums are likely to attract greater enrollment, and large manufacturers' rebates can help keep plan costs and premiums down. The issue is not rebates per se but rather what form those rebates take and how they affect beneficiary and program cost.

The program's cost data show a pronounced trend toward higher gross prices for therapies used by patients with the highest annual drug costs. The Medicare program pays for 74.5 percent of the total cost of the program, split between direct subsidies to the plans, reinsurance for the catastrophic phase of the benefit, and payment of cost sharing for low-income beneficiaries. The other 25.5 percent is covered by beneficiary premiums. As shown in Figure 4, the plans have maneuvered to secure more funding through reinsurance as opposed to premium subsidization. In 2020, reinsurance payments accounted for over 80 percent of the subsidies provided to Part D plans, up from just 35 percent in 2010.[26]

While the beneficiary premium is capped at 25.5 percent of program costs, there is no limit on the overall cost sharing that beneficiaries must pay. Cost-sharing amounts are based on the gross price charged for drugs

Figure 4. Medicare Drug Benefit Direct Subsidy and Reinsurance Payments

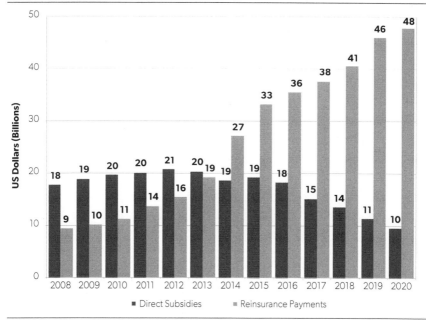

Source: Medicare Trustees, *The 2021 Annual Report of the Boards of Trustees of the Federal Hospital Insurance and Federal Supplementary Medical Insurance Trust Funds,* Centers for Medicare & Medicaid Services, August 2021, https://www.cms.gov/files/document/2021-medicare-trustees-report.pdf.

at the pharmacy, not the net price that takes rebates into account. Consequently, the structure of the Part D benefit design may inadvertently provide an incentive for shifting more costs onto the beneficiaries in the form of higher cost sharing. Higher cost sharing might make the beneficiaries more price sensitive and thus more willing to consider less costly therapies and interventions. On the other hand, some patients may find it difficult to pay the high prices, which could lead them to stop using therapies that would improve their health status.

Although Part D's incentive has led to rapid escalation of the government's reinsurance costs above the catastrophic threshold, its competitive design has effectively held down monthly premiums for the beneficiaries. In 2022, the average monthly premium for the coverage will be $33, which is remarkable given that it was $32.20 in 2006, when the program began, and has never been higher than $35.63 per month (in 2017).[27]

The Department of Veterans Affairs. The Department of Veterans Affairs (VA) runs an integrated health system serving about nine million former members of the US armed forces. Most of the care is provided through facilities owned and operated by the VA and by clinicians who are directly employed by the agency.

For many years, the VA used formularies established by its many dispersed pharmacies to negotiate prices from drug manufacturers. Those arrangements were disrupted by the 1990 Medicaid rebate provisions, which led many drug companies to cancel the preferential prices they had extended to the VA, fearing that those discounts would also need to be extended to the entire Medicaid program.

In 1992, Congress responded to the canceled discounts by placing a ceiling on prices for the VA, the Department of Defense health system, the Public Health Services, and the Coast Guard. (These four federal agencies are sometimes referred to as the "big four.") Drug companies are required to agree to these price ceilings as a condition of their participation in Medicaid.

The 1992 law specifies that these four purchasers can buy prescription drugs at prices that are no higher than the "nonfederal AMP," less a 24 percent discount. The nonfederal AMP is the AMP for all purchasers, not counting federal entities and federal programs. This price ceiling is roughly equal to the price the Medicaid program typically pays for branded drugs, after the required rebate is included in the net price. If a drug has a "best price" for a nonfederal purchaser that is lower than the nonfederal AMP minus 24 percent, then the big four can purchase that drug at the lower price. As with Medicaid, the law also increases the discounting that applies if a drug has price inflation exceeding the Consumer Price Index.[28]

Beyond this ceiling, the VA also was exempted from the Medicaid best-price calculation, which freed the agency to once again aggressively negotiate prices with manufacturers. In 1997, the VA moved to a single national formulary for all its pharmaceutical purchases. This change substantially increased the agency's leverage in price negotiations with manufacturers.

Several studies have shown that the VA generally gets lower prices for prescription drugs compared to other large purchasers. One study found that the VA paid an average of 38 percent of the average price paid for branded products, as measured by a survey of retail pharmacy invoices.[29]

The Broad Context for Pharmaceutical Pricing

Three aspects of the pharmaceutical market—beyond the intellectual property and market entry rules—affect the way drugs are priced.[30] First, the fixed costs for getting a product to market, including the research necessary to develop it and obtain approval from the FDA, are high. Second, the market is notoriously risky. Many product development efforts fail. Third, once a drug is approved and production begins, the marginal cost of producing an additional unit of the product is generally quite low relative to the product's overall fixed costs.

Thus, manufacturers must set their prices high enough to compensate investors for the fixed costs of product development, cover the losses from investments that do not produce revenue, and provide an appropriate risk-adjusted rate of return on invested capital. If the return on investment in drug development falls too low, capital will move naturally to other markets with higher returns.

Limited competition and the prevalence of third-party payment contribute to escalating drug prices for branded products. Patents and regulatory hurdles make it costly for other companies to develop alternative therapies and can substantially delay market entry for lower-price competitors. Pressure from consumers for lower prices is also attenuated since the primary purchasers are public and private insurance plans that require limited cost sharing from plan enrollees. Payments from patients account for only about 14 percent of drug costs at retail pharmacies.[31]

Demand for drugs also depends on physicians' prescribing patterns. As noted throughout this volume, patients usually accept their physicians' recommendations and do not act as autonomous decision makers. That applies in the prescription drug market as much as with medical care more generally.

There is no fixed formula for determining prices for prescription drugs that properly balance access and affordability for the patients. In many countries, governments take the lead in setting prices to counteract the leverage of drug manufacturers, but, in doing so, they could be undercutting investment in effective therapies (and relying on other countries—the US—to offset their underpayments). Governments operate within political constraints and are generally under pressure to deliver tangible benefits to voters in the short term, with less attention to considerations that might affect public welfare over longer periods. Consequently, there is built into the political process a tendency to push prices as low as possible—and possibly below the levels needed to incentivize product development.

An alternative to government-set prices is the use of private-sector agents acting on behalf of large numbers of consumers. This is the model used in Medicare's Part D benefit. Private plans negotiate prices with drug manufacturers and can pit companies with competing products against each other to get better discounts. This approach to drug pricing attempts to counteract drug companies' leverage with the leverage that comes from consolidating the demand side of the market. The resulting prices are reached through voluntary agreement rather than government fiat. That helps ensure returns on investment are sufficient to encourage new product development.

The Difficult Problem of Pricing for Therapies with No Effective Competition

Even when there is no generic competition for a branded prescription drug because of intellectual property protection, physicians often can prescribe appropriate clinical alternatives that may be less expensive. Typically, more than one product is available to treat a given condition. A new therapy may be an improvement over an existing drug, but its cost may not match the added value it provides. By pitting competing therapies against each other, insurers and other purchasers can counter the pricing leverage of brand manufacturers.

From time to time, however, products are brought to the market for which there are no competing alternatives to keep pricing in check. If a therapy is also in high demand among patients because of its clinical value, then the manufacturer has even more pricing power. As Joseph Newhouse noted, when insurance (public or private) is paying rather than the patient, manufacturers of products with significant clinical value and no competition face little resistance from consumers in setting the profit-maximizing price.[32]

Policymakers are faced with the dilemma of enforcing policies to counter monopoly pricing without unduly discouraging innovation. The

US generally, and the Medicare program in particular, does not currently have an answer for this economic problem. Other high-income countries have in place processes that limit pricing for such products. These policies, with appropriate modifications, may have some application in the US.

Drug Pricing in a Global Context

The US and other high-income countries face the challenge of establishing pricing mechanisms that balance the competing objectives of fostering innovation with equitable and affordable access to care. The Medicare program relies on a market-based approach that allows manufacturers to voluntarily price their products in negotiations with private purchasers. In all other countries with advanced economies, central governments have put in place processes and policies that limit manufacturers' ability to set prices on their own.

According to the Council of Economic Advisers (in a report written during the Trump administration), the US accounts for 46 percent of all sales of drug products under patent protection but contributes more than 70 percent of the profits for those products.[33] This is primarily due to higher prices for most branded products in the US. HHS conducted a similar review of drug prices paid in the US and 16 other countries with advanced economies and found that the US pays prices for the 27 top-selling drugs in Medicare Part B that are 1.8 times the prices paid, on average, in other countries.[34]

Some high-income countries—including Australia, France, Germany, and the UK—use clinical evaluations as part of their price negotiations with drug manufacturers. The UK and Germany are often cited for inclusion in pricing schemes that reference other countries because their clinical evaluation efforts are viewed as highly credible.

In the UK, prices are set mainly through complex voluntary agreements with drug manufacturers that tie prices to limits on profits and invested capital. Before a new product is covered by the National Health Service (NHS), it undergoes a clinical effectiveness review through the National Institute for Health and Care Excellence (NICE).[35] Such reviews include an estimate of the added value of new products in extending longevity and improving the quality of life, known as quality-adjusted life years (QALYs). QALYs provide a metric for assessing whether a new therapy is cost-effective and eligible for inclusion in the NHS budget. NICE reviews all new therapies expected to have a major effect on total NHS spending.

Germany also commissions clinical assessments of new therapies, but it takes a different approach to price negotiations. Drug companies voluntarily set their prices for the first year of a new product without interference or negotiation with insurers. Negotiations to set prices for the second and subsequent years are conducted with an association representing not-for-profit "sickness funds" that provide health coverage to most German citizens.

At product launch, manufacturers are required to submit a report justifying their products' clinical value with outcomes data, which are reviewed with other available data. If a review concludes that a new therapy leads to no clinical improvement over an existing treatment, the drug would be paid a reference price in the second and subsequent years on the market that is tied to the existing standard for treatment. If a review concludes that a new product offers added clinical value, then it is put into one of three categories—major, considerable, or minor—to indicate the significance of the added benefit.[36]

After the clinical review, manufacturers engage in price negotiations with the association of sickness funds. If they cannot agree on a price based on that information, the decision is left to an arbitration system. The manufacturers do not have to agree to the arbitrators' pricing decisions, but that requires pulling their products from the German market. Although unusual, this has happened several times over the past decade.[37]

The Medicare program does not have a formal process for incorporating clinical evaluations into pricing policy for pharmaceutical products. However, in 2010, as part of the ACA, Congress created the nongovernmental Patient-Centered Outcomes Research Institute (PCORI) to conduct comparative effectiveness research on drugs, medical devices, and medical procedures. That law, along with prior funding provided by the economic stimulus measure of 2009, has significantly added to the public investment in this type of research.[38]

In addition to the PCORI, the Institute for Clinical and Economic Review (ICER) is a nonprofit private research organization that conducts clinical and cost evaluations of pharmaceutical products and other health care products and services. Insurers and other purchasers of drug products increasingly use the ICER's work as part of their price negotiations, but it has no official role in drug pricing for government programs.[39]

Balancing Improved Pricing Discipline with Innovation

The pricing of pharmaceutical products is a difficult subject for public officials because society has an interest in both medical progress and affordable access to beneficial treatments. Patent protection provides a strong financial incentive for innovators to develop new medications, but high prices could limit patient access to effective care. Federal law's long-standing protection of intellectual property is an important reason the US remains the world's largest and most dynamic economy for biopharma innovation.

The question for public officials is how to create the right balance of incentives, restraint, regulation, and public subsidies to achieve a combination that delivers the best overall results. The policies now in place are coming under increasing pressure because growing numbers of voters believe they are not striking the right balance.

The current mix of policies was assembled over a long period—and not systematically. Legal and regulatory changes have been made on an ad hoc basis to correct for the perceived problems of the moment. The result is a complex mix of public purchasing rules that works in some ways but that also produces distortions and problematic side effects. Among other things, the current mandatory discounts required for Medicaid, 340B-covered entities, and large federal purchasers have left a smaller slice of the market to face higher, unregulated prices. Enrollees in employer-sponsored plans and other private insurance are now paying much higher prices than those who gain access through the mandatory public discounts, which is likely one reason for growing discontent.

As policymakers consider what might be done to strike a new balance of laws and regulations affecting the market for prescription drugs, the following can provide an outline for how to proceed.

Encouraging Supply Competition. Manufacturers of pharmaceutical products have maximum leverage over pricing when they face little or no competition. Patent law and exclusivity rights are the primary reasons manufacturers gain pricing power. But government regulation can also affect how quickly a product will face competition from another effective therapy. It is important to encourage generic competition as much as possible. But it is also crucial to have more than one brand-name therapy available during the period of patent protection to prevent full monopoly pricing power for one manufacturer.

In recent years, the FDA has announced several measures aimed at speeding the introduction of competing products. The agency also should look at what can be done with research funding to speed up the development of competing therapies when one product dominates a drug class.

Making Sense of Discounting. There is a strong temptation for policymakers to ensure that public programs and the beneficiaries participating in them have access to drugs at discounted prices. However, guaranteed discounts for one or several purchasers are likely to mean even higher prices for those who do not benefit from public regulation. The overall goal should be to strengthen countervailing pressure that can be brought to bear on pricing on behalf of all purchasers and consumers, not just a favored segment of the market.

One option would be to consolidate consumer demand through competing nongovernmental third parties that would negotiate prices on behalf of large numbers of public and private insurance enrollees. Privately negotiated prices on behalf of millions of consumers can better balance the interests of both the supply and demand sides of the markets, particularly when an effective brand-name therapy is still under patent protection and no competing alternative therapy is on the horizon.

Using Clinical Data to Inform Pricing. Although Congress created the PCORI in 2010, the US does not explicitly incorporate clinical evaluations into its payment policies for Medicare. Clinical assessments of therapies can be controversial. They necessarily involve judgments, assumptions, and hard data, and it is difficult to assemble a process that all parties view as neutral and fair.

Nonetheless, better and more broadly disseminated clinical assessments can add value to the pricing environment in the US, especially in situations that involve a clinically important therapy in which no effective alternative is available to patients and purchasers. In those circumstances, the only way to assess value is by looking at the actual clinical benefits for patients. ICER is increasingly seen as providing credible reviews that can be used by all purchasers of these products.

The US could move toward a more systematic use of these data by building the following new procedures into pricing policy in Medicare Part B.

Identify Important Products with No Effective Competition. The HHS secretary should be required to identify any new product that is about to be covered under Medicare Part B for which no comparable treatment course is currently available. For these drugs, there would be a clinical assessment of the product's value to patient health that would help inform pricing negotiations between private-sector vendors working under contract with Part B and the drug manufacturers.

Assess Clinical Value. HHS should create an advisory panel composed of experts from academia, industry, and medicine. This panel would analyze available clinical information on the therapies that the secretary identifies as lacking effective competition. Sources for this assessment should include research organizations such as PCORI and ICER, other academic centers, governmental agencies, and relevant agencies in other countries (such as NICE and the clinical evaluation bodies in Australia, France, and Germany). The manufacturers would also submit clinical evidence to the panel. The panel would determine the range of clinical value estimates globally and determine if there is a general consensus on which to base an assessment of a product's benefits for patient health.

Publish Findings. The panel should publish a report on its findings that would inform negotiations between the Part B vendors and the manufacturers.

Conduct Ongoing Clinical Data Collection and Review. Following the launch of a product, clinical data on patient outcomes should be collected to inform subsequent pricing negotiations.

This approach would lead to more systematic use of clinical evaluation in the pricing of Part B drugs, but it is unlikely to satisfy either critics or defenders of existing policy. Critics would prefer government price setting based on clinical assessments rather than relying on a more market-oriented process. Defenders of the status quo would raise concerns about the objectivity of the clinical evaluation process. What is proposed here is intended to strike a balance. Explicitly accounting for clinical value can bring an objective basis to privately negotiated prices and avoid the risks to pharmaceutical development that arbitrary price cutting by the government would entail.

An Unusual Slice of an Unusual Market

As noted in Chapter 1, the market for medical services and products suffers from defects that can be addressed only by effective public policy. Prescription drugs come with the further complication of intellectual property protection. It makes for a complex environment that requires a balanced approach.

The US stands nearly alone in the developed world in steering clear of explicit price setting for these products, for good reason. Setting prices centrally, based on political considerations, carries the substantial risk of under-investing in future therapies.

But there is the opposite risk, too, which is that the system can become so compromised that patients and taxpayers end up paying far more than they should for products with clinical benefits that fall short of what is claimed.

The US can do better, starting with Medicare, which is a large purchaser of these products. Instead of setting arbitrary price limits, the government should help the market identify the real clinical value of therapies as they compare to alternative ways of treating patients. Collecting and broadcasting that information by itself will have a substantial disciplining effect.

Notes

1. This chapter draws from two previously published reports, both of which were coauthored by Joseph Antos, the Wilson H. Taylor Scholar in Health Care and Retirement Policy at the American Enterprise Institute. See Joseph Antos and James C. Capretta, "Prescription Drug Pricing: An Overview of Legal, Regulatory, and Market Environment," American Enterprise Institute, July 23, 2018, https://www.aei.org/research-products/report/prescription-drug-pricing-an-overview-of-the-legal-regulatory-and-market-environment/; and Joseph Antos and James C. Capretta, "Reforming Medicare Payments for Part B Drugs," American Enterprise Institute, June 3, 2019, https://www.aei.org/research-products/report/reforming-medicare-payments-for-part-b-drugs/.

2. Paul Demko, "Politico-Harvard Poll: Congress Should Focus on Reducing Drug Pricing," *Politico*, September 25, 2017, https://www.politico.com/story/2017/09/25/politico-harvard-poll-congress-should-focus-on-reducing-drug-prices-243109.

3. US Senate, "The Constitution of the United States of America: Analysis and Interpretation," 2017, https://www.govinfo.gov/content/pkg/GPO-CONAN-2017/pdf/GPO-CONAN-2017.pdf.

4. US Patent and Trademark Office, "The US Patent System Celebrates 212 Years," April 2002.

5. Edward Walterscheid, "'Within the Limits of the Constitutional Grant': Constitutional Limitations on the Patent Power," *Journal of Intellectual Property* 9, no. 2 (April 2002), https://digitalcommons.law.uga.edu/cgi/viewcontent.cgi?referer=&httpsredir=1&article=1367&context=jipl.

6. Congressional Research Service, "The Hatch-Waxman Act: A Primer," September 28, 2016, https://www.everycrsreport.com/reports/R44643.html.

7. Judith Johnson, "Biologics and Biosimilars: Background and Key Issues," Congressional Research Service, October 27, 2017, https://sgp.fas.org/crs/misc/R44620.pdf.

8. Medicare Payment Advisory Commission, "Medicare Part B Drug and Oncology Payment Policy Issues," June 15, 2016, https://www.medpac.gov/recommendation/medicare-part-b-drug-and-oncology-payment-policy-issues-june-2016/; and Medicare Payment Advisory Commission, "Report to the Congress: Medicare and the Health Care Delivery System," June 15, 2016, https://www.medpac.gov/wp-content/uploads/import_data/scrape_files/docs/default-source/reports/june-2016-report-to-the-congress-medicare-and-the-health-care-delivery-system.pdf.

9. Food and Drug Administration, "Biosimilar Product Information," February 25, 2022, https://www.fda.gov/drugs/biosimilars/biosimilar-product-information.

10. Congressional Budget Office, "Prescription Drug Pricing in the Private Sector," January 2007, https://www.cbo.gov/sites/default/files/110th-congress-2007-2008/reports/01-03-prescriptiondrug.pdf.

11. Congressional Budget Office, "Prescription Drug Pricing in the Private Sector."

12. Congressional Budget Office, "Prescription Drug Pricing in the Private Sector."

13. Congressional Budget Office, "Prescription Drug Pricing in the Private Sector."

14. Medicare Payment Advisory Commission, "Medicare Part B Drug Payment Policy Issues," June 15, 2017, https://www.medpac.gov/recommendation/medicare-part-

b-drug-payment-policy-issues-june-2017/; and Medicare Payment Advisory Commission, "Medicare and the Health Care Delivery System," June 15, 2017, https://www.medpac.gov/wp-content/uploads/import_data/scrape_files/docs/default-source/press-releases/june2017_pressrelease.pdf.

15. Medicare Payment Advisory Commission, "Medicare Part B Drug Payment Policy Issues"; and Medicare Payment Advisory Commission, "Medicare and the Health Care Delivery System."

16. Medicaid and CHIP Payment and Access Commission, "Medicaid Payment for Outpatient Prescription Drugs," March 2018, https://www.macpac.gov/wp-content/uploads/2015/09/Medicaid-Payment-for-Outpatient-Prescription-Drugs.pdf.

17. Congressional Budget Office, "How the Medicaid Rebate on Prescription Drugs Affects Pricing in the Pharmaceutical Industry," January 1996, https://www.cbo.gov/sites/default/files/104th-congress-1995-1996/reports/1996doc20.pdf.

18. Centers for Medicare & Medicaid Services, "Medicaid Pharmacy Supplemental Rebate Agreements (SRA)," September 2021, https://www.medicaid.gov/medicaid-chip-program-information/by-topics/prescription-drugs/downloads/xxxsupplemental-rebates-chart-current-qtr.pdf.

19. Andrew W. Mulcahy et al., "The 340B Prescription Drug Discount Program: Origins, Implementation, and Post-Reform Future," RAND Corporation, 2014, https://www.rand.org/pubs/perspectives/PE121.html.

20. Mulcahy et al., "The 340B Prescription Drug Discount Program."

21. Mulcahy et al., "The 340B Prescription Drug Discount Program."

22. Medicare Payment Advisory Commission, "Medicare Part B Drug Payment Policy Issues"; and Medicare Payment Advisory Commission, "Medicare and the Health Care Delivery System."

23. Juliette Cubanski and Anthony Damico, "Medicare Part D: A First Look at Medicare Prescription Drug Plans in 2022," Kaiser Family Foundation, November 2, 2021, https://www.kff.org/medicare/issue-brief/medicare-part-d-a-first-look-at-medicare-prescription-drug-plans-in-2022/.

24. Kaiser Family Foundation, "An Overview of the Medicare Part D Prescription Drug Benefit," October 13, 2021, https://www.kff.org/medicare/fact-sheet/an-overview-of-the-medicare-part-d-prescription-drug-benefit/.

25. Centers for Medicare & Medicaid Services, "Medicare Part D-Direct and Indirect Remuneration," January 19, 2017, https://www.cms.gov/newsroom/fact-sheets/medicare-part-d-direct-and-indirect-remuneration-dir.

26. Medicare Trustees, *The 2021 Annual Report of the Boards of Trustees of the Federal Hospital Insurance and Federal Supplementary Medical Insurance Trust Funds*, Centers for Medicare & Medicaid Services, August 31, 2021, https://www.cms.gov/files/document/2021-medicare-trustees-report.pdf.

27. Centers for Medicare & Medicaid Services, "CMS Releases 2022 Projected Medicare Part D Average Premium," July 29, 2021, https://www.cms.gov/newsroom/news-alert/cms-releases-2022-projected-medicare-part-d-average-premium; and Congressional Research Service, "Medicare Part D Prescription Drug Benefit," December 18, 2020, https://sgp.fas.org/crs/misc/R40611.pdf.

28. Mike McCaughan, "Prescription Drug Pricing: Veterans Health

Administration," *Health Affairs*, August 10, 2017, https://www.healthaffairs.org/do/10.1377/hpb20171008.000174/full/.

29. US Department of Veterans Affairs, "An Assessment of the Department of Veteran Affairs Supply Purchasing System," McKinsey & Company, September 1, 2015, https://www.va.gov/opa/choiceact/documents/assessments/Assessment_J_Supplies.pdf.

30. Joseph P. Newhouse, "How Much Should Medicare Pay for Drugs?," *Health Affairs* 23, no. 1 (January 2004): 89–102, https://www.healthaffairs.org/doi/pdf/10.1377/hlthaff.23.1.89.

31. Centers for Medicare & Medicaid Services, "National Health Expenditure Data, Historical Tables: Table 16," 2018, https://www.cms.gov/Research-Statistics-Data-and-Systems/Statistics-Trends-and-Reports/NationalHealthExpendData/NationalHealthAccountsHistorical.

32. Newhouse, "How Much Should Medicare Pay for Drugs?"

33. Council of Economic Advisers, "Reforming Biopharmaceutical Pricing at Home and Abroad," February 2018, https://trumpwhitehouse.archives.gov/wp-content/uploads/2017/11/CEA-Rx-White-Paper-Final2.pdf.

34. Office of the Assistant Secretary for Planning and Evaluation, "Comparison of US and International Prices for Top Medicare Part B Drugs by Total Expenditure," US Department of Health and Human Services, October 25, 2018, https://aspe.hhs.gov/sites/default/files/private/pdf/259996/ComparisonUSInternationalPricesTopSpendingPartBDrugs.pdf.

35. Steven Morgan, "Summaries of National Drug Coverage and Pharmaceutical Pricing Policies in 10 Countries: Australia, Canada, France, Germany, the Netherlands, New Zealand, Norway, Sweden, Switzerland, and the U.K." (working paper, Commonwealth Fund, New York, 2016), https://www.commonwealthfund.org/sites/default/files/2018-09/Steven%20Morgan%2C%20PhD_Ten%20Country%20Pharma%20Policy%20Summaries_2016%20Vancouver%20Group%20Meeting.pdf.

36. Daniel Bahr and Thomas Huelskoetter, "Comparing the Effectiveness of Drugs: The German Experience," Center for American Progress, May 21, 2014, https://cdn.americanprogress.org/wp-content/uploads/2014/05/PharmaReform.pdf.

37. James C. Robinson, Dimitra Panteli, and Patricia Ex, "Reference Pricing in Germany: Implications for U.S. Pharmaceutical Pricing," Commonwealth Fund, February 4, 2019, https://www.commonwealthfund.org/publications/issue-briefs/2019/jan/reference-pricing-germany-implications.

38. Amanda K. Sarata, "Funding for ACA-Established Patient-Centered Outcomes Research Trust Fund (PCORTF) Expires in FY2019," Congressional Research Service, December 20, 2018, https://sgp.fas.org/crs/misc/IN11010.pdf.

39. Peter J. Neumann and Joshua T. Cohen, "America's 'NICE'?," Health Affairs Forefront, March 12, 2018, https://www.healthaffairs.org/do/10.1377/hblog20180306.837580/full/.

8

The Physician Workforce

The objective of a functioning market for medical services is to help consumers see meaningful price differences among the practitioners and facilities offering the services they need, but those price differences will not surface if the competition is held back by an insufficient number of competing suppliers. Put another way, if there are too few physicians, patients may not have many options when they need care.

Unfortunately, the history of the nation's system for regulating and credentialing doctors is a cause for concern in this regard, as the physicians themselves are in control of these processes. Excessive barriers to entry could lead to a level of competition that is below what would be beneficial to consumers and below what might be achievable with the right policies.

The Context of the Status Quo

The United States has high expenditures for medical care compared to other industrialized countries. Among the 36 members of the Organisation of Economic Co-operation and Development (OECD), the US ranks first in terms of spending as a percentage of gross domestic product (GDP), at 17.1 percent in 2017. The next highest-spending country, Switzerland, devoted only 12.3 percent of its GDP to health expenses that same year.[1]

Further, US physicians have incomes well in excess of what their peers earn in other advanced economies. For instance, in 2019, US physicians were expected to earn an average income of $313,000, compared to $163,000 for their counterparts in Germany and $108,000 in France.[2]

Several factors might explain why US doctors command higher salaries than physicians practicing in other rich countries do. Among other things, medical training and licensure are more expensive in the US than

JAMES C. CAPRETTA   177

elsewhere, with medical school graduates typically carrying large student loan debts into their residencies and first years of medical practice. Medical training in other countries is less expensive because national governments often heavily subsidize it. For instance, in the US, three-fourths of 2019 medical school graduates had student loan debts, with a median debt level of $200,000.[3] By contrast, in Germany, most newly minted physicians have incurred no debt for their medical school education because state governments pay for their tuition.[4]

Qualified candidates for medical school have other career options too. The medical sector is competing with other fields for talented students and therefore must offer competitive compensation levels when taking into account the many factors considered when career tracks are chosen.

While these factors play a role in high physician fees, so too does the interplay of demand for medical services with available supply. In a fully unregulated medical services market, with low barriers to entry for practitioners, one would expect supply to adjust as necessary to meet demand and thus lead to pricing that both sides of each transaction find satisfactory.

But the market for medical care in the US is anything but unregulated. Public policies (at both the federal and state levels) play important roles in how the market functions. In particular, public policies that restrict the available supply of physician services may drive up consumer prices. All else being equal, fees for physician services will be lower when there is wide availability of competing practitioners. A study from 2015 showed that pricing for many common physician procedures was 8–26 percent higher in markets with high levels of consolidation among physicians groups compared to markets with more numerous and independent practices.[5]

In the US and elsewhere, public policy in health care must balance the need to provide patients with a level of quality that might not exist in an unregulated market with the goal of making the care they receive as inexpensive as possible. Given the high cost of physician services in the US, it is appropriate to consider whether current policies could be adjusted to boost available supply without harming the quality of care provided to patients.

Figure 1. Active Physicians per 100,000 US Population

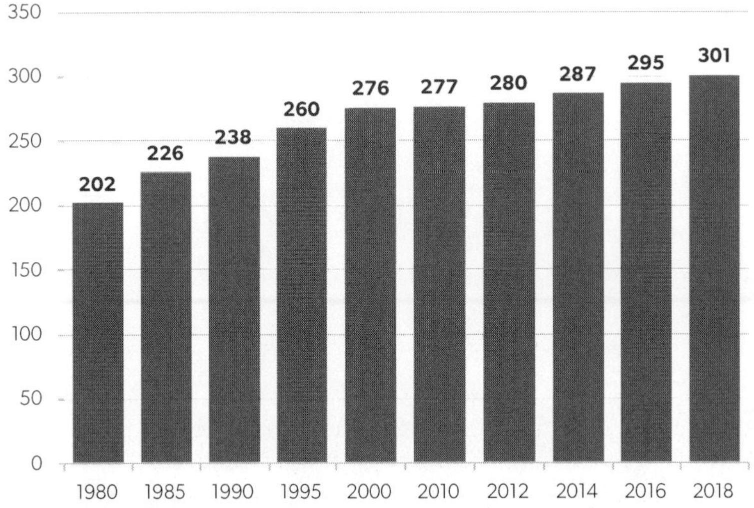

Source: Federation of State Medical Boards, *U.S. Medical Regulatory Trends and Actions: 2018,* 2018, https://www.fsmb.org/siteassets/advocacy/publications/us-medical-regulatory-trends-actions.pdf; and Edward S. Salsberg and Gaetano J. Forte, "Trends in the Physician Workforce," *Health Affairs* 21, no. 5 (2020), https://www.healthaffairs.org/doi/pdf/10.1377/hlthaff.21.5.165.

A Topline Perspective

As shown in Figure 1, in recent decades, the US has experienced a steady increase in the ratio of physicians to the potential patient population. In 2018, there were 301 active physicians for every 100,000 residents, up nearly 50 percent since 1980. All other factors being equal, a higher ratio indicates more readily available services.

While the ratio has been rising in the US, it is still below levels seen in other high-income countries. As shown in Figure 2, in 2019 and 2020, the US had fewer active physicians relative to the size of its population than did Germany, Italy, Australia, France, the UK, and Canada.[6]

Periodically, the American Association of Medical Colleges (AAMC)— the association representing the interests of accredited medical schools and academic medical centers—commissions an analysis comparing the expected census of practicing physicians against a measure of patient demand. The latest forecast, from April 2019, projects rising demand,

Figure 2. US Physician Ratio (per 100,000 Population) Compared to Other High-Income Countries, 2019–20

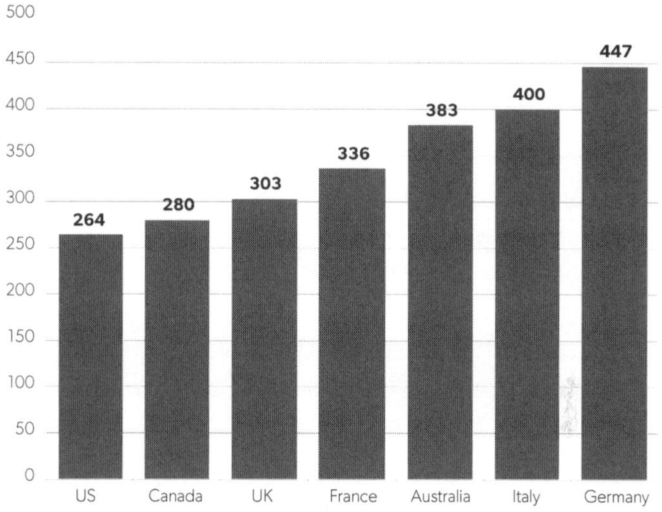

Source: Organisation of Economic Co-operation and Development, "Doctors," 2022, https://data. oecd.org/healthres/doctors.htm.

mainly from an aging and growing population, outpacing the growth in the physician workforce, such that there would be a shortfall of between 46,900 and 121,900 physicians in 2032.[7] The AAMC uses this analysis to press for expanded federal financial support of residency training. Other studies have looked at potential shortfalls of primary care physicians, certain specialists, and rural practitioners.

Projections of this kind are highly uncertain because of the many assumptions on which they are built. They also do not incorporate possible adaptive behavior by the existing workforce, the larger health systems responsible for meeting their patients' needs, or the organizations responsible for educating and training the future physician workforce.

The AAMC's projections from two decades ago illustrate the unreliability of these static forecasts. In 1997, there was growing concern in the physician community and among academic medical centers of an impending oversupply of doctors. The AAMC and its affiliated institutions issued a recommendation to Congress to cap the number of residency slots funded by Medicare to slow the pipeline of newly trained physicians coming into the market.[8] Congress obliged and imposed a cap in the 1997 Balanced Budget Act, which remains in place today. The AAMC and other organizations that were worried about oversupply two decades ago are now warning of an impending shortage and want Congress to remove the cap they helped put in place in the 1990s.

Ideally, the government should not be involved in planning the size of the physician workforce. Rather, the overall structure that controls the physician pipeline should be flexible and adaptive enough to respond to signals of greater patient demand for access to care, albeit with a fairly long delay due to the time it takes to become a licensed physician. This analysis focuses on the existing system and whether it is accommodating enough to adjust to patients' changing needs no matter what variables come into play.

Aggregate physician counts might not even tell the whole story. The availability of physician services depends also on practitioners' productivity. US physicians might be capable of adequately serving a larger population based on longer work hours, better technology, and other factors. Even so, the relatively high prices patients must pay for physician services in the US indicate that additional supply might help ease the financial pressures that are leading some policymakers and candidates for political office to support a more active role for the government in regulating clinician fees.

The balance of this chapter examines the federal and state policies that influence, but do not fully determine, the supply side of the physician market. These policies have evolved slowly over the past century and a half as medical care became more sophisticated and effective and the physician community became more organized and assertive in claiming for itself a preeminent role in policing the profession and setting the rules for admitting new members.

Origins and Evolution of the Current System

The US Constitution reserves to the states all powers not enumerated for the federal government. An important consequence of this ordering of governmental authority has been the primacy of states in the regulation of medical practice. The current state-based system of medical licensure and medical school regulation can be traced to the organizational strength that mainstream physicians developed in the latter half of the 19th century.

In the mid-1800s, the US was a battleground for competing theories of effective medical care, with mainstream medicine (as then understood and practiced) being challenged by homeopathic care (focused on natural remedies and recuperation) and eclecticism (focused on plant-based remedies and steam baths), all three of which captured a significant share of dedicated practitioners and patients. The competing camps were supported by scores of schools that trained their adherents, many of which were for-profit and fully exempt from any governmental regulation.

Mainstream physician care suffered in this era largely because of its ineffectiveness; in the early part of the century, physicians were administering therapies that were poisonous and harmful and continued to perform procedures, such as bloodletting, that were painful for patients and detrimental to their health.[9]

The landscape began to change with the formation of the American Medical Association (AMA) in 1847 and the growing use and acceptance of the scientific method to determine effective medical care. From its inception, the AMA and its affiliated state bodies prioritized screening to weed out unqualified practitioners and establishing quality standards for the schools educating physicians.

Organized medicine quickly became a powerful force in state legislatures. (See Table 1 for a list of historical milestones in the evolution of the physician licensure process.) In 1859, North Carolina established a state medical board for oversight of the profession, and in 1876, both California and Texas passed laws creating boards of examiners to issue licenses and examine the qualifications of persons claiming to be physicians. Many states pursued similar policies in the ensuing years. From 1875 to 1915, state legislatures passed more than 400 separate laws governing medical practice, with increasing emphasis on licensure, competency exams, and oversight of the schools issuing medical degrees.[10]

A new and decisive phase began with the Flexner report in 1910.[11] The Carnegie Foundation (at the urging of the AMA and others) commissioned Abraham Flexner, an educator and not a physician, to survey the state of medical education in the United States. His report, which directed withering criticism at the for-profit school system that had proliferated in the

Table 1. Notable Periods and Milestones in the Licensure System for US Physicians

Year	Milestone
1847	The American Medical Association is founded.
1876	The American Association of Medical Colleges is formed.
1875–1915	States enact 400 laws regulating licensure and practice.
1910	The Flexner report is released.
1912	The Federation of State Medical Boards is formed.
1942	The Liaison Committee for Medical Education is formed.
1947	The AAMC sponsors the first Medical College Admission Test.
1968	Eight states start using the first national licensing exam.
1979	A standardized exam is adopted nationwide.
1992	The US Medical Licensing Exam is instituted.

Source: Author.

19th century, transformed the medical education landscape and set a philosophical course for medical school curricula, clinical training, and physician licensure that has been the foundation for American medicine over the past century.[12]

The Flexner report placed every medical school reviewed into three categories: those seen as providing a scientifically sound education, on par with the best schools in Europe, particularly in Germany; those that were deficient but could be salvaged; and those that were hopeless and should be closed. Flexner put scores of medical schools into this third category, which ultimately led to their demise.[13]

The enduring influence of Flexner's study is threefold. First, it established that academic medical training in the US should be tied directly to scientific inquiry and evidence. In practical terms, this meant that medical education should be centered on an understanding of what science, in the laboratory, reveals about effective medical care.

Second, it placed academic medical centers, tied to the nation's most prestigious universities, at the pinnacle of US health care. The institutions that met Flexner's standards for medical training and scientific inquiry became the driving forces for advances in medical understanding and practice. The nation's top physicians gravitated to these institutions for their training and then stayed and practiced medicine at the growing network of inpatient hospital facilities that developed around them.

Third and crucially, Flexner's findings became the predicate for a medical school and residency credentialing system that controls physicians' entry into medical practice.

In the years after Flexner issued his findings and recommendations, states moved quickly to write licensing requirements that recognized only graduates of accredited medical schools, with the AMA (and, subsequently, additional bodies affiliated with the medical profession) establishing the certification criteria. In short order, only graduates of these accredited schools were allowed to take the exams run by state medical boards that became significant steps in the licensure process. From 1906 to 1944, the number of medical schools in the US producing newly educated physicians fell from 162 to 69.[14]

Basic Framework for Physician Licensure in the US

The traditional pathway to becoming a licensed physician involves multiple steps and takes many years to complete. (See Figure 3.)

Medical licenses are issued by state medical boards, which are empowered by state legislatures to enforce professional standards on practitioners. This licensure system establishes the educational, training, and examination process that candidates must navigate before they can operate independent practices and care for patients without supervision.

For students residing in the US, the starting point for a career as a physician is admission to a qualified school. Since 1942, the Liaison Committee on Medical Education (LCME) has established the criteria for accrediting the nation's medical schools.[15] The LCME is a joint enterprise of the AMA and the AAMC.[16] The committee is comprised of 19 members: 15 medical doctors (MDs) who either are in practice or serve as educators in medical schools, two current medical school students, and two nonphysicians. The AMA and AAMC nominate 14 of the 19 members, with the other five coming from candidates appointed by the LCME itself.

Figure 3. Basic Physician Licensure Framework for US Medical Schools

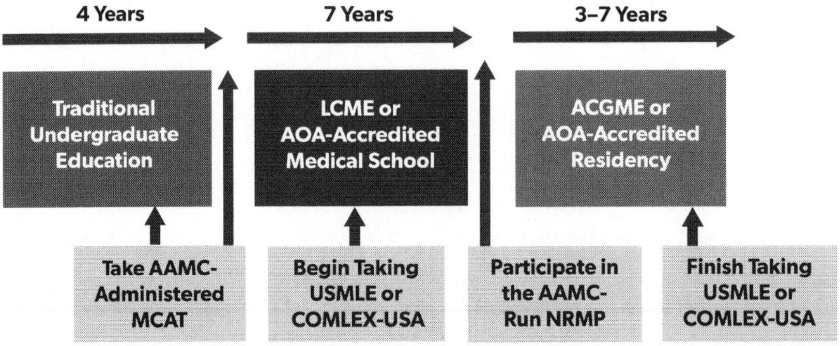

4 Years	7 Years	3–7 Years
Traditional Undergraduate Education	LCME or AOA-Accredited Medical School	ACGME or AOA-Accredited Residency
Take AAMC-Administered MCAT	Begin Taking USMLE or COMLEX-USA	Participate in the AAMC-Run NRMP	Finish Taking USMLE or COMLEX-USA

AAMC = American Association of Medical Colleges
AOA = American Osteopathic Association
COMLEX = Comprehensive Osteopathic Medical Licensing Examination
LCME = Liaison Committee for Medical Education
MCAT = Medical College Admission Test
NRMP = National Residency Match Program
USMLE = United States Medical Licensing Examination

Source: Federation of State Medical Boards, *U.S. Medical Regulatory Trends and Actions: 2018*, 2018, https://www.fsmb.org/siteassets/advocacy/publications/us-medical-regulatory-trends-actions.pdf.

Admission to an LCME-accredited medical school requires taking the Medical College Admission Test, which is a standardized test developed and administered by the AAMC.

Institutional accreditation is crucial to the process because, in the aftermath of the Flexner report, most states stipulated that conferring a medical license is predicated on graduation from an accredited institution. Further, graduation from an accredited school makes candidates eligible to take the standardized US Medical Licensing Exam, which is also a necessary step for licensure by the state medical boards.[17]

Although there are exceptions, the typical path to medical school admission presumes completion of a traditional four-year undergraduate college education. Thus, it usually takes eight years of school-based education to obtain both an undergraduate and a medical degree.

States also require medical school graduates to enter into an approved residency training program, for a minimum of three years and perhaps seven or more depending on the specialization.[18] In the fourth year of medical school, students participate in an elaborately structured residency assignment program that matches interested students with available residency slots. The students specify their preferences, and an algorithm matches them with residency programs in a manner that is supposed to maximize overall student and residency program satisfaction.[19]

Residency program accreditation began in 1972 with the establishment of the Liaison Committee for Graduate Medical Education, which transitioned into the American Council for Graduate Medical Education (ACGME) in 1981. The ACGME was founded by five sponsoring organizations: the American Board of Medical Specialties, the American Hospital Association, the AMA, the AAMC, and the Council of Medical Specialty Societies.

In recent years, the ACGME and the American Osteopathic Association (AOA) have jointly accredited the residency programs for allopathic and osteopathic physicians. Beginning with the academic year starting July 1, 2020, the ACGME accredits residency training for both branches of medical school education. Consequently, the sponsoring organizations for the ACGME now also include the AOA and the American Association of Colleges of Osteopathic Medicine.

Although states generally do not require further board certification by specialty societies as a condition of licensure, these certifications are increasingly important to the professional viability of physicians wishing to practice in the relevant specialties. Hospitals often require board certifications before granting physicians admitting privileges, and these certifications are crucial for admittance to referral networks that allow practices to build stable patient populations.[20]

Foreign-Born Physicians and International Medical Graduates

The US is heavily dependent on foreign-born physicians and graduates (both US- and foreign-born) of medical schools located outside the US and Canada.[21] Currently, 29 percent of US-based physicians are foreign-born, including 22 percent who are foreign-born and remain non-US citizens even as they care for patients in every corner of the country.[22] Physicians attending non-US medical schools are particularly important to ensuring

Figure 4. Practicing Physicians in the US by Medical School Location, 2020

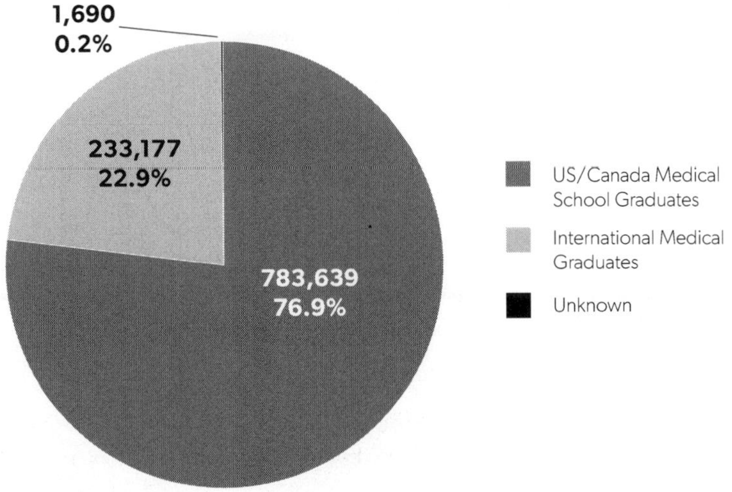

1,690
0.2%

233,177
22.9%

783,639
76.9%

US/Canada Medical School Graduates

International Medical Graduates

Unknown

Source: Aaron Young et al., "FSMB Census of Licensed Physicians in the United States, 2020," *Journal of Medical Regulation* 107, no. 2 (2021), https://www.fsmb.org/siteassets/advocacy/publications/2020-physician-census.pdf.

access to care in underserved areas and are more likely than are their US-educated counterparts to become primary care physicians.[23]

The typical pathway for non–US citizens to become practicing, US-based physicians is to attend medical school outside the US and Canada and then participate in a US-based residency program as a condition of securing an unrestricted license from state medical boards. Graduates of medical schools outside the US and Canada are known as international medical graduates (IMGs). As shown in Figure 4, in 2020, 23 percent of practicing US physicians are IMGs.

IMGs can be US citizens or foreign-born, non–US citizens. Many IMGs have attended schools in the Caribbean, which has become a destination for students looking for lower-cost medical education options and those unable to secure admittance to a US-based school.

In 2017, of the more than 93,000 native US citizens who were participating in US-based residency programs, 9 percent were IMGs (Figure 5). There were also more than 10,000 foreign-born US citizens in these residency

Figure 5. Physicians in Residency Programs by Medical School Type and US Residency Status, 2017

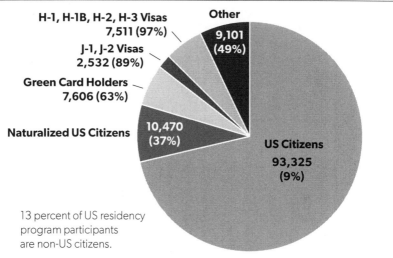

H-1, H-1B, H-2, H-3 Visas
7,511 (97%)

J-1, J-2 Visas
2,532 (89%)

Green Card Holders
7,606 (63%)

Naturalized US Citizens
10,470 (37%)

Other
9,101 (49%)

US Citizens
93,325 (9%)

13 percent of US residency program participants are non-US citizens.

Note: Figures in parentheses are the percentages of physicians in each category of US residency status who are IMGs.
Source: Sarah E. Brotherton and Sylvia I. Etzel, "Graduate Medical Education, 2017–2018," *Journal of the American Medical Association* 210, no. 10 (September 11, 2018): 1051–70, https://jamanetwork.com/journals/jama/fullarticle/2702121.

programs, of whom 37 percent were IMGs. More than 13 percent of residents were foreign-born, non–US citizens who were participating in these programs under various immigration authorities provided in federal law.

Figure 6 depicts the complex residency program and immigration law processes that foreign-born IMGs must navigate to obtain licenses from state medical boards. First, they must graduate from medical schools that have been certified by the Educational Commission for Foreign Medical Graduates (ECFMG), an organization created by the medical and teaching hospital community to oversee the qualifications of foreign-born physicians for practice in the US. ECFMG certification is a necessary condition for IMGs to enter US-based residency training.[24] IMGs cannot satisfy US licensing requirements with residency training in non-US teaching facilities. ECFMG certification is also required for advancing to step three of the medical licensing exam.

Figure 6. The Residency Process

* Primary Options:
H-1B: Employer-initiated for temporary skilled foreign workers
J-1: Temporary training to obtain skills beneficial to an applicant's home country

ECFMG = Educational Commission for Foreign Medical Graduates
NRMP = National Residency Match Program
USMLE = United States Medical Licensing Examination

Source: Federation of State Medical Boards, *U.S. Medical Regulatory Trends and Actions: 2018,* 2018, https://www.fsmb.org/siteassets/advocacy/publications/us-medical-regulatory-trends-actions. pdf; and Silva Mathema, *Immigrant Doctors Can Help Lower Physician Shortages in Rural America,* Center for American Progress, July 2019, https://cdn.americanprogress.org/content/uploads/2019/ 07/29074013/ImmigrantDoctors-report.pdf.

Foreign-born IMGs have essentially two paths to temporary legal status that will allow them to complete their residency requirements in the US. Under the J-1 program, the ECFMG can sponsor candidates who would like to attend a US-based residency program with the stated intention of returning to their home country for at least two years after finishing their clinical training. Upon fulfillment of their two-year commitment, they can then apply for an alternative visa status that might allow them to return to work in the US as a practicing physician.[25]

J-1 visa holders have the option to apply for a Conrad 30 waiver, which would allow them to skip the two-year commitment in their home countries. The Conrad 30 waiver program was created to allow qualified IMGs to provide care in areas of the US with insufficient access to physician services, particularly in rural communities. States sponsor the IMGs under the Conrad 30 program, which gets its name from the authorization of up to 30 waivers per year per state.[26] Participants must commit to serving at least three years at a health care facility in an underserved area, after which they can apply for either temporary or permanent residency status.[27]

The other option for IMGs wishing to conduct their training in a US-based residency program is the H-1B visa program, which is aimed at bringing to the US foreign-born workers with specialized employment skills. Employers sponsor applicants, who must enter a lottery for one of the available annual visas, which are capped by law. However, higher education institutions, nonprofit organizations affiliated with exempt higher education institutions, and nonprofit and governmental research organizations are exempt from the H-1B cap.[28] These exemptions allow many IMGs to obtain visas for their residency training, as the institutions are generally affiliated with universities. However, after finishing their residency rotations, foreign-born IMGs must reenter the H-1B lottery to secure a visa that will allow them to work for a sponsoring employer.[29]

There are far more IMGs interested in attending US-based residency programs than there are available residency slots. As of July 2014, 9,326 IMGs were eligible but not yet assigned to a residency program through the National Residency Match Program.[30]

Public Subsidies and Policies for Graduate Medical Education

Whatever influence the federal government has over the pipeline of physicians is tied to its role in providing subsidies for required residency programs at accredited institutions. Federal support for this training—called graduate medical education (GME)—is provided mainly through Medicare, Medicaid, and the Department of Veterans Affairs (VA). As shown in Table 2, in 2015 (the last year for which data are available), total federal spending on GME was $14.5 billion, according to the Government Accountability Office (GAO). Total federal and state support for GME, which includes the state share of Medicaid GME spending, was $16.3 billion.[31]

Medicare's GME provisions provide, by far, the largest amount of support to institutions engaged in residency training. Medicare has been supporting residency training since the program began providing insurance coverage to beneficiaries in July 1966. When Medicare was enacted in 1965, the key committees writing the initial legislation explicitly included payments for residency training in the program's mandate, on the grounds that the institutions providing educational services to residents are, generally,

Table 2. Government Support for GME, 2015

Program	US Dollars (Billions)
Medicare	
Direct Graduate Medical Education	3.7
Indirect Medical Education	6.6
Medicaid (Federal Share Only)	2.4
Department of Veterans Affairs	1.5
Other Federal	0.3
Total Federal	**14.5**
Medicaid (State Share)	1.8
Total Federal and State	**16.3**

Source: Government Accountability Office, "Physician Workforce: HHS Needs Better Information to Comprehensively Evaluate Graduate Medical Education Funding," March 2018, https://www.gao.gov/assets/700/690581.pdf.

some of the best facilities in the country, and Congress wanted Medicare beneficiaries to have access to them. Further, the law's authors believed Medicare should shoulder its fair share of the costs of an educational system that has system-wide benefits.[32]

While the states, through their medical boards, have taken the lead in requiring approved residency training for physicians, the federal government has reinforced the essential role of accredited institutions by stipulating that Medicare GME funds can be paid only to institutions approved for residency training by either the ACGME or the AOA.[33] Beyond this accreditation requirement, however, the federal government has taken a hands-off approach to residency program oversight. Funding is provided with few demands for relevant data, to the point that several outside organizations have pointed to the paucity of information about program outcomes as a critical failure of current GME operations.[34]

Before the enactment of Medicare's prospective payment system in 1983, the program paid hospitals based on cost. Hospitals reported expenses associated with their residency programs, and Medicare sent payments based on its share of a facility's inpatient admissions.

With the prospective payment system, Medicare moved away from reimbursing facilities based on cost and instead calculated fixed-rate payments based on the diagnoses of the patients admitted for inpatient care—the so-called diagnosis-related groups (DRGs). The new DRG payments were calculated to specifically exclude the costs associated with residency training.

To continue subsidizing the "bedside" education of physicians, Congress created two separate add-on funding streams for academic hospitals to run in tandem with the prospective payment system. First, the program pays institutions based on the direct costs of employing residents—called Direct Graduate Medical Education (DGME). This spending is supposed to offset expenses such as the salary stipends paid to residents, the salaries of the physicians supervising them, and associated overhead costs.[35] Second, since 1983, Medicare has also paid hospitals for the indirect costs of running a residency program—the so-called indirect medical education (IME) subsidy.

Medicare makes DGME payments to facilities on a per-resident basis, using base year costs starting in October 1983 as a reference point. The base year amount is indexed to inflation. Medicare pays for an approved number of residents per hospital using a formula that incorporates the percentage of total patient days in the hospital that were attributed to Medicare beneficiaries.[36]

IME payments are supposed to address the added costs hospitals incur, separate and apart from directly paying for residents and their supervising physicians. The contention is that these hospitals have added costs that nonteaching facilities do not incur, such as additional tests that residents may order as they are trained in their specialties and the costs associated with duplication of effort when residents work alongside a supervising physician.

The IME payment is calculated as an add-on to the regular Medicare DRG rates, equal to roughly 5.5 percent of the base amount. The Medicare Payment Advisory Commission estimates that the actual added, indirect cost of residency training is only 2.2 percent of teaching hospitals' expenses. In 2015, paying hospitals an add-on of 2.2 percent, instead of 5.5 percent, would have reduced Medicare spending by $3.5 billion annually.[37]

As noted previously, in 1997, at the urging of academic medical centers and the physician community, Congress capped the number of residency slots that are eligible for Medicare subsidization each year. Each hospital may apply for payments but only up to the number of residents on staff as of 1996. New training programs are exempt from a cap for five years, and the law allows for redistribution among facilities when residency slots go unused or when hospitals with residency programs cease operations.

Medicare's payments to teaching facilities are significant on a per-resident basis. According to analysts at the Congressional Research Service, total Medicare DGME and IME payments in 2015 were $11.1 billion, for a resident census (on a full-time-equivalent basis) of 85,700. Thus, on average, Medicare sent approximately $129,000 per resident per year to the nation's teaching hospitals.[38]

In addition to Medicare, teaching hospitals in most states receive add-on payments from Medicaid. These payments are optional and fully at the discretion of state governments. They are also opaque and hard to track, as, historically, the federal government has collected little information from the states on GME costs and outcomes. The most useful information on Medicaid's role in GME comes from organizations that have conducted ad hoc surveys of the states. According to the GAO, 44 states provided some GME support to teaching hospitals in 2015, at a combined federal-state cost of $4.2 billion.[39] This spending occurred with little federal oversight or accountability.

The VA directly finances training for 43,000 residents annually in its 11,000 hospitals. The purpose is to support the physician workforce generally throughout the country and specifically in the VA system. The average cost per resident was $139,000 in 2015—well above Medicare's rate. The VA incurs costs directly with stipend payments to residents and provides additional direct and indirect GME support in a manner similar to Medicare's payments to non-VA facilities.[40]

More GME Funding Is Not the Answer

There has been an ongoing debate about the rationale and efficacy of public GME funding for nearly three decades. In the 1990s, the AAMC and politicians representing the primary institutional recipients of public funding—including Sens. Pat Moynihan (D-NY) and Edward Kennedy

(D-MA)—pushed for a new federal GME trust fund, financed with levies on all insurance plans. The argument was that ensuring a top-flight physician workforce, through educational and training requirements, was in the interest of all users of health care, not just enrollees in Medicare. Therefore, all participants in health insurance plans, public and private, should share in the burden of financing the costs of training this workforce. The trust fund idea was introduced as legislation and was featured in a report from the Institute of Medicine.[41]

The push for a publicly funded GME trust fund foundered, in part, because of disagreement regarding the underlying rationale for an active federal role in financing residency expenses. The national government does not provide comparable levels of support for the training costs of other high-skilled professions. Absent public subsidies, residency programs would continue; they provide value both to the physician candidates who improve their income prospects and to the institutions that employ them because they can charge for the services their residents provide to patients.

Economic theory would indicate that the residents, not the institutions that employ them, incur the costs of their training, in the form of adjustments to the stipends they receive from the teaching hospitals where they work. Put another way, residents earn salaries equal to their net value to their employers, which is equal to the revenue they generate less the costs of their training.

Teaching hospitals might pay their residents somewhat more than their current net value if the training they provided were an investment producing a later return, in the form of even higher rates of billed services. But once physicians complete their residency requirements, they are under no obligation to remain working at the teaching facilities where they were trained. Because teaching hospitals are not guaranteed to capture the value of the training they provide, they pass on the full costs to the residents themselves.[42]

After Congress cut funding for both DGME and IME in the 1997 Balanced Budget Act, one might have expected resident salaries to fall, reflecting an increase in the net training cost to teaching hospitals. Instead, resident salaries continued to increase in the ensuing years. One possible explanation is that teaching hospitals treat government GME payments as general support funds untethered to the costs of their residency training programs. The general lack of auditable financial and programmatic data for GME spending supports this hypothesis.[43]

The AAMC and other advocates of the existing system of GME subsidies argue that public funding must increase to address the supposed physician shortage coming in 2032, and the 1997 cap on residency slots should be removed as well. But if the incidence of residency costs falls on the residents themselves, as the evidence suggests, and current GME funding does not factor directly into what residents are paid, then indiscriminate increases in Medicare GME payments will only subsidize the teaching institutions without altering the overall incentives that determine the number of residency slots.

The view that federal funding and aggregate residency enrollment is not strongly correlated is also supported by the trend in residency enrollment. Despite the cap imposed in federal law, the total number of residency slots at accredited institutions grew by 27 percent in the years after the cap went into effect.[44] The new slots provide evidence that sponsoring residency training is financially beneficial to teaching hospitals, regardless of Medicare's GME payments.

While it is difficult to justify increased GME funding to influence the overall numbers of physicians entering residency training, there is some justification for having separate DGME payments from Medicare to teaching hospitals, as a matter of fairness for the facilities. Medicare's system of regulated payment rates does not allow hospitals to set the prices they charge for the services they provide to Medicare beneficiaries, which limits their ability to collect fees that fully take advantage of the services their residents provide to patients. Medicare DGME payments are a way to accommodate the diminished pricing flexibility hospitals have when financing the costs of residency training.[45]

The rationale for retaining current Medicare IME spending is on weaker ground. Numerous analyses have demonstrated that the current formula for paying institutions for the indirect, higher costs of care associated with residency training far exceeds their actual costs.

The Role of the Medicare Fee Schedule

While government oversight and licensing requirements influence the supply of physicians in the US, so too does the expected income physician candidates can earn once they enter the profession. Prospective medical students must weigh the costs of securing an unrestricted license to practice medicine, measured both in direct out-of-pocket costs and time lost to earning a wage in an alternative profession, against the expected financial return they will reap on their acquired skills once they can see and bill patients directly.

Government policy also influences this income side of the medical profession calculus. In particular, the fees paid for individual physician services in Medicare are the most important factors in determining the earnings of the profession. The Medicare fee schedule (MFS)—the product of a long and complex legislative history—is used by not only the federal government to pay for physician services but also many private payers.

For the most part, private payers set higher fees than Medicare does, but they often use the MFS as the starting point, sometimes by simply paying a multiple of what the MFS would pay for the same services. Private insurers find the MFS useful in part because, without it, they would be forced to separately negotiate prices for the thousands of codes physicians use to bill for their services. The federal imprimatur also gives it credibility.[46]

The widespread use of the MFS for compensating physicians is important and relevant to the question of overall supply because of its well-known flaws. When created in legislation that originally passed in 1989, the MFS was supposed to help steer higher levels of compensation toward physicians providing primary care and common services to patients, such as internists and family medicine practitioners. But the actual effect was the opposite. Specialists who earn most of their fees from the procedures they perform have been able to boost their incomes substantially under the MFS by increasing the volume of services for which they bill both Medicare and private payers. Primary care physicians have far less ability to adjust their incomes in this manner, as the bulk of their time is spent directly in communication with their patients.

Over time, the influence of the MFS on physician incomes has created a marked difference in earning power across specialties, as shown in Figure 7.

Figure 7. Average Annual Physician Compensation, 2020

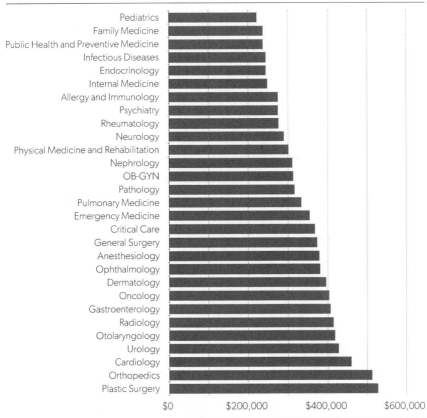

Source: Lindsay Wilcox, "Physician Salary Report 2021: Compensation Steady Despite COVID-19," Weatherby Healthcare, May 26, 2021, https://weatherbyhealthcare.com/blog/annual-physician-salary-report.

In 2020, family medicine physicians earned less than half of the incomes of orthopedic and plastic surgeons.

Unsurprisingly, this large variation in expected earnings translates directly into career decisions. Many analysts argue the nation already suffers from a shortage of primary care practitioners. Assuming that is true, an obvious and important reason would be that primary care physicians will, over their professional working careers, earn millions of dollars less than physicians who chose to become specialists.[47]

Toward a More Flexible and Adaptable Pipeline
of Prospective Physicians

The ideal system of educating and training the future physician workforce would be flexible and adaptable enough to adjust automatically to changes in patient demand, without the need for agreement among federal or state policymakers on modifications to subsidy levels, available educational or training slots, or other regulatory requirements. Reliance on the efficacy and timeliness of government planning to produce the right number of physicians, at the right time, to meet market requirements is an invitation for large numbers of frustrated, underserved, and overcharged patients.

No system will be fully driven by unregulated market signals (due to the need for enforcing high standards on the profession). However, reforms that lowered the cost of obtaining a physician license, sent compensation signals based more on market realities, placed oversight of the profession in more independent hands, and facilitated immigration of larger numbers of talented and foreign-born physicians all would be improvements over the status quo.[48]

Reform of Public GME Support. The federal government's financial support of GME should be modified not to cut overall costs but to address the major shortcomings of today's payment methods.

First, Medicare, Medicaid, and VA funding for GME should be combined into one common funding stream. This will ensure that public subsidies are directed at meeting a single set of objectives, with clear goals and expected outcomes.

Second, this funding should be adjusted to provide greater direct benefits to the residents themselves, rather than the institutions employing them. As noted, current GME funding is not strongly correlated with resident salaries. Government GME support could make entering the physician market less costly by providing vouchers directly to residents, perhaps in a manner that supplements stipends or reduces student loan balances. Not all GME funding can be redirected in this manner, but certainly the amount of IME spending that is in excess of what can be justified by cost assessments should be eliminated and replaced with direct support for the residents.

Third, GME funds that support teaching institutions should be more flexible, to allow nonhospital institutions to compete for the funds. The current system encourages excessive reliance on hospital-based residency training even though most physician care now takes place in ambulatory settings.

Promotion of Medical Oversight with Fewer Ties to the Profession. Professional associations tied to active clinicians and powerful academic health centers have essentially designed the United States's credentialing and licensing systems for physicians. This process is overseen by the individual states, with the federal government playing only a small role through its funding of GME.

The federal government has the power to exert more leadership over this process through its large financial commitment to GME. While centralizing the entire process is not the answer, as that would not lessen the political pressures that reinforce the status quo, the federal government could use the leverage its funding provides to steer state governments toward a more balanced and neutral system of professional oversight. For instance, the federal government could stipulate that GME funds are to be sent only to institutions approved by a credentialing system that is more independent of persons or organizations with economic ties to the profession.

Development of a Market-Based MFS Based on Price Transparency Initiatives. An effective price transparency effort, as recommended in Chapter 2, could also provide the basis for introducing market pricing into the MFS.

So far, price transparency requirements have been focused on hospitals and insurers. This agenda could be expanded to require physicians to disclose their prices for various services. The government should standardize what is being priced to allow consumers to make apples-to-apples comparisons, which will intensify competition and bring costs down. These disclosed prices could then be used to modify and adjust the MFS.

Adjusting the MFS in this way would bring stronger market signals to Medicare's physician payment system, which in turn would influence the rates set by commercial insurers. As physician incomes adjust based on the competition that price transparency would bring, talented students considering a medical profession will get more market-driven signals regarding their likely earned incomes, which could help ensure the supply of services matches more closely with the services patients need.

Testing and Promotion of a Shorter Education Time Frame. Other industrialized countries have lower cost barriers to entering the physician profession, either because medical schools are subsidized or because it takes fewer years to earn a degree and satisfy on-the-job training requirements. In Germany, for example, state governments finance medical education for students, and the process begins after completion of secondary school. There is a two-year, preclinical educational phase, focused on the basic scientific knowledge necessary for the profession. That is followed by four years of clinical training, more akin to the education received in US medical schools.[49] In total, it takes six years to earn the necessary degrees to become a licensed physician in Germany.

The US has experimented with a shortened pathway to a medical degree, focused mainly on completion of medical school in three, rather than four, years. The government heavily promoted a three-year MD during World War II, to address the wartime physician shortage, and again in the 1970s, to lower costs. Since 2010, nine schools (less than 10 percent of the overall number) have been offering three-year medical degrees, mainly to candidates seeking to become primary care physicians.[50]

The federal government should encourage states and their medical oversight bodies to test a model of medical education that more closely follows the German approach of beginning just after high school.[51] This would allow more coordination of a traditional undergraduate education with a medical school curriculum and perhaps open up the possibility of a six-year time frame for securing both degrees. Residency training would still be required, but the overall costs of becoming a licensed physician would fall, which would make the pipeline of physician candidates more flexible and responsive to other market signals.

Create a More Liberalized Pathway to H-1B Visas for Qualified Physicians and Physician Candidates. Immigration policy has been highly contentious in the US for more than a decade, but policymakers agree more on the benefits of welcoming high-skilled workers than on other questions. The US has plenty of experience with a high percentage of physicians who were born and educated elsewhere, and yet the immigration laws still prohibit large numbers of qualified physician candidates from coming to the US.

Congress should amend current immigration law to either exempt physician candidates from the current H-1B cap altogether (beyond the exemption that already applies to certain organizations, including teaching hospitals attached to higher education institutions) or create a new, separate allocation for the physician profession to allow greater numbers of willing immigrants to come to the US and care for patients. This policy could be combined with incentives to encourage these immigrants to practice, at least for some minimum period, in areas that have limited access to physician services.

Aiming Higher (and for More Supply)

The current system of regulating the physician workforce, led by the states and centered on state medical boards, has deep historical roots and generally has served the nation well. Even so, it could be improved. The quality of care provided to patients is, for the most part, high, and medical care is continually improving. But the system of credentialing practitioners is rigid, controlled by incumbents, and thus slow to adjust as needed to the changing demands of the patient population. The restricted supply it creates in many cases impairs the functioning of the market and thus leads to higher prices.

The federal government, without usurping the role of the states, should provide stronger leadership over this process by using the funds provided for GME as a catalyst for reform. There should be more distance between the economic interests of existing practitioners and institutions and decision-making bodies that issue licenses to physician candidates. Further, the government should loosen its immigration laws to allow as many qualified and talented physicians who want to come to the US to do so, as there would be tangible benefits for the patients they would serve.

Notes

1. Organisation for Economic Co-operation and Development, "Health Expenditure and Financing Database," 2020, https://stats.oecd.org/Index.aspx?ThemeTreeId=90.

2. Advisory Board, "How Much Are US Doctors Paid? (Hint: A Lot More Than in the Rest of the World.)," September 24, 2019, https://www.advisory.com/daily-briefing/2019/09/24/international-physician-compensation.

3. American Association of Medical Colleges, "Medical Student Education: Debt, Costs, and Loan Repayment Fact Card," October 2019, https://store.aamc.org/downloadable/download/sample/sample_id/296/.

4. Dmitry Zavlin et al., "A Comparison of Medical Education in Germany and the United States: From Applying to Medical School to the Beginnings of Residency," *German Medical Science* 15, no. 15 (September 2017), https://www.ncbi.nlm.nih.gov/pmc/articles/PMC5617919/.

5. Daniel R. Austin and Laurence C. Baker, "Less Physician Practice Competition Is Associated with Higher Prices Paid for Common Procedures," *Health Affairs* 34, no. 10 (October 2015), https://www.healthaffairs.org/doi/full/10.1377/hlthaff.2015.0412.

6. The Organisation for Economic Co-operation and Development (OECD) data for the US do not match the data from the Federation of State Medical Boards (FSMB), possibly because the OECD's definition of "active physician" excludes some doctors who are included in the FSMB total.

7. Tim Dall et al., "The Complexities of Physician Supply and Demand: Projections from 2017 to 2032," Association of American Medical Colleges, April 2019, https://aamc-black.global.ssl.fastly.net/production/media/filer_public/31/13/3113ee5c-a038-4c16-89af-294a69826650/2019_update_-_the_complexities_of_physician_supply_and_demand_-_projections_from_2017-2032.pdf.

8. Council on Graduate Medical Education, *International Medical Graduates, the Physician Workforce, and GME Reform: Eleventh Report*, March 1998, https://www.hrsa.gov/sites/default/files/hrsa/advisory-committees/graduate-medical-edu/reports/archive/1998-March.pdf.

9. Ronald Hamowy, "The Early Development of Medical Licensing Laws in the United States, 1875–1900," *Journal of Libertarian Studies* (October 1979), https://cdn.mises.org/3_1_5_0.pdf.

10. Hamowy, "The Early Development of Medical Licensing Laws in the United States, 1875–1900."

11. Abraham Flexner, *Medical Education in the United States and Canada*, Carnegie Foundation, 1910, http://archive.carnegiefoundation.org/publications/pdfs/elibrary/Carnegie_Flexner_Report.pdf.

12. Thomas P. Duffy, "The Flexner Report—100 Years Later," *Yale Journal of Biology and Medicine* 84 (September 2011): 269–76, https://www.ncbi.nlm.nih.gov/pmc/articles/PMC3178858/pdf/yjbm_84_3_269.pdf.

13. Duffy, "The Flexner Report—100 Years Later."

14. Reuben A. Kessel, "The A.M.A. and the Supply of Physicians," *Law and Contemporary Problems* (Spring 1970), https://scholarship.law.duke.edu/cgi/viewcontent.cgi?article=3288&context=lcp.

15. The Liaison Committee on Medical Education (LCME) is the accrediting body for allopathic medical schools conferring medical doctor (MD) degrees. Schools for osteopathic medicine, which confer doctor of osteopathy (DO) degrees, are accredited by the American Osteopathic Association Commission on Osteopathic College Accreditation. The curricula for MD and DO degrees are similar. The two branches of the medical profession have their roots in different traditions, with allopathic training focused on laboratory-based diagnoses and osteopathy focused on holistic and primary care. These distinctions have become less meaningful over time as views among adherents of the two branches—and their approaches to educating and training physician candidates—have converged.

16. Donald G. Kassebaum, "Origin of the LCME, the AMA-AAMC Partnership for Accreditation," *Academic Medicine* 67, no. 2 (February 1992), https://journals.lww.com/academicmedicine/abstract/1992/02000/origin_of_the_lcme,_the_aamc_ama_partnership_%20for.5.aspx.

17. Federation of State Medical Boards, *U.S. Medical Regulatory Trends and Actions: 2018*, 2018, https://www.fsmb.org/siteassets/advocacy/publications/us-medical-regulatory-trends-actions.pdf.

18. Federation of State Medical Boards, *U.S. Medical Regulatory Trends and Actions*.

19. Alvin E. Roth, "The Origins, History, and Design of the Resident Match," *Journal of the American Medical Association* 289, no. 7 (February 19, 2003): 909–12, https://jamanetwork.com/journals/jama/fullarticle/195998.

20. Jill Eden, Donald Berwick, and Gail Wilensky, eds., *Graduate Medical Education That Meets the Nation's Health Needs* (Washington, DC: National Academies Press, 2014), https://www.nap.edu/read/18754/chapter/1.

21. Uniform accreditation standards for US and Canadian medical schools began with the Flexner report in 1910. Since 1942, the LCME has accredited Canadian medical schools. Graduates of Canadian schools have been treated identically to graduates of US medical schools for purposes of the residency matching program and licensure requirements. Today, the LCME accreditation process for medical schools in Canada is run in coordination with the Committee on Accreditation of Canadian Medical Schools (CACMS). In 2014, a coordination agreement between the LCME and CACMS allowed the CACMS to establish standards applicable to Canadian schools. Disagreements over accreditation decisions by the LCME and CACMS are resolved by a joint review committee. Graduates of Canadian schools are not included in US counts of IMGs. For example, see Barbara Sibbald, "Made-in-Canada Accreditation Coming for Medical Schools," *Canadian Medical Association Journal* 186, no. 2 (February 2014), https://www.ncbi.nlm.nih.gov/pmc/articles/PMC3903760/.

22. Lisa Rapaport, "U.S. Relies Heavily on Foreign-Born Healthcare Workers," Reuters, December 4, 2018, https://www.reuters.com/article/us-health-professions-us-noncitizens/u-s-relies-heavily-on-foreign-born-healthcare-workers-idUSKBN1O32FR.

23. Padmini D. Ranasinghe, "International Medical Graduates in the US Physician Workforce," *Journal of the American Osteopathic Association* 115 (April 2015): 236–41, https://jaoa.org/article.aspx?articleid=2213422.

24. Ranasinghe, "International Medical Graduates in the US Physician Workforce."

25. Silva Mathema, *Immigrant Doctors Can Help Lower Physician Shortages in Rural*

America, Center for American Progress, July 2019, https://cdn.americanprogress.org/content/uploads/2019/07/29074013/ImmigrantDoctors-report.pdf.

26. Mathema, *Immigrant Doctors Can Help Lower Physician Shortages in Rural America*.

27. US Citizenship and Immigration Services, "Conrad 30 Waiver Program," May 15, 2020, https://www.uscis.gov/working-united-states/students-and-exchange-visitors/conrad-30-waiver-program.

28. US Citizenship and Immigration Services, "Conrad 30 Waiver Program."

29. Mathema, *Immigrant Doctors Can Help Lower Physician Shortages in Rural America*.

30. Ranasinghe, "International Medical Graduates in the US Physician Workforce."

31. Government Accountability Office, "Physician Workforce: HHS Needs Better Information to Comprehensively Evaluate Graduate Medical Education Funding," March 2018, https://www.gao.gov/assets/700/690581.pdf.

32. US House of Representatives, "Social Security Amendments of 1965 Volume 1," March 1965, https://www.ssa.gov/history/pdf/Downey%20PDFs/Social%20Security%20Amendments%20of%201965%20Vol%201.pdf.

33. Medicare also provides educational support for dental and podiatric training in institutions accredited by the relevant oversight bodies. For example, see Marco A. Villagrana, "Medicare Graduate Medical Education Payments: An Overview," Congressional Research Service, February 19, 2019, https://fas.org/sgp/crs/misc/IF10960.pdf.

34. Eden, Berwick, and Wilensky, *Graduate Medical Education That Meets the Nation's Health Needs*.

35. Elayne J. Heisler et al., "Federal Support for Graduate Medical Education: An Overview," Congressional Research Service, December 27, 2018, https://fas.org/sgp/crs/misc/R44376.pdf.

36. Heisler et al., "Federal Support for Graduate Medical Education."

37. Mark Miller, "Graduate Medical Education Payments," Medicare Payment Advisory Commission, February 20, 2015.

38. Heisler et al., "Federal Support for Graduate Medical Education."

39. Government Accountability Office, "Physician Workforce."

40. Heisler et al., "Federal Support for Graduate Medical Education."

41. Institute of Medicine, *On Implementing a National Graduate Medical Education Trust Fund* (Washington, DC: National Academies Press, 1997), https://www.nap.edu/catalog/5771/on-implementing-a-national-graduate-medical-education-trust-fund.

42. Amitabh Chandra, Dhurv Khullar, and Gail R. Wilensky, "The Economics of Graduate Medical Education," *New England Journal of Medicine* 370 (June 2014): 2357–60, https://www.nejm.org/doi/full/10.1056/NEJMp1402468.

43. Chandra, Khullar, and Wilensky, "The Economics of Graduate Medical Education."

44. Heisler et al., "Federal Support for Graduate Medical Education."

45. Sean Nicholson, *Medicare Hospital Subsidies: Money in Search of a Purpose* (Washington, DC: AEI Press, 2002), https://www.aei.org/wp-content/uploads/2011/10/20040218_book168.pdf.

46. Jeffrey Clemens and Joshua D. Gottlieb, "In the Shadow of a Giant: Medicare's Influence on Private Physician Payments," *Journal of Political Economy* 125, no. 1 (February 2017): 1–39, https://www.journals.uchicago.edu/doi/pdfplus/10.1086/689772.

47. Bruce Steinwa et al., *Medicare Graduate Medical Education Funding Is Not*

Addressing the Primary Care Shortage: We Need a Radically Different Approach, USC-Brookings Schaeffer Initiative for Health Policy, December 2018, https://www.brookings.edu/wp-content/uploads/2018/12/Steinwald_Ginsburg_Brandt_Lee_Patel_GME-Funding_12.3.181.pdf.

48. Many other analysts and expert bodies have made recommendations to improve the system of educating and training physicians. The recommendations in this chapter echo some of the concepts found in this earlier work. In particular, the Medicare Payment Advisory Commission has made numerous sensible recommendations for reform over many years, and the 2014 report from the Institute of Medicine included a comprehensive set of recommendations that are similar in their overall direction to what is proposed here. For example, see Medicare Payment Advisory Commission, *Aligning Incentives in Medicare*, June 2010, https://www.medpac.gov/wp-content/uploads/import_data/scrape_files/docs/default-source/reports/Jun10_EntireReport.pdf; and Eden, Berwick, and Wilensky, *Graduate Medical Education That Meets the Nation's Health Needs*.

49. Zavlin et al., "A Comparison of Medical Education in Germany and the United States."

50. Christine C. Schwartz et al., "Comprehensive History of 3-Year and Accelerated Medical School Programs: A Century in Review," *Medical Education Online* 23, no. 1 (December 2018), https://www.ncbi.nlm.nih.gov/pubmed/30376794.

51. Tim Rice, "Why America Faces a Doctor Shortage," *City Journal*, September 26, 2018, https://www.city-journal.org/why-america-faces-doctor-shortage-16194.html.

9

Political and Administrative Considerations

Health policy is not implemented in an apolitical vacuum. As discussed in Chapter 1, market failures in the health sector force political leaders in all countries to actively supervise both their insurance systems and how care is delivered to patients. The question is the nature of those interventions, not whether they will occur, and how they might be expected to evolve and change over time when taken up in the context of a particular form of government and within a nation's political culture.

Put another way, when weighing the merits of alternative policies, one must consider not just stylized simulations but also what will likely happen when policies are pursued and implemented in the real world, with periodic elections, governance structures, and systems and cultures of public administration. Among other things, government agencies tasked with implementing policies in the health sector often must do so with purposeful limits on their operational capacities (and budgets), imperfect information, and heavy pressure and oversight from elected leaders.

When health policy questions are viewed this way, the task of finding the right formula becomes even more challenging. Setting a promising course requires accounting for the political and administrative context in which specific policies are to be implemented and the implications of that context for expected results over time.

Political and public administration considerations are particularly relevant to the policy debate in the United States. The nation's Constitution disperses power and is designed to frustrate sudden and dramatic change in any direction, and US political culture and history are infused with distrust of centralized authority. At the same time, federal administrative agencies have become centers of substantial power in their own right. Once created, the tendency is for them to grow and accumulate authority and develop agendas that would further entrench their roles and expand their influence.

Most likely, for the foreseeable future, the US will retain a mixed public-private health system, with substantial regulation and subsidization existing alongside private-sector enterprises and decision-making that is beyond the reach of government. A properly regulated (and structured) market is perfectly compatible with this reality and would not suffer from some of the political and administrative handicaps of system-wide price regulations. Even so, reliance on market incentives must be accepted and tried first before it can prove its worth, which means skeptical voters will need to be convinced.

The Forces Aligned Against Dramatic Change

The basic structure of US health care has changed less over recent decades than one might have expected given the visibility and frequency of calls for far-reaching reform. Notably, employer-sponsored insurance persists as the dominant source of private coverage even though both market and single-payer advocates are, to varying degrees, dissatisfied with its role and influence. In 2019, job-based insurance covered 56 percent of the overall population, which was down only modestly from 62 percent in 1987.[1]

Inertia and incumbency are powerful forces in most policy realms but especially in health care because of the political salience of the issue. Consumers who are comfortable with their insurance and the care they receive are risk averse and not eager to trade in what they have for untested alternatives. To gain popular support, sponsors of proposed changes must accept that upending the status quo for too many people will doom what they are trying to achieve.

Further, the nation's mixed, public-private system has left ample room for private enterprises to grow and become central participants in both the insurance and service-delivery markets. These include large national and regional insurance plans, for-profit and not-for-profit health systems, major academic health centers, and global pharmaceutical companies. These and many other health-sector entities have substantial constituencies of their own—and political leverage. Their natural resistance to disruption is a large impediment blocking sweeping change.

Voters, too, prefer gradualism, although their frustration with high costs makes them open to hearing about systemic change. For instance, for many years, a large fraction of the electorate has expressed support for Medicare for All, which is shorthand for conversion of the nation's insurance system into a single, publicly administered plan. A Kaiser Family Foundation poll conducted in 2020 showed support for this switch at above 50 percent of voters. However, when those same respondents were presented with the direct consequence of this policy—namely, that it would lead to the elimination of private insurance altogether—opposition rose to 58 percent.[2]

The public's aversion to abrupt change to their personal insurance situations also protects existing government subsidies and regulations and thus severely limits what might be rolled back when proponents of deregulation are in charge. For instance, in 2017, Republicans opposed to some features of the Affordable Care Act (ACA) attempted to replace it with a more decentralized and state-focused plan, with fewer guarantees for consumers. They failed in part because the Congressional Budget Office (CBO) estimated their plans would end insurance protection for many millions of Americans.[3] Public subsidization of insurance and medical care is more often liberalized over time rather than pulled back.

The nation's constitutional structure reinforces the tendency toward caution. With a separately elected president, House, and Senate, along with an independent Supreme Court and federal judiciary, power is widely dispersed, which makes abrupt and large-scale change rare. Major policy breakthroughs do occur, but only when the forces are perfectly aligned to circumvent the normal barriers, which usually only happens in a crisis or its aftermath.

The COVID-19 pandemic is certainly an epic, worldwide calamity. It has been the most disruptive global event in decades and will alter fundamental aspects of American society and international arrangements. Even so, its effect on US health care may be modest.

When the crisis began, some observers thought (and some hoped) it might be otherwise. In particular, there was a sense that the United States's uneven public health response might open the door to a more centrally managed health system, along the lines of Medicare for All.

That now seems unlikely, in part because countries with nationalized health systems (France, Spain, the UK, and many others) have not fared much better. A centralized health system was not a predictor of a better pandemic response and may have left some countries with insufficient capacity to handle the crisis.

All of this suggests that, even in the wake of the COVID-19 pandemic, the US is most likely to continue down the path it has been on for many years, which is one of incremental modification to the nation's vast and diverse insurance and care delivery networks. The only question is whether the direction of reform is toward stricter payment regulation (building mainly on what Medicare does today) or toward a functioning market bolstered with guardrails and consumers incentives, which would facilitate price discipline with less ongoing intervention by public agencies.

Extending the Price Regulation Net

While both voters and the health sector would resist Medicare for All on the grounds that it would entail intolerable disruption, steps in the same general direction could encounter less resistance. In particular, advocates of greater government control are likely to have better success with an agenda focused mainly on extending the reach of public regulations that control the prices of medical services.

That is certainly the expectation of political leaders in Colorado, Nevada, and Washington state. In each, state officials have been pursuing similarly gradualist price regulation agendas under the banner of standing up a "public option." In recent political debates, the public option—which connotes a voluntary, publicly administered insurance plan—has been offered as a moderate alternative to mandatory Medicare for All. In these states, however, the idea has undergone a transformation. Instead of a new insurance plan, which has proved too difficult substantively and politically to advance, officials have designed new regulations that apply to private insurers already offering coverage in their markets.[4] In effect, the states are compelling these insurers to offer new plans—dubbed the "public option"—which incorporate, to varying degrees, additional public controls on the prices paid for various services.

The difficulty each state encountered in taking these first steps points to both the long odds Medicare for All and other disruptive changes face and the characteristics of reforms that can take hold politically and then become more consequential over time. Political leaders in each of the relevant states began with more ambitious ideas, but those were recalibrated to navigate the political forces that defined their initial ideas as impossible to enact. In the end, the plans that passed were not frontal assaults on private insurance or on those delivering medical services. Rather, they were extensions of an existing, and relatively trusted, source of payment limits (as found in Medicare) to insurance that would be managed by existing private insurers. To secure passage of these measures in the relevant state legislatures, officials were forced to compromise with hospital and physician groups to accommodate their demands for payments well above Medicare's rates for the same services.

Nationally, the Biden administration is attempting to navigate similar political currents. The president supports creating a new, federally administered public option, but that idea faces long odds due to stiff opposition from insurers, hospitals, and physician groups.[5] However, some variation of what is now being tried in the three states with "public option" schemes might be possible. Instead of creating a public competitor to the private insurance industry, Congress might be able to inject more price regulation (again using Medicare as the model and starting point) into privately administered plans.

Many voters will not complain. Public regulation of medical care prices can occur without canceling their private coverage. Nor does it lead inexorably to disruptions in the availability of physicians to enrollees in the affected plans. Further, the benefits are obvious. With public authorities imposing cost controls, consumers would be relieved of the responsibility of trying to find savings themselves and grateful if the result were lower premiums and reduced cost-sharing expenses when they used services.

Several possibilities are available for imposing new price limits. The most prominent would be introducing direct Medicare price setting for prescription drugs. (The Biden administration calls this Medicare "negotiation.") The US Department of Health and Human Services would be given the authority to bargain with drug manufacturers over their prices, which, in practical terms, means the federal government would have the authority to stipulate prices if an unbridgeable difference emerges (which would be likely). The existence of this fallback authority would hand all the leverage to federal officials.

The administration also could take a page from the states implementing public options by requiring private insurers offering coverage in the ACA-regulated market to offer plans meeting more stringent payment requirements. Like the state-sponsored public option plans, the new coverage could have ceilings on prices pegged to what Medicare pays today for the same services and provide for a cushion above 100 percent of Medicare to counter the stiff opposition that would emerge from hospital and physician associations.

Flattering Cost Estimates

Public regulation of pricing in the health sector has a major political advantage over market-leaning reforms: The government's official cost estimates usually confirm that tighter payment rules will deliver substantial savings, while the effects of market reforms are uncertain at best and potentially costly under some circumstances, especially when they involve replacing existing public controls.

This role of cost estimating in the political viability of competing plans is a major, if poorly understood, factor in national health policy debates. Congress's official scorekeeping agency—the CBO—is responsible for providing projections for proposed legislation and has long taken the view that if federal agencies are given the authority to impose price limits on spending for services, in Medicare or elsewhere, the effect will be a reduction in costs, as intended. Moreover, the potential downsides of such measures, such as reductions in the quality of services and perhaps less timely care, are only discussed in accompanying narratives that have much less political salience than do easily understood tables showing substantial cost reductions.

An additional factor favoring pricing limits is the ease with which they can be estimated, as they usually involve straightforward comparisons of new, and lower, prices with those that are in effect without the new limits. Modeling market reforms is a more difficult and uncertain exercise because it must estimate the effects of changed incentives on the pricing behavior of those entities supplying insurance and medical services to patients. Proponents of using competitive pricing in health care have been

advised regularly over the years that estimating their plans will be too difficult to complete quickly and thus will only be undertaken at all if they
can be realistically enacted. The result is a sort of catch-22: Market advocates are left to make the case for their plans without the benefit of official
cost projections, which means their ideas are taken less seriously in policy
debates and thus less likely to be estimated by the CBO.

The lure of government savings from price controls is powerful too.
In budget bills going back four decades, Congress has regularly tightened
Medicare's and Medicaid's payments for all manner of medical services
and used the savings for deficit reduction or, even more frequently, to pay
for benefit liberalizations of some kind. The cumulative effect has been to
restrain publicly set rates for services far more than has occurred in private
insurance.

The overall effect of these incentives in federal budget policy is now a
yawning gap between the prices paid by public and private insurance—a
gap that some elected officials now believe should be closed by extending public rates into the private sector (such as through the state public
option plans discussed previously). If done nationally, the federal government would see financial benefits because lower private-sector premiums
reduce subsidies for coverage provided through the ACA-regulated market
and lessen the federal tax break conferred on job-based insurance.

Congress and state legislatures can cut expenses further by tightening
certain payment screws in Medicare and Medicaid. Among other things,
Medicare could set pricing limits for its purchases of prescription drugs
and lower what it pays when program enrollees join Medicare Advantage
plans (the private insurance options in Medicare).[6]

The political advantages of strict price regulations in health care pro-
foundly affect the national policy debate. Advocates of market reforms
often fail to even offer alternative ideas because of the barriers that unfa-
vorable scoring erects. Among other things, the media tends to assign
great importance and credibility to official cost estimates and discount
the potential value of reforms that are offered without the validation that
comes from the CBO. The result is that market advocates have often lost
debates even before the first bills are introduced.

The only major obstacle slowing the march to full public regulation of
health-sector pricing is the affected industries. Major insurers and health

systems, along with physician groups, drug companies, and many other enterprises, fight proposals that would allow the government to further tighten public regulation of what they are paid. They contend that artificially lowering their prices distorts the market and leads to degradations in the quality of the services they can provide to their plan enrollees and patients.

And they are not powerless, as demonstrated by their relative success in heading off even stricter pricing limits for their services and products. Even so, the overall direction of policy is clear enough and has been toward tighter control at the federal level. One reason is that price control proponents can sometimes use the prospect of consumer savings, and perhaps more generous benefits, to push past the opposition. The most probable reform scenario for the overall health system, then, is for continued movement, perhaps in fits and starts, toward full public regulation of medical care prices.

The Administrative State in Practice

The generally favorable politics pushing price regulation forward does not imply optimal results will follow when the rules are implemented or that the downsides will be minor and therefore go unnoticed. The federal government, and the states, have been writing complex payment rules in medical care for decades, primarily through Medicare and Medicaid, and the overall record is mixed. Pricing limits can reduce spending as advertised in most (although not all) instances, but the connection to sensible allocations of resources is tenuous.

A major factor is that the rules are watched most closely by the industries affected by them, and they hire armies of lawyers and lobbyists to help them secure adjustments in the details that will determine their fate. Over time, the rules tend to cater to incumbents.

One important reason for this is that the regulatory agency responsible for writing the rules—the Centers for Medicare & Medicaid Services (CMS)—is sensitive politically to charges that its decisions could spell the doom of whole businesses. The regulated entities are fully aware of the leverage this gives them, which they exploit by eliciting pressure from their elected representatives. Not infrequently, the pressure on Congress to protect certain enterprises leads to rifleshot interventions in the regulatory process, which is a further signal to CMS to not go too far when setting the terms of payment. The overall result is an incentive structure for setting the fees that tries to thread a needle: payments low enough to hit budget targets but not so low that the nation's vast networks of facilities and practitioners cannot continue business as usual.

The list of payment rules in effect in Medicare is now lengthy and covers inpatient hospital stays, physician fees, outpatient procedures, psychiatric hospitals, hospices, clinical labs, physician-administered drugs, dialysis services, rehabilitation care, skilled nursing facilities, graduate medical education programs, accountable care organizations, and privately administered Medicare Advantage plans. Each rule is its own unique labyrinth, with complex wrinkles added regularly to address the inevitable anomalous circumstances that arise in a large and expansive country with great geographic and demographic diversity.

The payment rule covering physician fees illustrates the broader tendencies of the administrative process. Originally created in legislation passed in 1989, the fee schedule for physicians and related practitioners establishes payments for each individual service, with adjustments for geography and other variations in input costs. The 1989 reform moved away from a cost-based system and tried to establish objective criteria for payment based on the intensity and skill required to provide the services. The basis for payment is summed up in "relative value units," which were originally thought to reward physicians providing time-intensive primary care services rather than procedures.[7]

A much-discussed feature of the fee schedule is the role physicians themselves play in determining its basic building blocks. In particular, when trying to value individual services, the law allows for input from relative value scale update committees (RUCs), which are staffed by physicians and central to determining which specialists will see fee increases and which will see decreases.[8] Not surprisingly, physicians' direct role in this process has tended to protect the incomes of those receiving the highest total payments today.

RUCs are a dramatic example of a phenomenon that is common (if usually more hidden) throughout the regulated payment system, which is that the regulators tend to work, directly and indirectly, with those whom the regulated systems will affect. To a point, this is understandable, because usually the industry itself has the relevant data the government needs to make adjustments and refinements to the rules. (This also explains why many of the rules include data collection and submission mandates.)

On the other hand, it should be obvious that these arrangements and relationships create substantial opportunities for regulatory capture, with the affected industries becoming excessively influential in setting the terms for their regulated payments. The predictable result is a tendency toward rigidity and a slowness to adapt and change over time. Most problematically, the regulations become a source of protection for incumbents, by providing a minimum source of income if the government's rules are satisfied and establishing higher minimum requirements (such as with data collection and submission) that require upfront investments and thus become barriers to new entrants.

The (Market) Price Is Right

A substantial additional problem is the potential for large discrepancies between the regulated prices and those that would emerge in a functioning market. Without market failure, market prices are efficient because they allow resources to move naturally to maximize value for consumers and producers. With nonmarket prices, some services may not get paid what they would with proper incentives and thus may be underprovided. (With lower-than-optimal prices, some suppliers would exit the market.) On the other hand, some services may get overpaid and thus oversupplied.

The long road to competitive bidding for durable medical equipment (DME) and related products in Medicare illustrates the importance of market pricing and the barriers that existing regulated rates can erect to sensible improvements.

DME helps patients better manage their diagnoses and conditions. Examples include wheelchairs, prosthetics, orthotics, glucose testing strips, and machines that aid patients with sleep apnea. Historically, Medicare paid for DME using an administrative process based on cost reporting from the industry. Many studies showed that, over time, these fees were well above market rates for the same products because Medicare's fee schedule did not keep up with technological advances and reductions in manufacturing expenses.[9]

For decades, analysts called for replacing the administrative fees with prices based on competitive bids. Not surprisingly, the DME industry fought these initiatives fiercely, with some success. In 1997, Congress tasked CMS (then known as the Health Care Financing Administration) with testing competitive bidding for DME, which was then followed by a provision passed in 2003 that required the switch for certain categories of products. However, it was not until 2011 that CMS finally went beyond a demonstration and actually began paying for large amounts of DME based on competitive bids.

The results were instantaneous and impressive.

- From 2011 to 2017, spending on DME and related items subject to competitive bidding fell by 62 percent, from $7.5 billion to $2.8 billion. Over the same period, Medicare spending for those DME products that were exempted from competitive bidding rose by 44 percent.[10]

- CMS has estimated total government savings from competitive bidding for DME at $25.7 billion from 2013 to 2022. Beneficiaries are expected to experience a reduction in their out-of-pocket costs of $17.1 billion over the same period.[11]

- The prices secured for CMS through competitive bidding were in line with the prices paid by the largest commercial purchasers, which indicates they were competitive and reflective of market realities.[12]

- Rental prices for the continuous positive airway pressure machines, which are needed to treat sleep apnea, fell by 45 percent when subjected to competitive bidding.[13]

Critics of market pricing will argue that DME is a special case, and they have a point. The products are more easily interchangeable than are most medical services provided by hospitals or physicians and thus lend themselves to a bidding process that relies on standardization to eliminate significant quality differences among the competing products and suppliers.

This argument, which is valid, actually points to what is required more generally to make market pricing work throughout the health sector. A functioning market will not emerge spontaneously. It requires structure that only the government can provide through sensible regulation, including standardization of what is being priced so that consumers and insurance plans can compare apples to apples. DME is readily amenable to these requirements. While it will take more work to write the rules that allow market pricing for other medical services and products, it is not an impossible challenge (as discussed in Chapter 2), and the payoff would be substantial.

Resiliency

The DME experience also points to an important potential advantage that market pricing may have over regulated rates: resiliency to political interference.

It is difficult to insulate the administrative process from the influence of the affected parties because those parties have recourse to their elected representatives, who, in turn, can interfere with regulatory decisions. As described previously, this dynamic is fundamental to explaining the current process of writing and updating payment rules in the medical sector.

A structured market would not be exempt from political meddling, as is apparent from the DME example. For decades, studies showed how much could be saved through competitive bidding, yet the industry was successful (and still is to some degree) in stalling reform and limiting its scope.

Once an effective market is in place, however, the political leverage flips to what is in current law and regulation. One factor is that competitive bidding creates new "winners" who themselves become impediments to undoing the reform.

Moreover, the cost cutting an effective market can produce will create a new baseline against which administered pricing will then be compared. Even if some in Congress were inclined to interfere and push for favorable rates through regulations, the costs involved would become a hurdle. CMS also would find it much easier to fend off pleas for regulatory adjustments if market pricing is already producing reliable savings for taxpayers and patients.

Selling Markets

The biggest barrier to moving gradually in a market-based direction is consumer skepticism: Most Americans believe the medical care market is irrational and thus incapable of producing affordable prices. Indeed, their expectation is that market reforms would be more likely to cause them harm than reduce their costs.

The only way market advocates can overcome this significant barrier is by writing their reform plans to eliminate all, or nearly all, financial risks for the consumers themselves and pledging to share a large portion of whatever savings materialize with them.

The political challenge was on display during the 2012 presidential campaign, when competition in Medicare was being debated. Nongovernmental analyses of the premium support model (a form of market competition in Medicare) showed some beneficiaries would pay higher, not lower, premiums if the reform were implemented, largely because it was assumed that these beneficiaries would remain enrolled in the traditional program in areas with much less expensive private alternatives. The potential for overall savings and net savings for most beneficiaries was significant because private plans were expected to be more efficient than government-managed insurance. But those potential gains were lost in the firestorm over the premium hikes that some beneficiaries might incur.[14]

There are other obstacles too. Distrust of profit-making is a common perspective among voters when considering alternative health system arrangements, which makes it difficult to build support for market reforms. Further, while providers of medical services oppose government-enforced payment reductions, they are not eager to be forced into a strongly competitive marketplace either. Their first inclinations are always to push for policies that protect the status quo from their perspective and erect barriers to further competition from market entrants.

Overcoming these obstacles will be challenging. To do so, the emphasis of market-based reform must be to deliver financial benefits to consumers, with no real possibility of large losses for anyone. In other words, voters must see the advent of market pricing as having only financial upsides and thus perhaps worth giving an opportunity to work.

Preventing the possibility of losses should be possible in most cases. If, for instance, a market reform could reduce premiums or pricing for targeted services by 10 percent, part of the savings might come from charging more to consumers who choose high-cost options. Instead of leaving those consumers worse off, however, a reform plan will have a better chance of gaining the necessary political support if there is a hold harmless for the consumers who stay with their current options and savings for those who switch.

Further, reform should include guarantees to protect consumers from abrupt changes. For instance, with premium support in Medicare, beneficiaries who live in high-cost areas and might otherwise face substantially higher premiums should be guaranteed to experience increases in their premiums that do not exceed an acceptable threshold (such as 5 percent annually). This limit would reduce the savings from the initial reform but might allow it to get a fair hearing and then proceed, after which it might then be amended to produce more robust budgetary savings.

The reason these compromises are necessary should be clear enough. They allow market reforms to get a fair hearing in public debates; without them, these schemes are unlikely to gain acceptance and may never be introduced.

Once in place, however, market reforms will become part of the existing system and therefore much more likely to survive political challenges. As they produce positive results, their reach and scope also can be expanded.

A Public-Private Health System

Critics of US health policy often mischaracterize it by tying it to laissez-faire ideology. It is more accurate to describe what exists as a nonsystem, without any overall organizing principle guiding its direction.

US health care is heavily regulated, and the government runs large public insurance programs to ensure an equitable level of access to care for all citizens and legal residents. At the same time, the US allows a much larger role for private enterprises (including for-profit companies) in both its insurance and service delivery networks than do other countries.

The resulting mix of public and private roles is neither fish nor fowl; health care is not fully controlled by public regulation and decision-making, as is the case in other high-income countries, nor is it disciplined by effective market incentives. No one is fully satisfied with how the current mix is performing.

The available choices for next steps, constrained by political reality, come down to this: better and more comprehensive price regulations, written and enforced by the federal government (with some assistance by the states) or better rules for the market to allow effective and competitive pricing to surface from the suppliers of services and products. A combination of the two approaches could also be pursued.

Stricter controls of prices and spending through regulation have a clearer path, but that does not mean a functioning market is beyond reach. It is possible to move in a market-friendly direction with gradual reforms that, like competitive bidding for Medicare-financed DME, rely on structured markets to maximize the pressure for lower prices.

It will be challenging politically to implement such a plan, but it would be worth the effort. The United States's openness to private enterprise and incentives in the health sector should be seen not as a liability but as an asset that has yet to be fully exploited. Stronger market discipline, facilitated with the right public regulation, is required to direct the energy of the private sector toward cost discipline and improved quality. That is within reach with the right changes. Once in place, market incentives can then deliver in US health care the productivity improvements that are needed to slow escalating costs and give consumers appropriate value for what they are required to spend.

Notes

1. US Census Bureau, "Health Insurance Historical Tables-HHI Series," 2020, https://www.census.gov/data/tables/time-series/demo/health-insurance/historical-series/hic.html; and Katherine Keisler-Starkey and Lisa N. Bunch, "Health Insurance Coverage in the United States: 2019," US Census Bureau, September 2020, https://www.census.gov/content/dam/Census/library/publications/2020/demo/p60-271.pdf.

2. Kaiser Family Foundation, "Public Opinion on Single-Payer, National Health Plans, and Expanding Access to Medicare Coverage," October 16, 2020, https://www.kff.org/slideshow/public-opinion-on-single-payer-national-health-plans-and-expanding-access-to-medicare-coverage/.

3. Congressional Budget Office, "H.R. 1628: American Health Care Act of 2017," May 24, 2017, https://www.cbo.gov/system/files/115th-congress-2017-2018/costestimate/hr1628aspassed.pdf.

4. James C. Capretta, "Colorado's Standardized Health Benefit Plan," State of Reform, August 2, 2021, https://stateofreform.com/news/colorado/2021/08/colorados-standardized-health-benefit-plan/.

5. Biden for President, "Biden-Sanders Unity Task Force Recommendations," August 2020, https://joebiden.com/wp-content/uploads/2020/08/UNITY-TASK-FORCE-RECOMMENDATIONS.pdf.

6. For a description of prescription drug policies favored by many in Congress, see Ron Wyden, "Principles for Drug Pricing Reform," US Senate, Committee on Finance, June 2021, https://www.finance.senate.gov/imo/media/doc/062221%20SFC%20Drug%20Pricing%20Principles.pdf.

7. Medicare Payment Advisory Commission, "Physician and Other Health Professional Payment System," November 2021, https://www.medpac.gov/wp-content/uploads/2021/11/medpac_payment_basics_21_physician_final_sec.pdf.

8. Government Accountability Office, "Medicare Physician Payment Rates: Better Data and Greater Transparency Could Improve Accuracy," May 2015, https://www.gao.gov/assets/gao-15-434.pdf.

9. Paulette C. Morgan, "Medicare Durable Medical Equipment: The Competitive Bidding Program," Congressional Research Service, June 26, 2013, https://www.everycrsreport.com/files/20130626_R43123_06589524b9a48d90aa589cc3a8f513bd5dd39e2e.pdf.

10. Brian O'Donnell, Eric Rollins, and James Mathews, "Competitive Bidding Reduced Medicare Spending on Diabetes Testing Supplies Without Negatively Affecting Beneficiary Outcomes," Health Affairs Forefront, April 8, 2020, https://www.healthaffairs.org/do/10.1377/hblog20200326.122054/full/.

11. David Newman, Eric Barrette, and Katharine McGraves-Lloyd, "Medicare Competitive Bidding Program Realized Price Savings for Durable Medical Equipment Purchases," Health Affairs 36, no. 8 (August 2017), https://www.healthaffairs.org/doi/full/10.1377/hlthaff.2016.1323.

12. Newman, Barrette, and McGraves-Lloyd, "Medicare Competitive Bidding Program Realized Price Savings for Durable Medical Equipment Purchases."

13. Hui Ding, Mark Duggan, and Amanda Starc, "Getting the Price Right? The Impact of Competitive Bidding in the Medicare Program" (working paper, National Bureau of Economic Research, Cambridge, MA, February 2021), https://www.nber.org/papers/w28457.

14. For an example of the analyses that were used to criticize premium support, see Zirui Song, David M. Cutler, and Michael E. Chernew, "Potential Consequences of Reforming Medicare into a Competitive Bidding System," *Journal of the American Medical Association* 308, no. 5 (August 1, 2012), https://jamanetwork.com/journals/jama/article-abstract/1273025.

Appendix A. References

Aaron, Henry, Joseph Antos, Loren Adler, James C. Capretta, Matthew Fiedler, Paul Ginsburg, Benedic Ippolito, and Alice Rivlin. 2019. "Letter to the Honorable Lamar Alexander on Slowing the Rate of Increase of Health Care Costs." Brookings Institution. March 1. https://www.brookings.edu/wp-content/uploads/2019/03/AEI_Brookings_Letter_Attachment_Cost_Reducing_Health_Policies.pdf.

Advisory Board. 2019. "How Much Are US Doctors Paid? (Hint: A Lot More Than in the Rest of the World.)." September 24. https://www.advisory.com/daily-briefing/2019/09/24/international-physician-compensation.

Alexander, Diane, and Molly Schnell. 2019. "The Impacts of Physician Payments on Patient Access, Use, and Health." Working Paper. National Bureau of Economic Research. July 2019. https://www.nber.org/system/files/working_papers/w26095/w26095.pdf.

American Academy of Actuaries. 2018. "Estimating the Potential Health Care Savings of Reference Pricing." November. https://www.actuary.org/sites/default/files/files/publications/ReferencePricing_11.2018.pdf.

American Association of Medical Colleges. 2019. "Medical Student Education: Debt, Costs, and Loan Repayment Fact Card." October. https://store.aamc.org/downloadable/download/sample/sample_id/296/.

American Council for Graduate Medical Education. "Member Organizations." https://www.acgme.org/About-Us/Member-Organizations/.

Antos, Joseph, and James C. Capretta. 2019. "Reforming Medicare Payments for Part B Drugs." American Enterprise Institute. June 3. https://www.aei.org/research-products/report/reforming-medicare-payments-for-part-b-drugs/.

———. 2019. "The Center for Medicare and Medicaid Innovation Has Too Much Power." RealClearPolicy. December. https://www.realclearpolicy.com/articles/2018/12/28/the_center_for_medicare_and_medicaid_innovation_has_too_much_power_110969.html.

———. 2018. "Prescription Drug Pricing: An Overview of the Legal, Regulatory, and Market Environment." American Enterprise Institute. July 23. https://www.aei.org/research-products/report/prescription-drug-pricing-an-overview-of-the-legal-regulatory-and-market-environment/.

Archibald, Nancy, Michelle Soper, Leah Smith, Alexandra Kruse, and Joshua Wiener. 2019. *Integrating Care Through Dual Eligible Special Needs Plans (D-SNPs): Opportunities and Challenges.* US Department of Health and Human Services. April. https://aspe.hhs.gov/sites/default/files/migrated_legacy_files/188071/MMI-DSNP.pdf.

Ario, Joel, and Kevin McAvey. 2018. "Transparency in Health Care: Where We Stand and What Policy Makers Can Do Now." Health Affairs Forefront. July 11. https://www.healthaffairs.org/do/10.1377/hblog20180703.549221/full/.

Armour, Stephanie, and Anna Wilde Mathews. 2019. "Hospitals, Insurers Set to Resist Price Transparency Proposal." *Wall Street Journal.* March. https://www.wsj.com/articles/hospitals-insurers-set-to-resist-price-transparency-proposal-11552343346.

Arrow, Kenneth. 1963. "Uncertainty and the Welfare Economics of Medical Care." *American Economic Review* 53, no. 5 (December): 941–73. https://web.stanford.edu/~jay/health_class/Readings/Lecture01/arrow.pdf.

Artiga, Samantha, and Maria Diaz. 2019. "Health Coverage and Care of Undocumented Immigrants." Kaiser Family Foundation. July 15. https://www.kff.org/racial-equity-and-health-policy/issue-brief/health-coverage-and-care-of-undocumented-immigrants/.

Austin, Daniel R., and Laurence C. Baker. 2015. "Less Physician Practice Competition Is Associated with Higher Prices Paid for Common Procedures." *Health Affairs* 34, no. 10 (October). https://www.healthaffairs.org/doi/full/10.1377/hlthaff.2015.0412.

Baghdadi, Ramsey. 2017. "Medicaid Best Price." *Health Affairs.* August. https://www.healthaffairs.org/do/10.1377/hpb20171008.000173/full/healthpolicybrief_173.pdf.

Bahr, Daniel, and Thomas Huelskoetter. 2014. "Comparing the Effectiveness of Drugs: The German Experience." Center for American Progress. May 21. https://cdn.americanprogress.org/wp-content/uploads/2014/05/PharmaReform.pdf.

Baicker, Katherine, Sarah L. Taubman, Heidi L. Allen, Mira Berstein, Jonathan H. Gruber, Joseph P. Newhouse, Eric C. Schneider, Bill J. Wright, Alan M. Zaslavsky, and Amy N. Finkelstein. 2013. "The Oregon Experiment—Effect of Medicaid on Clinical Outcomes." *New England Journal of Medicine* 368 (May): 1713–22. https://www.nejm.org/doi/full/10.1056/NEJMsa1212321.

Barua, Bacchus, and Mackenzie Moir. 2019. "Waiting Your Turn: Wait Times for Health Care in Canada, 2019 Report." Fraser Institute. https://www.fraserinstitute.org/sites/default/files/waiting-your-turn-2019-rev17dec.pdf.

Berenson, Robert A., Jonathan H. Sunshine, David Helms, and Emily Lawton. 2015. "Why Medicare Advantage Plans Pay Hospitals Traditional Medicare Prices." *Health Affairs* 34, no. 8 (August): 1289–95. https://www.healthaffairs.org/doi/pdf/10.1377/hlthaff.2014.1427.

Biden for President. 2020. "Biden-Sanders Unity Task Force Recommendations." August. https://joebiden.com/wp-content/uploads/2020/08/UNITY-TASK-FORCE-RECOMMENDATIONS.pdf.

Bipartisan Policy Center. 2015. "Medicare Benefit Modernization." April. https://bipartisanpolicy.org/wp-content/uploads/2017/02/BPC-Medicare-Benefit-Modernization.pdf.

Boccuti, Cristina. 2016. "Paying a Visit to the Doctor: Current Protections for Medicare Patients When Receiving Physician Services." Kaiser Family Foundation. November 30. https://www.kff.org/medicare/issue-brief/paying-a-visit-to-the-doctor-current-financial-protections-for-medicare-patients-when-receiving-physician-services/.

Bower, Anthony, and Peter Kolchinsky. 2018. "Unintended Consequences of 'Fairness': Critically Examining the Idea of the U.S. Referencing EU Prices." October. https://medium.com/the-biotech-social-contract/https-medium-com-the-biotech-social-contract-kolchinsky-tbsc-8-2717553ccefe.

Brot-Goldberg, Zarek C., Amitabh Chandra, Benjamin R. Handel, and Jonathan T. Kolstad. 2015. "What Does a Deductible Do? The Impact of Cost-Sharing on Health Care Prices, Quantities, and Spending Dynamics." Working Paper. National Bureau of Economic Research. October. https://www.nber.org/papers/w21632.pdf.

Brotherton, Sarah E., and Sylvia I. Etzel. 2018. "Graduate Medical Education, 2017–2018." *Journal of the American Medical Association* 210, no. 10 (September 11): 1051–70. https://jamanetwork.com/journals/jama/fullarticle/2702121.

Cabral, Marika, and Neale Mahoney. 2017. "Externalities and Taxation of Supplemental Insurance: A Study of Medicare and Medigap." Working Paper. National Bureau of Economic Research. October. https://www.nber.org/system/files/working_papers/w19787/w19787.pdf.

California Health Care Foundation. 2018. "The ABCs of APCDs: How States Are Using Claims Data to Understand and Improve Care." November 8. https://www.chcf.org/publication/the-abcs-of-apcds/.

Capretta, James C. 2021. "Colorado's Standardized Health Benefit Plan." State of Reform. August 2. https://stateofreform.com/news/colorado/2021/08/colorados-standardized-health-benefit-plan/.

———. 2021. "Covering the Uninsured in the United States' Multi-Payer Health System." American Enterprise Institute. May 11. https://www.aei.org/research-products/report/covering-the-uninsured-in-the-united-states-multi-payer-health-system/.

———. 2021. "Evaluations of Four State-Run Dually Eligible Demonstrations." State of Reform. December 1. https://stateofreform.com/featured/2021/12/evaluations-of-our-state-run-dually-eligible-demonstrations/.

———. 2021. "Structured Markets: Disciplining Medical Care with Regulated Competition." American Enterprise Institute. March 31. https://www.aei.org/research-products/report/structured-markets-disciplining-medical-care-with-regulated-competition/.

———. 2019. "Toward Meaningful Price Transparency in Health Care." American Enterprise Institute. June 26. https://www.aei.org/research-products/report/toward-meaningful-price-transparency-in-health-care/.

———. 2018. "Rethinking Medicare." *National Affairs.* Spring. https://www.nationalaffairs.com/publications/detail/rethinking-medicare.

Centers for Medicare & Medicaid Services. 2022. "Medicare Costs at a Glance." https://www.medicare.gov/your-medicare-costs/medicare-costs-at-a-glance.

———. 2021. "CMS Releases 2022 Projected Medicare Part D Average Premium." July 29. https://www.cms.gov/newsroom/news-alert/cms-releases-2022-projected-medicare-part-d-average-premium.

———. 2021. "Medicaid Pharmacy Supplemental Rebate Agreements (SRA)." September. https://www.medicaid.gov/medicaid-chip-program-information/by-topics/prescription-drugs/downloads/xxxsupplemental-rebates-chart-current-qtr.pdf.

———. 2021. "Requirements Related to Surprise Billing; Part II Interim Final Rule with Comment Period." September 30. https://www.cms.gov/newsroom/fact-sheets/requirements-related-surprise-billing-part-ii-interim-final-rule-comment-period.

———. 2020. "2018 Actuarial Report on the Financial Outlook for Medicaid." April. https://www.cms.gov/files/document/2018-report.pdf.

———. 2020. "CMS Completes Historic Price Transparency Initiative." Press Release. October 29. https://www.cms.gov/newsroom/press-releases/cms-completes-historic-price-transparency-initiative.

———. 2020. "Dually Eligible Beneficiaries Under Medicare and Medicaid." February. https://www.cms.gov/Outreach-and-Education/Medicare-Learning-Network-MLN/MLNProducts/downloads/medicare_beneficiaries_dual_eligibles_at_a_glance.pdf.

———. 2018. "Budget Neutrality Policies for Section 1115(a) Medicaid Demonstration Policies." August 22. https://www.medicaid.gov/federal-policy-guidance/downloads/smd18009.pdf.

———. 2018. "Fiscal Year (FY) 2019 Medicare Hospital Inpatient Prospective Payment System (IPPS) and Long-Term Acute Care Hospital (LTCH) Prospective Payment System Final Rule (CMS-1694-F)." August. https://www.cms.gov/newsroom/fact-sheets/fiscal-year-fy-2019-medicare-hospital-inpatient-prospective-payment-system-ipps-and-long-term-acute-0.

———. 2018. "National Health Expenditure Data, Historical Tables: Table 16." https://www.cms.gov/Research-Statistics-Data-and-Systems/Statistics-Trends-and-Reports/NationalHealthExpendData/NationalHealthAccountsHistorical.

———. 2017. "Medicare Part D-Direct and Indirect Remuneration." January 19. https://www.cms.gov/newsroom/fact-sheets/medicare-part-d-direct-and-indirect-remuneration-dir.

———. 2015. "Medicare and Medicaid Milestones: 1937 to 2015." July. https://www.cms.gov/About-CMS/Agency-Information/History/Downloads/Medicare-and-Medicaid-Milestones-1937-2015.pdf.

———. 2013. "Dual Eligible Beneficiaries of Medicare and Medicaid: Characteristics, Health Care Spending, and Evolving Policies." June. https://www.cbo.gov/sites/default/files/113th-congress-2013-2014/reports/44308dualeligibles2.pdf.

———. "10 Steps to Making Public Standard Charges for Shoppable Services." https://www.cms.gov/files/document/steps-making-public-standard-charges-shoppable-services.pdf.

———. "Bundled Payments for Care Improvement Advanced: Frequently Asked Questions." https://innovation.cms.gov/Files/x/bpci-advanced-faqs.pdf.

———. "Conditions of Coverage (CfCs) and Conditions of Participations (CoPs)." https://www.cms.gov/Regulations-and-Guidance/Legislation/CFCsAndCoPs/index.html.

Chandra, Amitabh, Dhurv Khullar, and Gail R. Wilensky. 2014. "The Economics of Graduate Medical Education." *New England Journal of Medicine* 370 (June): 2357–60. https://www.nejm.org/doi/full/10.1056/NEJMp1402468.

Chernew, Michael, Zack Cooper, Eugene Larsen-Hallcok, and Fiona Scott Morton. 2019. "Are Health Care Services Shoppable? Evidence from the Consumption of Lower-Limb MRI Scans." Working Paper. National Bureau of Economic Research. January. https://www.nber.org/system/files/working_papers/w24869/w24869.pdf.

Clemens, Jeffrey, and Joshua D. Gottlieb. 2017. "In the Shadow of a Giant: Medicare's Influence on Private Physician Payments." *Journal of Political Economy* 125, no. 1 (February): 1–39. https://www.journals.uchicago.edu/doi/pdfplus/10.1086/689772.

Cogan, John F., R. Glenn Hubbard, and Daniel P. Kessler. 2008. "The Effect of Tax Preferences on Health Spending." Working Paper. National Bureau of Economic Research. January. https://www.nber.org/papers/w13767.pdf.

Competition and Markets Authority. 2015. "Productivity and Competition: A Summary of the Evidence." July 9. https://assets.publishing.service.gov.uk/government/uploads/system/uploads/attachment_data/file/909846/Productivity_and_competition_report_.pdf.

Congressional Budget Office. 2021. "10-Year Trust Fund Projections." February. https://www.cbo.gov/data/budget-economic-data#5.

———. 2021. "American Rescue Plan Act of 2021 (P.L. 117-2): Private Health Insurance, Medicaid, CHIP, and Medicare Provisions." April 27. https://crsreports.congress.gov/product/pdf/R/R46777.

———. 2021. "Budget and Economic Data." https://www.cbo.gov/data/budget-economic-data#1.

———. 2021. "Cost Estimate: Reconciliation Recommendations of the House Committee on Ways and Means." February 17. https://www.cbo.gov/system/files/2021-02/hwaysandmeansreconciliation.pdf.

———. 2021. "Federal Subsidies for Health Insurance Coverage for People Under Age 65: CBO and JCT's July 2021 Projections." July. https://www.cbo.gov/system/files/2021-08/51298-2021-07-healthinsurance.pdf.

———. 2021. "Reconciliation Recommendations of the House Committee on Ways and Means." February. https://www.cbo.gov/system/files/2021-02/hwaysandmeansreconciliation.pdf.

———. 2020. "Federal Subsidies for Health Insurance Coverage for People Under 65: 2020 to 2030." September. https://www.cbo.gov/system/files/2020-09/56571-federal-health-subsidies.pdf.

———. 2020. "Who Went Without Health Insurance in 2019, and Why?" September. https://www.cbo.gov/system/files/2020-09/56504-Health-Insurance.pdf.

———. 2018. "Exploring the Growth of Medicaid Managed Care." August. https://www.cbo.gov/system/files/2018-08/54235-MMC_chartbook.pdf.

———. 2017. "A Premium Support System for Medicare: Updated Analysis of Illustrative Options." October. https://www.cbo.gov/system/files/115th-congress-2017-2018/reports/53077-premiumsupport.pdf.

———. 2017. "H.R. 1628: American Health Care Act of 2017." May 24. https://www.cbo.gov/system/files/115th-congress-2017-2018/costestimate/hr1628aspassed.pdf.

———. 2016. "Federal Subsidies for Health Insurance Coverage for People Under Age 65: Tables from CBO's March 2016 Baseline." March. https://www.cbo.gov/sites/default/files/recurringdata/51298-2016-03-healthinsurance.pdf.

———. 2013. "Dual-Eligible Beneficiaries of Medicare and Medicaid: Characteristics, Health Care Spending, and Evolving Policies." June. https://www.cbo.gov/sites/default/files/113th-congress-2013-2014/reports/44308dualeligibles2.pdf.

———. 2007. "Prescription Drug Pricing in the Private Sector." January. https://www.cbo.gov/sites/default/files/110th-congress-2007-2008/reports/01-03-prescriptiondrug.pdf.

———. 1996. "How the Medicaid Rebate on Prescription Drugs Affects Pricing in the Pharmaceutical Industry." January. https://www.cbo.gov/sites/default/files/104th-congress-1995-1996/reports/1996doc20.pdf.

Congressional Research Service. 2022. "Health Insurance Premium Tax Credit and Cost-Sharing Reductions." February 3. https://crsreports.congress.gov/product/pdf/R/R44425.

———. 2021. "Medicaid: An Overview." February 22. https://sgp.fas.org/crs/misc/R43357.pdf.

———. 2020. "Medicaid's Federal Medical Assistance Percentage (FMAP)." July 29. https://sgp.fas.org/crs/misc/R43847.pdf.

———. 2020. "Medicare Part D Prescription Drug Benefit." December 18. https://fas.org/sgp/crs/misc/R40611.pdf.

———. 2016. "The Hatch-Waxman Act: A Primer." September 28. https://www.everycrsreport.com/reports/R44643.html.

————. 2012. "Medicaid and Federal Grant Conditions After *NFIB v. Sebelius*: Constitutional Issues and Analysis." July 17. https://crsreports.congress.gov/product/pdf/R/R42367.

Coulam, Robert, Roger Feldman, and Bryan Dowd. 2021. "Time to Save Money on Medicare Advantage: The Case for Competitive Bidding." Working Paper. University of Minnesota.

Council of Economic Advisers. 2018. "Reforming Biopharmaceutical Pricing at Home and Abroad." February. https://www.whitehouse.gov/wp-content/uploads/2017/11/CEA-Rx-White-Paper-Final2.pdf.

Council on Graduate Medical Education. 1998. *International Medical Graduates, the Physician Workforce, and GME Reform: Eleventh Report.* March. https://www.hrsa.gov/sites/default/files/hrsa/advisory-committees/graduate-medical-edu/reports/archive/1998-March.pdf.

Cubanski, Juliette, and Anthony Damico. 2021. "Medicare Part D: A First Look at Medicare Prescription Drug Plans in 2022." Kaiser Family Foundation. November 2. https://www.kff.org/medicare/issue-brief/medicare-part-d-a-first-look-at-medicare-prescription-drug-plans-in-2022/.

Curfman, Gregory D. 2017. "All-Payer Claims Databases After *Gobeille*." Health Affairs Forefront. March 3. https://www.healthaffairs.org/do/10.1377/hblog20170303.058995/full/.

Daemmrich, Arthur. 2009. "Where Is the Pharmacy to the World? International Regulatory Variation and Pharmaceutical Industry Location." Working Paper. Harvard Business School. https://www.hbs.edu/ris/Publication%20Files/09-118.pdf.

Dall, Tim, Ryan Reynolds, Kari Jones, Kitashree Chakrabarti, and Will Iacobucci. 2019. "The Complexities of Physician Supply and Demand: Projections from 2017 to 2032." Association of American Medical Colleges. April. https://aamc-black.global.ssl.fastly.net/production/media/filer_public/31/13/3113ee5c-a038-4c16-89af-294a69826650/2019_update_-_the_complexities_of_physician_supply_and_demand_-_projections_from_2017-2032.pdf.

Demko, Paul. 2017. "Politico-Harvard Poll: Congress Should Focus on Reducing Drug Pricing." *Politico.* September 25. https://www.politico.com/story/2017/09/25/politico-harvard-poll-congress-should-focus-on-reducing-drug-prices-243109.

Desai, Sunita, Laura A. Hatfield, Andrew L. Hicks, Anna D. Sinaiko, Michael E. Chernew, David Cowling, Santosh Gautam, Sze-jung Wu, and Ateev Mehrotra. 2017. "Offering a Price Transparency Tool Did Not Reduce Overall Spending Among California Public Employees and Retirees." *Health Affairs* 26, no. 8 (August). https://www.healthaffairs.org/doi/10.1377/hlthaff.2016.1636.

Ding, Hui, Mark Duggan, and Amanda Starc. 2021. "Getting the Price Right? The Impact of Competitive Bidding in the Medicare Program." Working Paper. National Bureau of Economic Research. February. https://www.nber.org/system/files/working_papers/w28457/w28457.pdf.

Dobson, Allen, Donald Moran, and Gary Young. 1992. "The Role of Federal Waivers in the Health Policy Process." *Health Affairs* 11, no. 4 (Winter). https://www.healthaffairs.org/doi/10.1377/hlthaff.11.4.72.

Dowd, Bryan E. 2005. "Coordinated Agency Versus Autonomous Consumers in Health Services Markets." *Health Affairs* 24, no. 6 (November/December). https://www.healthaffairs.org/doi/abs/10.1377/hlthaff.24.6.1501.

Drozd, Edward M., Deborah A. Healy, Leslie M. Greenwald, Melissa A. Morley, and Dianne Munevar. 2009. "Evaluation of the Competitive Acquisition Program for Part B Drugs." RTI International. December. https://www.cms.gov/Research-Statistics-Data-and-Systems/Statistics-Trends-and-Reports/Reports/downloads/CAPPartB_Final_2010.pdf.

Dubois, Pierre, Ashvin Gandhi, and Shoshana Vasserman. 2018. "Bargaining and International Reference Pricing in the Pharmaceutical Industry." November. https://scholar.harvard.edu/gandhi/files/dgv_pharma.pdf.

Duffy, Thomas P. 2011. "The Flexner Report—100 Years Later." *Yale Journal of Biology and Medicine* 84 (September): 269–76. https://www.ncbi.nlm.nih.gov/pmc/articles/PMC3178858/pdf/yjbm_84_3_269.pdf.

Eden, Jill, Donald Berwick, and Gail Wilensky, eds. 2014. *Graduate Medical Education That Meets the Nation's Health Needs.* Washington, DC: National Academies Press. https://www.nap.edu/read/18754/chapter/1.

Ellwood, Paul M., and Alain C. Enthoven. 1995. "'Responsible Choices': The Jackson Hole Group Plan for Health Reform." *Health Affairs* 14, no. 2 (Summer). https://www.healthaffairs.org/doi/pdf/10.1377/hlthaff.14.2.24.

Federal Reserve Economic Data. Website. https://fred.stlouisfed.org.

Federation of State Medical Boards. 2018. "Physician Census." https://www.fsmb.org/physician-census.

———. 2018. *U.S. Medical Regulatory Trends and Actions: 2018.* https://www.fsmb.org/siteassets/advocacy/publications/us-medical-regulatory-trends-actions.pdf.

Fein, Adam. 2017. "New Part B Buy-and-Bill Data: Physician Offices Are Losing to Hospital Outpatient Sites." Drug Channels. August. https://www.drugchannels.net/2017/08/new-part-b-buy-and-bill-data-physician.html.

Feldman, Roger, Bryan Dowd, and Robert Coulam. 2015. "Medicare's Role in Determining Prices Throughout the Health Care System." George Mason University. Mercatus Center. October. https://www.mercatus.org/system/files/Feldman-Medicare-Role-Prices-oct.pdf.

Feng, Zhanlian, Alison Vadnais, Emily Vreeland, Susan Haber, Joshua Wiener, and Bob Baker. 2019. *Analysis of Pathways to Dual Eligible Status.* US Department of Health and Human Services, Office of the Assistant Secretary for Planning and Evaluation. May. https://aspe.hhs.gov/sites/default/files/migrated_legacy_files//189226/DualStatus.pdf.

Finnegan, Joanne. 2017. "Orthopedic Practice Among the First to Pursue Bundled Payments with Private Payers." Fierce Healthcare. April 20. https://www.fiercehealthcare.com/practices/orthopedic-practice-among-first-private-groups-to-soon-offer-bundled-payments.

Flexner, Abraham. 1910. *Medical Education in the United States and Canada.* Carnegie Foundation. http://archive.carnegiefoundation.org/pdfs/elibrary/Carnegie_Flexner_Report.pdf.

Food and Drug Administration. 2022. "Biosimilar Product Information." https://www.fda.gov/drugs/biosimilars/biosimilar-product-information.

Fox, Peter D., and Peter R. Kongstvedt. 2013. "A History of Managed Health Care and Health Insurance in the United States." *Essentials of Managed Health Care.* 6th ed. Burlington, MA: Jones & Bartlett Learning. http://samples.jbpub.com/9781284043259/Chapter1.pdf.

Frizzera, Jim. "History of the Disproportionate Share Hospital (DSH) Program: 1981 to 2009." NHP Foundation. https://www.nhpf.org/library/handouts/Frizzera.slides_06-19-09.pdf.

Fronstin, Paul, and Edna Dretzka. 2018. "Consumer Engagement in Health Care: Findings from the 2018 EBRI/Greenwald & Associates Consumer Engagement in Health Care Survey." Employee Benefit Research Institute. December 20. https://www.ebri.org/docs/default-source/ebri-issue-brief/ebri_ib_468_cehcs-20dec18.pdf.

Fronstin, Paul, and Stephen A. Woodbury. 2020. "How Many Americans Have Lost Jobs with Employer Health Coverage During the Pandemic?" Commonwealth Fund. October. https://www.commonwealthfund.org/sites/default/files/2020-10/Fronstin_how_many_americans_lost_employer_coverage_pandemic_ib.pdf.

Frost, Amanda, and David Newman. 2016. "Spending on Shoppable Services in Health Care." Health Care Cost Institute. March. https://www.healthcostinstitute.org/images/easyblog_articles/110/Shoppable-Services-IB-3.2.16_0.pdf.

Fuchs, Beth C. 1997. "Managed Health Care: Federal and State Regulation." Congressional Research Service. October 8. https://www.everycrsreport.com/files/19971008_97-938_046b2240a0226328c280576158960ddffa38d14e.pdf.

Fuchs, Beth, and Lisa Potetz. 2011. "The Nuts and Bolts of Medicare Premium Support Proposals." Kaiser Family Foundation. June. https://www.kff.org/wp-content/uploads/2013/01/8191.pdf.

Garrett, Bowen, and Anuj Gangopadhyaya. 2020. "How the COVID-19 Recession Could Affect Health Insurance Coverage." Robert Wood Johnson Foundation and Urban Institute. May. https://www.rwjf.org/en/library/research/2020/05/how-the-covid-19-recession-could-affect-health-insurance-coverage.html.

Ginsburg, Paul B. 2007. "Shopping for Price in Medical Care." February. *Health Affairs.* https://www.healthaffairs.org/doi/pdf/10.1377/hlthaff.26.2.w208.

Goldin, Jacob, Ithai Z. Lurie, and Janet McCubbin. 2019. "Health Insurance and Mortality: Experimental Evidence from Taxpayer Outreach." Working Paper. National Bureau of Economic Research. December. https://www.nber.org/system/files/working_papers/w26533/w26533.pdf.

Goldman, Dana, and Darius Lakdawalla. 2018. "The Global Burden of Medical Innovation." University of Southern California. Leonard D. Schaeffer Center for Health Policy & Economics. January. https://healthpolicy.usc.edu/wp-content/uploads/2018/01/01.2018_Global%20Burden%20of%20Medical%20Innovation.pdf.

Goodman, John C. 2012. "HSAs Force Health Care Providers to Compete." *San Francisco Chronicle*. September 29. https://www.sfgate.com/opinion/article/HSAs-force-health-providers-to-compete-3905150.php.

Government Accountability Office. 2018. "Physician Workforce: HHS Needs Better Information to Comprehensively Evaluate Graduate Medical Education Funding." March. https://www.gao.gov/assets/gao-18-240.pdf.

———. 2017. "Drug Discount Program: Update on Agency Efforts to Improve 340B Program Oversight." July 18. https://www.gao.gov/assets/gao-17-749t.pdf.

———. 2015. "Medicare Physician Payment Rates: Better Data and Greater Transparency Could Improve Accuracy." May. https://www.gao.gov/assets/gao-15-434.pdf.

———. 2011. "Drug Pricing: Manufacturer Discounts in the 340B Program Offer Benefits, but Federal Oversight Needs Improvement." September. https://www.gao.gov/assets/gao-11-836.pdf.

———. 2011. "Health Care Price Transparency: Meaningful Price Information Is Difficult for Consumers to Obtain Prior to Receiving Care." September. https://www.gao.gov/assets/590/585400.pdf.

Gudiksen, Katie. 2018. "Are APCDs the Solution to Price Transparency in Healthcare?" Source on Healthcare Price & Competition. April 16. http://sourceonhealthcare.org/are-apcds-the-solution-to-price-transparency-in-healthcare/.

Hahn, Jim, and Kristin B. Blom. 2015. "The Medicare Access and CHIP Reauthorization Act of 2015." Congressional Research Service. November 10. https://sgp.fas.org/crs/misc/R43962.pdf.

Hamowy, Ronald. 1979. "The Early Development of Medical Licensing Laws in the United States, 1875–1900." *Journal of Libertarian Studies*. https://cdn.mises.org/3150.pdf.

Haviland, Amelia M., Matthew D. Eisenberg, Ateev Mehrotra, Peter J. Huckfeldt, and Neeraj Sood. 2015. "Do 'Consumer-Directed Health Plans' Bend the Cost Curve over Time?" Working Paper. National Bureau of Economic Research. March. https://www.nber.org/system/files/working_papers/w21031/w21031.pdf.

Health Care Cost Institute. 2019. "2017 Health Care Cost and Utilization Report." February. https://www.healthcostinstitute.org/images/pdfs/HCCI_2017_%20Health_%20Care_Cost_and_Utilization_Report_02.12.19.pdf.

Hearne, Jean. 2004. "Medicaid Disproportionate Share Payments." Congressional Research Service. January 15. http://research.policyarchive.org/395.pdf.

Heisler, Elayne J., Bryce H. P. Mendez, Alison Mitchell, Sidath Viranga Panangala, and Marco A. Villgrana. 2018. "Federal Support for Graduate Medical Education: An Overview." Congressional Research Service. December 27. https://fas.org/sgp/crs/misc/R44376.pdf.

Hempstead, Katherine, and Chapin White. 2019. "Plain Talk About Price Transparency." Health Affairs Forefront. March. https://www.healthaffairs.org/do/10.1377/hblog20190319.99794/full/.

Hill, Timothy B. 2018. "Letter to State Medicaid Director." August 22. https://www.medicaid.gov/federal-policy-guidance/downloads/smd18009.pdf.

Hinton, Elizabeth, Robin Rudowitz, Lina Stoylar, and Natalie Singer. 2020. "10 Things to Know About Medicaid Managed Care." Kaiser Family Foundation. October 29. https://www.kff.org/medicaid/issue-brief/10-things-to-know-about-medicaid-managed-care/.

Houses of Parliament. Parliamentary Office of Science and Technology. "Drug Pricing." 2010. https://www.parliament.uk/documents/post/postpn_364_Drug_Pricing.pdf.

Humphreys, Adrian. 2011. "Illegal Immigrants Have No Right to Free Health Care: Court." *National Post.* July 8. https://nationalpost.com/news/canada/illegal-immigrants-have-no-right-to-free-health-care-court.

Iglehart, John K. 1999. "Support for Academic Medical Centers—Revisiting the 1997 Balanced Budget Act." *New England Journal of Medicine* 321 (July): 299–304. https://www.nejm.org/doi/full/10.1056/NEJM199907223410424.

Institute of Medicine. 1997. *On Implementing a National Graduate Medical Education Trust Fund.* Washington, DC: National Academies Press. https://www.nap.edu/catalog/5771/on-implementing-a-national-graduate-medical-education-trust-fund.

Internal Revenue Service. 2021. "Internal Revenue Bulletin: 2021–35." August 30. https://www.irs.gov/irb/2021-35_IRB#REV-PROC-2021-36.

IQVIA Institute. 2019. "The Global Use of Medicine in 2019 and Outlook to 2023." January. https://www.iqvia.com/institute/reports/the-global-use-of-medicine-in-2019-and-outlook-to-2023.

Japsen, Bruce. 2016. "Private Exchange Growth Hits 8M, but Slows Among Large Employers." *Forbes.* January 20. https://www.forbes.com/sites/brucejapsen/2016/01/20/private-exchange-growth-hits-8m-but-slows-among-large-employers/?sh=15e9f2947652.

Johnson, Judith. 2017. "Biologics and Biosimilars: Background and Key Issues." Congressional Research Service. October 27. https://sgp.fas.org/crs/misc/R44620.pdf.

Johnson, Nick, Christopher S. Kunkel, and Annie Hallum. 2020. "Changing How Medicare and Medicaid Talk to Each Other." Milliman. March. https://www.milliman.com/-/media/milliman/pdfs/articles/changing_how_medicare_and_medicaid_talk_to_each_other.ashx.

Kaiser Family Foundation. 2022. "Status of State Action on the Medicaid Expansion Decision." February 24. https://www.kff.org/health-reform/state-indicator/state-activity-around-expanding-medicaid-under-the-affordable-care-act/?currentTimeframe=0&sortModel=%7B%22colId%22:%22Location%22,%22sort%22:%22asc%22%7D.

———. 2022. "Status of State Medicaid Expansion." January 18. https://www.kff.org/medicaid/issue-brief/status-of-state-medicaid-expansion-decisions-interactive-map/.

———. 2022. "Status of State Medicaid Expansion Decisions: Interactive Map." February 24. https://www.kff.org/medicaid/issue-brief/status-of-state-medicaid-expansion-decisions-interactive-map/.

———. 2021. "An Overview of the Medicare Part D Prescription Drug Benefit." October 13. https://www.kff.org/medicare/fact-sheet/an-overview-of-the-medicare-part-d-prescription-drug-benefit/.

———. 2021. *Employer Health Benefits: 2021 Annual Survey.* November 3. https://files.kff.org/attachment/Report-Employer-Health-Benefits-2021-Annual-Survey.pdf.

———. 2021. "State Health Facts: Total Number of Children Ever Enrolled in CHIP Annually." November. https://www.kff.org/other/state-indicator/annual-chip-enrollment/.

———. 2020. "Public Opinion on Single-Payer, National Health Plans, and Expanding Access to Medicare Coverage." October 16. https://www.kff.org/slideshow/public-opinion-on-single-payer-national-health-plans-and-expanding-access-to-medicare-coverage/.

———. 2020. "State Health Facts: Births Financed by Medicaid." https://www.kff.org/medicaid/state-indicator/births-financed-by-medicaid/.

———. 2019. "Public Opinion on Prescription Drugs and Their Prices: Poll Findings from 2015–2019 KFF Health Tracking Polls." February. https://www.kff.org/slideshow/public-opinion-on-prescription-drugs-and-their-prices/.

———. 2018. "Employer Health Benefits: 2018 Annual Survey." October. http://files.kff.org/attachment/Report-Employer-Health-Benefits-Annual-Survey-2018.

Kanavos, Panos, and Uwe Reinhardt. 2003. "Reference Pricing for Drugs: Is It Compatible with U.S. Health Care?" *Health Affairs* 22, no. 3 (May/June 2003). https://www.healthaffairs.org/doi/pdf/10.1377/hlthaff.22.3.16.

Kassebaum, Donald G. 1992. "Origin of the LCME, the AMA-AAMC Partnership for Accreditation." *Academic Medicine* 67, no. 2 (February): 85–87. https://journals.lww.com/academicmedicine/abstract/1992/02000/origin_of_the_lcme,_the_aamc_ama_partnership_for.5.aspx.

Keckley, Paul. 2018. "Price Transparency in Healthcare: What We've Learned, What's Ahead." Keckley Report. July 9. https://www.paulkeckley.com/the-keckley-report/2018/7/9/price-transparency-in-healthcare-what-weve-learned-whats-ahead.

Keisler-Starkey, Katherine, and Lisa N. Bunch. 2020. "Health Insurance Coverage in the United States: 2019." US Census Bureau. September. https://www.census.gov/content/dam/Census/library/publications/2020/demo/p60-271.pdf.

Kessel, Reuben A. 1970. "The A.M.A. and the Supply of Physicians." *Law and Contemporary Problems* (Spring). https://scholarship.law.duke.edu/cgi/viewcontent.cgi?article=3288&context=lcp.

Kronick, Richard. 2020. "Why Medicare Advantage Plans Are Overpaid by $200 Billion and What to Do About It." Health Affairs Forefront. January 29. https://www.healthaffairs.org/do/10.1377/forefront.20200127.293799/full/.

Kullgren, Jeffrey T., Betsy Q. Cliff, Chris D. Krenz, Helen Levy, Brady West, A. Mark Fendrick, Jonathan So, and Angela Fagerlin. 2019. "A Survey of Americans with High-Deductible Health Plans Identifies Opportunities to Enhance Consumer Behaviors." *Health Affairs* 38, no. 2 (March). https://www.healthaffairs.org/doi/abs/10.1377/hlthaff.2018.05018.

Kurani, Nisha, Giorlando Ramirez, Julie Hudman, Cynthia Cox, and Rabah Kamal. 2021. "Early Results from Federal Price Transparency Rule Show Difficulty in Estimating the Cost of Care." Peterson-KFF Health System Tracker. April 9. https://www.healthsystemtracker.org/brief/early-results-from-federal-price-transparency-rule-show-difficultly-in-estimating-the-cost-of-care/.

Lallemand, Nicole Cafarella. 2012. "Reducing Waste in Health Care." *Health Affairs*. December. https://www.healthaffairs.org/do/10.1377/hpb20121213.959735/full/healthpolicybrief_82.pdf.

Leu, Robert E., Frans F. H. Rutten, Werner Brouwer, Pius Matter, and Christian Rutschi. 2009. "The Swiss and Dutch Health Insurance Systems: Universal Coverage and Regulated Competitive Insurance Markets." Commonwealth Fund. January. https://www.commonwealthfund.org/publications/fund-reports/2009/jan/swiss-and-dutch-health-insurance-systems-universal-coverage-and.

Lewis, William W. 2004. "The Power of Productivity: Poor Countries Should Put Their Consumers First." *McKinsey Quarterly*, no. 2. https://econfaculty.gmu.edu/pboettke/workshop/spring05/Lewis.pdf.

Liaison Committee on Medical Education. "Appointment of LCME Members." https://lcme.org/about/meetings-members/.

Loehrer, Andrew P., Zirui Song, Alex B. Haynes, David C. Chang, Matthew M. Hutter, and John T. Mullen. 2016. "Impact of Health Insurance Expansion on the Treatment of Colorectal Cancer." *Journal of Clinical Oncology* 34, no. 34 (December): 4110–15. https://www.ncbi.nlm.nih.gov/pmc/articles/PMC5477821/.

Maini, Luca, and Fabio Pammoli. 2017. "Reference Pricing as Deterrent to Entry: Evidence from the European Pharmaceutical Market." December. https://scholar.harvard.edu/files/lucamaini/files/reference_pricing_as_a_deterrent_to_entry.pdf.

Martin, Kristi, and Jeremy Sharp. 2018. "Old Lesson for the New Medicare Part B Drug Payment Model." Commonwealth Fund. November. https://www.commonwealthfund.org/blog/2018/new-medicare-part-b-drug-payment-model.

Mathema, Silva. 2019. "Immigrant Doctors Can Help Lower Physician Shortages in Rural America." Center for American Progress. July. https://cdn.americanprogress.org/content/uploads/2019/07/29074013/ImmigrantDoctors-report.pdf.

McCaughan, Mike. 2017. "Prescription Drug Pricing: Veterans Health Administration." *Health Affairs*. August 10. https://www.healthaffairs.org/do/10.1377/hpb20171008.000174/full/.

McDermott, Daniel, and Cynthia Cox. 2021. "A Closer Look at the Uninsured Marketplace Population Following the American Rescue Plan Act." Kaiser Family Foundation. May 27. https://www.kff.org/private-insurance/issue-brief/a-closer-look-at-the-uninsured-marketplace-eligible-population-following-the-american-rescue-plan-act/.

Medicaid and CHIP Payment and Access Commission. 2021. "Federal Match Rate Exceptions." https://www.macpac.gov/federal-match-rate-exceptions/.

———. 2021. "Federal Match Rates for Medicaid Administrative Activities." https://www.macpac.gov/federal-match-rates-for-medicaid-administrative-activities/.

———. 2021. *MACSTATS: Medicaid and CHIP Date Book.* December. https://www.macpac.gov/wp-content/uploads/2021/12/MACStats-Medicaid-and-CHIP-Data-Book-December-2021.pdf.

———. 2018. "Medicaid Payment for Outpatient Prescription Drugs." March. https://www.macpac.gov/wp-content/uploads/2015/09/Medicaid-Payment-for-Outpatient-Prescription-Drugs.pdf.

———. 2018. "State Children's Health Insurance Program (CHIP)." February. https://www.macpac.gov/wp-content/uploads/2018/02/State-Children's-Health-Insurance-Program-CHIP.pdf.

———. 2017. "Federal Requirements and State Options: Benefits." March. https://www.macpac.gov/wp-content/uploads/2017/03/Federal-Requirements-and-State-Options-Benefits.pdf.

———. 2017. "Federal Requirements and State Options: Eligibility." March. https://www.macpac.gov/wp-content/uploads/2017/03/Federal-Requirements-and-State-Options-Eligibility.pdf.

Medicare Payment Advisory Commission. 2021. "Health Care Spending and the Medicare Program: A Data Book." July. https://www.medpac.gov/wp-content/uploads/import_data/scrape_files/docs/default-source/data-book/july2021_medpac_data-book_sec.pdf.

———. 2021. "Hospital Acute Inpatient Services Payment System." November. https://www.medpac.gov/wp-content/uploads/2021/11/medpac_payment_basics_21_hospital_final_sec.pdf.

———. 2021. "Medicare Advantage Program Payment System." November. https://www.medpac.gov/wp-content/uploads/2021/11/medpac_payment_basics_21_ma_final_sec.pdf.

———. 2021. "Medicare Payment Policy." March. http://medpac.gov/docs/default-source/reports/mar21_medpac_report_to_the_congress_sec.pdf.

———. 2021. "Physician and Other Health Professional Payment System." November. https://www.medpac.gov/wp-content/uploads/2021/11/medpac_payment_basics_21_physician_final_sec.pdf.

———. 2020. "Health Care Spending and the Medicare Program: A Data Book." July. http://www.medpac.gov/docs/default-source/data-book/july2020_databook_entirereport_sec.pdf.

———. 2020. "Physician and Other Health Professional Payment System." October. http://www.medpac.gov/docs/default-source/payment-basics/medpac_payment_basics_20_physician_final_sec.pdf.

———. 2017. "Medicare and the Health Care Delivery System." June 15. https://www.medpac.gov/wp-content/uploads/import_data/scrape_files/docs/default-source/press-releases/june2017_pressrelease.pdf.

———. 2017. "Medicare Part B Drug Payment Policy Issues." June 15. https://www.medpac.gov/recommendation/medicare-part-b-drug-payment-policy-issues-june-2017/.

———. 2017. "Part B Drug Payment Systems." October. http://www.medpac.gov/docs/default-source/payment-basics/medpac_payment_basics_17_partb_final.pdf.

———. 2016. "Medicare Part B Drug and Oncology Payment Policy Issues." June 15. https://www.medpac.gov/recommendation/medicare-part-b-drug-and-oncology-payment-policy-issues-june-2016/.

———. 2010. *Aligning Incentives in Medicare.* June. http://www.medpac.gov/docs/default-source/reports/Jun10_EntireReport.pdf.

Medicare Trustees. 2021. *The 2021 Annual Report of the Boards of Trustees of the Federal Hospital Insurance and Federal Supplementary Medical Insurance Trust Funds.* Centers for Medicare & Medicaid Services. August 31. https://www.cms.gov/files/document/2021-medicare-trustees-report.pdf.

Mehrotra, Ateev, Michael E. Chernew, and Anna D. Sinaiko. 2018. "Promise and Reality of Price Transparency." *New England Journal of Medicine* 278 (April): 1348–54. https://www.nejm.org/doi/full/10.1056/NEJMhpr1715229.

Mehrotra, Ateev, Katie M. Dean, Anna D. Sinaiko, and Neeraj Sood. 2017. "Americans Support Price Shopping for Health Care, but Few Actually Seek Out Price Information." *Health Affairs* 36, no. 8 (August). https://www.healthaffairs.org/doi/pdf/10.1377/hlthaff.2016.1471.

Mercer. 2015. "Cost Transparency Missing Link in Health Care Consumerism." January 28. https://www.mercer.us/our-thinking/healthcare/cost-transparency-missing-link-in-health-care-consumerism.html.

Merlis, Mark. 2007. "Health Care Price Transparency and Price Competition." National Health Policy Forum. March. https://www.nhpf.org/library/background-papers/BP_PriceTransparency_03-28-07.pdf.

Meyer, Harris. 2019. "Hospital Develops Package Prices to Lure Cash-Paying Patients." *Modern Healthcare*. February. https://www.modernhealthcare.com/article/20190202/TRANSFORMATION04/190129925/hospital-develops-package-prices-to-lure-cash-paying-patients.

Miller, Mark. 2015. "Graduate Medical Education Payments." Medicare Payment Advisory Commission. February 20. https://www.nhpf.org/uploads/Handouts/Miller-slides_02-20-15.pdf.

Millman, Joel. 2006. "How the Amish Drive Down Medical Costs." *Wall Street Journal*. February 21. https://www.wsj.com/articles/SB114048909124578710.

Mitchell, Alison. 2018. "Federal Financing for the State Children's Health Insurance Program (CHIP)." Congressional Research Service. May 23. https://sgp.fas.org/crs/misc/R43949.pdf.

Moore, Judith D., and David G. Smith. 2005. "Legislating Medicaid: Considering Medicaid and Its Origins." *Health Care Financing Review* 27, no. 2 (Winter). https://www.ncbi.nlm.nih.gov/pmc/articles/PMC4194918/pdf/hcfr-27-2-045.pdf.

Morgan, Paulette C. 2013. "Medicare Durable Medical Equipment: The Competitive Bidding Program." Congressional Research Service. June 26. https://www.everycrsreport.com/files/20130626_R43123_06589524b9a48d90aa589cc3a8f513bd5dd39e2e.pdf.

Morgan, Steven. 2016. "Summaries of National Drug Coverage and Pharmaceutical Pricing Policies in 10 Countries: Australia, Canada, France, Germany, the Netherlands, New Zealand, Norway, Sweden, Switzerland, and the U.K." Working Paper. Commonwealth Fund. https://www.commonwealthfund.org/sites/default/files/2018-09/Steven%20Morgan%2C%20PhD_Ten%20Country%20Pharma%20Policy%20Summaries_2016%20Vancouver%20Group%20Meeting.pdf.

Morse, Susan. 2021. "Final Rule Ups Financial Penalties to Hospitals That Ignore Price Transparency Regulation." *Healthcare Finance*. November 3. https://www.healthcarefinancenews.com/news/final-rule-cms-ups-financial-penalties-hospitals-ignore-price-transparency-regulation.

Mulcahy, Andrew W., Courtney Armstrong, Jeffrey Lewis, and Soeren Mattke. 2014. "The 340B Prescription Drug Discount Program: Origins, Implementation, and Post-Reform Future." RAND Corporation. https://www.rand.org/pubs/perspectives/PE121.html.

Musumeci, MaryBeth. 2021. "Medicaid Provisions in the American Rescue Plan Act." Kaiser Family Foundation. March 18. https://www.kff.org/medicaid/issue-brief/medicaid-provisions-in-the-american-rescue-plan-act/.

National Council of State Legislatures. 2017. "Enacted State Legislation: Transparency and Disclosure of Health Costs." March. http://www.ncsl.org/research/health/transparency-and-disclosure-health-costs.aspx#Legislation.

National Institute for Health Care Management Foundation. 2017. "The Concentration of U.S. Health Care Spending." July. https://www.nihcm.org/categories/concentration-of-us-health-care-spending.

Neumann, Peter J., and Joshua T. Cohen. 2018. "America's 'NICE'?" Health Affairs Forefront. March 12. https://www.healthaffairs.org/do/10.1377/hblog20180306.837580/full/.

Newhouse, Joseph P. 2004. "How Much Should Medicare Pay for Drugs?" *Health Affairs* 23, no. 1 (January): 89–102. https://www.healthaffairs.org/doi/pdf/10.1377/hlthaff.23.1.89.

Newman, David, Eric Barrette, and Katharine McGraves-Lloyd. 2017. "Medicare Competitive Bidding Program Realized Price Savings for Durable Medical Equipment Purchases." *Health Affairs* 36, no. 8 (August). https://www.healthaffairs.org/doi/pdf/10.1377/hlthaff.2016.1323.

Nicholson, Sean. 2002. *Medicare Hospital Subsidies: Money in Search of a Purpose.* Washington, DC: AEI Press. https://www.aei.org/research-products/book/medicare-hospital-subsidies/.

Obama, Barack. 2009. "Remarks by the President to a Joint Session of Congress on Health Care." September 9. https://obamawhitehouse.archives.gov/the-press-office/remarks-president-a-joint-session-congress-health-care.

O'Donnell, Brian, Eric Rollins, and James Mathews. 2020. "Competitive Bidding Reduced Medicare Spending on Diabetes Testing Supplies Without Negatively Affecting Beneficiary Outcomes." Health Affairs Forefront. April 8. https://www.healthaffairs.org/do/10.1377/hblog20200326.122054/full/.

Office of the Assistant Secretary for Planning and Evaluation. 2018. "Comparison of US and International Prices for Top Medicare Part B Drugs by Total Expenditure." US Department of Health and Human Services. October 25. https://aspe.hhs.gov/sites/default/files/private/pdf/259996/ComparisonUSInternationalPricesTopSpendingPartBDrugs.pdf.

Organisation of Economic Co-operation and Development. 2022. "Doctors." https://data.oecd.org/healthres/doctors.htm.

———. 2020. "Health Expenditure and Financing." February. https://stats.oecd.org/Index.aspx?DataSetCode=SHA.

———. 2020. Health Expenditure and Financing Database. https://stats.oecd.org/Index.aspx.

———. 2018. "Pharmaceutical Reimbursement and Pricing in Germany." June. http://www.oecd.org/els/health-systems/Pharmaceutical-Reimbursement-and-Pricing-in-Germany.pdf.

Pear, Robert. 2019. "Hospitals Must Now Post Prices. But It May Take a Brain Surgeon to Decipher Them." *New York Times*. January. https://www.nytimes.com/2019/01/13/us/politics/hospital-prices-online.html.

Peterson Foundation. 2019. "What Are the Trends Slowing Wage Growth and Fueling Income Inequality?" July 30. https://www.pgpf.org/blog/2019/07/what-are-the-trends-slowing-wage-growth-and-fueling-income-inequality.

Pham, Kevin. 2019. "America Outperforms Canada in Surgery Wait Times—and It's Not Even Close." Foundation for Economic Education. July 17. https://fee.org/articles/america-outperforms-canada-in-surgery-wait-times-and-its-not-even-close/.

Polite, Blase, Rena M. Conti, and Jeffrey C. Ward. 2015. "Reform of the Buy-and-Bill System for Outpatient Chemotherapy Care Is Inevitable: Perspectives from an Economist, a Realpolitik, and an Oncologist." American Society of Clinical Oncology Educational Book. https://www.ncbi.nlm.nih.gov/pmc/articles/PMC4594838/.

Rae, Matthew, Cynthia Cox, Gary Claxton, and Daniel McDermott. 2021. "How the American Rescue Plan Act Affects Subsidies for Marketplace Shoppers and People Who Are Uninsured." Kaiser Family Foundation. March 25. https://www.kff.org/health-reform/issue-brief/how-the-american-rescue-plan-act-affects-subsidies-for-marketplace-shoppers-and-people-who-are-uninsured/.

Rae, Matthew, Daniel McDermott, Larry Levitt, and Gary Claxton. 2020. "Long-Term Trends in Employer-Based Coverage." Peterson Foundation and Kaiser Family Foundation. April 3. https://www.healthsystemtracker.org/brief/long-term-trends-in-employer-based-coverage/.

Ramirez, Edith. 2013. "The Relationship Between Competition, Productivity, and Economic Growth: The Case of the United States." Federal Trade Commission. September 3. https://www.ftc.gov/system/files/documents/public_statements/579931/140902lacfperuspeech.pdf.

Ranasinghe, Padmini D. 2015. "International Medical Graduates in the US Physician Workforce." *Journal of the American Osteopathic Association* 115 (April): 236–41. https://jom.osteopathic.org/.

Rapaport, Lisa. 2018. "U.S. Relies Heavily on Foreign-Born Healthcare Workers." Reuters. December 4. https://www.reuters.com/article/us-health-professions-us-noncitizens/u-s-relies-heavily-on-foreign-born-healthcare-workers-idUSKBN1O32FR.

Reinhardt, Uwe. 2014. "Health Care Price Transparency and Economic Theory." *Journal of the American Medical Association* (October). https://jamanetwork.com/journals/jama/article-abstract/1917413.

Rice, Tim. 2018. "Why America Faces a Doctor Shortage." *City Journal*. September 26. https://www.city-journal.org/why-america-faces-a-doctor-shortage-16194.html.

Robinson, James C., and Timothy T. Brown. 2013. "Increases in Consumer Cost-Sharing Redirect Patient Volumes and Reduce Hospital Prices for Orthopedic

Surgery." *Health Affairs* 32, no. 8 (September): 1392–97. https://bcht.berkeley.edu/sites/default/files/reference-pricing-impact.pdf.

Robinson, James C., Timothy T. Brown, and Christopher Whaley. 2017. "Reference Pricing Changes the 'Choice Architecture' of Health Care for Consumers." *Health Affairs* 36, no. 3 (March): 524–30. https://www.healthaffairs.org/doi/pdf/10.1377/hlthaff.2016.1256.

Robinson, James C., Dimitra Panteli, and Patricia Ex. 2019. "Reference Pricing in Germany: Implications for U.S. Pharmaceutical Pricing." Commonwealth Fund. February. https://www.commonwealthfund.org/publications/issue-briefs/2019/jan/reference-pricing-germany-implications.

Rohrer, Kristin, and Lauren Dundes. 2016. "Sharing the Load: Amish Healthcare Financing." *Healthcare* 4, no. 4 (December): 92. https://www.ncbi.nlm.nih.gov/pmc/articles/PMC5198134/.

Rosso, Ryan J. 2019. "The Affordable Care Act's (ACA's) Employer Shared Responsibility Provisions (ESRP)." Congressional Research Service. January 9. https://fas.org/sgp/crs/misc/R45455.pdf.

Rosso, Ryan J., and Patricia A. Davis. 2018. "Medicare and Budget Sequestration." Congressional Research Service. February. https://fas.org/sgp/crs/misc/R45106.pdf.

Roth, Alvin E. 2003. "The Origins, History, and Design of the Resident Match." *Journal of the American Medical Association* 289, no. 7 (February 19): 909–12. https://jamanetwork.com/journals/jama/fullarticle/195998.

Roy, Avik. 2019. "What Medicare Can Learn from Other Countries on Drug Pricing." Foundation for Research on Equal Opportunity. January. https://freopp.org/what-medicare-can-learn-from-other-countries-on-drug-pricing-bf298d390bc5.

Rudowitz, Robin, Elizabeth Williams, Elizabeth Hinton, and Rachel Garfield. 2021. "Medicaid Financing: The Basics." Kaiser Family Foundation. May 7. https://www.kff.org/report-section/medicaid-financing-the-basics-issue-brief/.

Ruggeri, Kai, and Ellen Nolte. 2013. "Pharmaceutical Pricing: The Use of External Reference Pricing." RAND Corporation. https://www.rand.org/content/dam/rand/pubs/research_reports/RR200/RR240/RAND_RR240.pdf.

Russell, Neal James, Lisa Murphy, Laura Nellums, Jonathan Broad, Sarah Boutros, Nando Sigona, and Delan Davakumar. 2019. "Charging Undocumented Migrant Children for NHS Healthcare: Implications for Child Health." *British Medical Journal* 104, no. 8 (August). https://adc.bmj.com/content/archdischild/104/8/722.full.pdf.

Salsberg, Edward S., and Gaetano J. Forte. 2002. "Trends in the Physician Workforce, 1980–2000." *Health Affairs* 21, no. 5 (September/October): 165–73. https://www.healthaffairs.org/doi/pdf/10.1377/hlthaff.21.5.165.

Sarata, Amanda K. 2018. "Funding for ACA-Established Patient-Centered Outcomes Research Trust Fund (PCORTF) Expires in FY2019." Congressional Research Service. December 20. https://fas.org/sgp/crs/misc/IN11010.pdf.

Sawyer, Bradley, and Gary Claxton. 2019. "How Do Health Expenditures Vary Across the Population?" Peterson-KFF Health System Tracker. January 16. https://www.healthsystemtracker.org/chart-collection/health-expenditures-vary-across-population/.

Schechter, Asher. 2016. "'There Is Regulatory Capture, but It Is by No Means Complete.'" Promarket. March 15. https://promarket.org/2016/03/15/there-is-regulatory-capture-but-it-is-by-no-means-complete/.

Schwartz, Christine C., Aparna S. Ajjarapu, Chris D. Stamy, and Debra A. Schwinn. 2018. "Comprehensive History of 3-Year and Accelerated Medical School Programs: A Century in Review." Medical Education Online 23, no. 1 (December). https://pubmed.ncbi.nlm.nih.gov/30376794/.

Semigran, Hannah L., Rebecca Gourevitch, Anna D. Sinaiko, David Cowling, and Ateev Mehrotra. 2017. "Patient Views on Price Shopping and Price Transparency." American Journal of Managed Care 23, no. 6 (June). https://www.ajmc.com/journals/issue/2017/2017-vol23-n6/patients-views-on-price-shopping-and-price-transparency.

Shirk, Cynthia. 2008. "Shaping Medicaid and SCHIP Through Waivers: The Fundamentals." National Health Policy Forum, no. 64 (July). https://www.nhpf.org/library/background-papers/BP64_MedicaidSCHIP.Waivers_07-22-08.pdf.

Shrank, William H., Teresa L. Rogstad, and Natasha Parekh. 2019. "Waste in the US Health Care System: Estimated Costs and Potential for Savings." Journal of the American Medical Association 322, no. 15 (October): 1501–9. https://jamanetwork.com/journals/jama/article-abstract/2752664.

Sibbald, Barbara. 2014. "Made-in-Canada Accreditation Coming for Medical Schools." Canadian Medical Association Journal 186, no. 2 (February). https://www.ncbi.nlm.nih.gov/pmc/articles/PMC3903760/.

Social Security Administration. 2019. "Average Wage Index Series." https://www.ssa.gov/oact/cola/AWI.html#Series.

Sommers, Benjamin D., Atul A. Gawande, and Katherine Baicker. 2017. "Health Insurance Coverage and Health—What the Recent Evidence Tells Us." New England Journal of Medicine 377 (August): 586–93. https://www.nejm.org/doi/full/10.1056/NEJMsb1706645.

Song, Ziriu, David M. Cutler, and Michael E. Chernew. 2012. "Potential Consequences of Reforming Medicare into a Competitive Bidding System." Journal of the American Medical Association 308, no. 5 (August 1). https://jamanetwork.com/journals/jama/article-abstract/1273025.

Steinwald, Bruce, Paul Ginburg, Caitlin Brandt, Sobin Lee, and Kavita Patel. 2018. Medicare Graduate Medical Education Funding Is Not Addressing the Primary Care Shortage: We Need a Radically Different Approach. USC-Brookings Schaeffer Initiative for Health Policy. December. https://www.brookings.edu/wp-content/uploads/2018/12/Steinwald_Ginsburg_Brandt_Lee_Patel_GME-Funding_12.3.181.pdf.

Sturny, Isabelle. 2020. "International Health Care System Profiles: Switzerland." Commonwealth Fund. June 5. https://www.commonwealthfund.org/international-health-policy-center/countries/switzerland.

Tax Policy Center. 2019. "Historical Average Federal Tax Rates for All Households." July. https://www.taxpolicycenter.org/statistics/historical-average-federal-tax-rates-all-households.

Tozzi, John. 2018. "Priced Out of Health Insurance, Americans Rig Their Own Safety Nets." Bloomberg. August 22. https://www.bloomberg.com/news/features/2018-08-22/priced-out-of-health-insurance-americans-rig-their-own-safety-nets.

US Census Bureau. 2020. "Health Insurance Historical Tables-HHI Series." https://www.census.gov/data/tables/time-series/demo/health-insurance/historical-series/hic.html.

———. 2014. "Health Insurance Coverage in the United States: 2013." September. https://www2.census.gov/library/publications/2014/demographics/p60-250.pdf.

———. "Historical Health Insurance Tables." https://www2.census.gov/programs-surveys/demo/tables/health-insurance/time-series/original/orghihistt1.txt.

US Citizenship and Immigration Services. 2014. "Conrad 30 Waiver Program." https://www.uscis.gov/working-united-states/students-and-exchange-visitors/conrad-30-waiver-program.

US Department of Health and Human Services. 2021. "Trends in the US Uninsured Population: 2010 to 2020." February 11. https://aspe.hhs.gov/sites/default/files/private/pdf/265041/trends-in-the-us-uninsured.pdf.

———. 2018. "Comparisons of U.S. and International Prices for Top Medicare Part B Drugs by Total Expenditure." Office of the Assistant Secretary for Planning and Evaluation. October. https://aspe.hhs.gov/system/files/pdf/259996/ComparisonUSInternationalPricesTopSpendingPartBDrugs.pdf.

———. 2018. "Medicare Program; International Pricing Index Model for Medicare Part B Drugs." *Federal Register* 83, no. 210 (October 30): 54546–61. https://www.govinfo.gov/content/pkg/FR-2018-10-30/pdf/2018-23688.pdf.

———. 2018. "National Health Expenditure Data, Historical Tables, Table 16." Centers for Medicare & Medicaid Services. https://www.cms.gov/Research-Statistics-Data-and-Systems/Statistics-Trends-and-Reports/NationalHealthExpendData/NationalHealthAccountsHistorical.html.

———. 2016. "Medicare Part B Drugs: Pricing and Incentives." Office of the Assistance Secretary for Planning an Evaluation. March. https://aspe.hhs.gov/pdf-report/medicare-part-b-drugs-pricing-and-incentives.

———. 2015. "Part B Payments for 340B-Purchased Drugs." Office of Inspector General. November. https://oig.hhs.gov/oei/reports/oei-12-14-00030.pdf.

US Department of Veterans Affairs. 2015. "An Assessment of the Department of Veteran Affairs Supply Purchasing System." McKinsey & Company. September 1. https://www.va.gov/opa/choiceact/documents/assessments/Assessment_J_Supplies.pdf.

US Departments of Health and Human Services, Treasury, and Labor. 2018. "Reforming the Health Care System Through Choice and Competition." December. https://www.hhs.gov/sites/default/files/Reforming-Americas-Healthcare-System-Through-Choice-and-Competition.pdf.

US House of Representatives. 1965. "Social Security Amendments of 1965 Volume 1." March. https://www.ssa.gov/history/pdf/Downey%20 PDFs/Social%20Security%20 Amendments%20of%201965%20Vol%201.pdf.

US Patent and Trademark Office. 2002. "The US Patent System Celebrates 212 Years." April.

US Senate. 2017. "The Constitution of the United States of America: Analysis and Interpretation." https://www.govinfo.gov/content/pkg/GPO-CONAN-2017/pdf/GPO-CONAN-2017.pdf.

Uyehara, Esther, and Margaret Thomas. 1975. "Health Maintenance Organization and the HMO Act of 1973." RAND Corporation. December. https://www.rand.org/content/dam/rand/pubs/papers/2009/P5554.pdf.

Villagrana, Marco A. 2019. "Medicare Graduate Medical Education Payments: An Overview." Congressional Research Service. February 19. https://fas.org/sgp/crs/misc/IF10960.pdf.

Walterscheid, Edward. 2002. "'Within the Limits of the Constitutional Grant': Constitutional Limitations on the Patent Power." *Journal of Intellectual Property* 9, no. 2 (April). https://digitalcommons.law.uga.edu/cgi/viewcontent.cgi?referer=&httpsredir=1&article=1367&context=jipl.

Wammes, Joost, Niek Stadhouders, and Gert Westert. 2020. "International Health Care System Profiles: Netherlands." Commonwealth Fund. June 5. https://www.commonwealthfund.org/international-health-policy-center/countries/netherlands.

Weigel, Dave. 2017. "Freedom Caucus Backs ACA 'Repeal and Replace' That Counts on Private Coverage." *Washington Post*. February 15. https://www.washingtonpost.com/news/powerpost/wp/2017/02/15/freedom-caucus-ready-for-obamacare-replacement-that-expands-hcas-bans-abortion-funding/.

Whaley, Christopher M., Lan Vu, Neeraj Sood, Michael E. Chernew, Leanne Metcalfe, and Ateev Mehrotra. 2019. "Paying Patients to Switch: Impact of a Rewards Program on Choice of Providers, Price, and Utilization." *Health Affairs* 38, no. 3 (March). https://www.healthaffairs.org/doi/pdf/10.1377/hlthaff.2018.05068.

Wheeler, Chris, and Russ Taylor. 2021. "New Year, New CMS Price Transparency Rule for Hospitals." Health Affairs Forefront. January 19. https://www.healthaffairs.org/do/10.1377/hblog20210112.545531/full/.

White, Chapin, and Megan Eguchi. 2014. "Reference Pricing: A Small Piece of the Health Care Puzzle." National Institute for Health Care Reform. October. http://nihcr.org/wp-content/uploads/2016/07/Research_Brief_No._18.pdf.

White, Chapin, Paul B. Ginsburg, Ha T. Tu, James D. Reschovsky, Joseph M. Smith, and Kristie Liao. 2014. "Healthcare Price Transparency: Policy Approaches and Estimated Impacts on Spending." West Health Policy Center. http://www.westhealth.org/wp-content/uploads/2015/05/Price-Transparency-Policy-Analysis-FINAL-5-2-14.pdf.

Wilcox, Lindsay. 2021. "Physician Salary Report 2021: Compensation Steady Despite COVID-19." Weatherby Healthcare. May 26. https://weatherbyhealthcare.com/blog/annual-physician-salary-report.

Wyden, Ron. 2021. "Principles for Drug Pricing Reform." US Senate. Committee on Finance. June. https://www.finance.senate.gov/imo/media/doc/062221%20SFC%20Drug%20Pricing%20Principles.pdf.

Young, Aaron, Humayun J. Chaudhry, Xiaomei Pei, Katie Arnhart, Michael Dugan, and Kenneth B. Simmons. 2021. "FSMB Census of Licensed Physicians in the United States, 2020." *Journal of Medical Regulation* 107, no. 2. https://www.fsmb.org/siteassets/advocacy/publications/2020-physician-census.pdf.

Young, Christen Linke, James C. Capretta, Stan Dorn, David Kendall, and Joseph Antos. 2020. "How to Boost Health Insurance Enrollment: Three Practical Steps That Merit Bipartisan Support." Health Affairs Forefront. August 17. https://www.healthaffairs.org/do/10.1377/hblog20200814.107187/full/.

Zavlin, Dmitry, Kevin T. Jubbal, Jonas G. Noé, and Bernd Gansbacher. 2017. "A Comparison of Medical Education in Germany and the United States: From Applying to Medical School to the Beginnings of Residency." *German Medical Science* 15, no. 15 (September). https://www.ncbi.nlm.nih.gov/pmc/articles/PMC5617919/.

Appendix B. Source Reports

All the chapters in this volume are adaptations of previously published American Enterprise Institute reports. The original reports are cited below.

Chapter 1: The Structured Markets Framework

James C. Capretta, "Structured Markets: Disciplining Medical Care with Regulated Competition," American Enterprise Institute, March 31, 2021, https://www.aei.org/research-products/report/structured-markets-disciplining-medical-care-with-regulated-competition/.

Chapter 2: Price Transparency

James C. Capretta, "Toward Meaningful Price Transparency in Health Care," American Enterprise Institute, June 26, 2019, https://www.aei.org/research-products/report/toward-meaningful-price-transparency-in-health-care/.

Chapter 3: Medicare

James C. Capretta, "Market-Based Medicare Would Set US Health Care on a Better Course," American Enterprise Institute, July 7, 2021, https://www.aei.org/research-products/report/market-driven-medicare-would-set-us-health-care-on-a-better-course/.

Chapter 4: Medicaid and the Children's Health Insurance Program

James C. Capretta, "A Medicaid and Children's Health Insurance Program Primer and Reform Outline," American Enterprise Institute, January 31, 2022, https://www.aei.org/research-products/report/a-medicaid-and-childrens-health-insurance-program-primer-and-reform-outline/.

Chapter 5: Employer-Sponsored Insurance

James C. Capretta, "The Future of Employer-Sponsored Health Insurance," American Enterprise Institute, November 19, 2020, https://www.aei.org/research-products/report/the-future-of-employer-sponsored-health-insurance/.

Chapter 6: Covering the Uninsured

James C. Capretta, "Covering the Uninsured in the United States' Multi-Payer Health System," American Enterprise Institute, May 11, 2021, https://www.aei.org/research-products/report/covering-the-uninsured-in-the-united-states-multi-payer-health-system/.

Chapter 7: Prescription Drug Pricing

Joseph Antos and James C. Capretta, "Prescription Drug Pricing: An Overview of Legal, Regulatory, and Market Environment," American Enterprise Institute, July 23, 2018, https://www.aei.org/research-products/report/prescription-drug-pricing-an-overview-of-the-legal-regulatory-and-market-environment/.

Joseph Antos and James C. Capretta, "Reforming Medicare Payments for Part B Drugs," American Enterprise Institute, June 3, 2019, https://www.aei.org/research-products/report/reforming-medicare-payments-for-part-b-drugs/.

Chapter 8: The Physician Workforce

James C. Capretta, "Policies Affecting the Number of Physicians in the US and a Framework for Reform," American Enterprise Institute, March 12, 2020, https://www.aei.org/research-products/report/policies-affecting-the-number-of-physicians-in-the-us-and-a-framework-for-reform/.

Chapter 9: Political and Administrative Considerations

James C. Capretta, "The Political Economy of Health Reform: Price Regulation vs. Regulated Competition," American Enterprise Institute, September 13, 2021, https://www.aei.org/research-products/report/the-political-economy-of-health-reform-price-regulation-vs-regulated-competition/.

About the Author

James C. Capretta is a senior fellow and holds the Milton Friedman Chair at the American Enterprise Institute, where he studies health care, entitlement, and US budget policy and global trends in aging, health, and retirement programs. Capretta also serves as a senior adviser to the Bipartisan Policy Center. He previously served in senior positions at the Office of Management and Budget and on the staff of the Senate Budget Committee.